# Informal Urbanization in Latin America

Various kinds of informal and extra-legal settlements—commonly called shanty-towns, favelas, or barrios—are the prevailing type of urban land use in much of the developing world. United Nations estimates suggest that there are close to 900 million people living in squatter communities worldwide, with the number expected to increase in the coming decades.

*Informal Urbanization in Latin America* investigates prevailing strategies for addressing informal settlements, which started to shift away from large-scale slum clearance to on-site upgrading in Latin America over the last 40 years, by improving public spaces, infrastructure and facilities. The cases in this book range from one micro intervention (the Villa Tranquila Project in Buenos Aires) to three large-scale government-run projects: the celebrated Favela Bairro Program in Rio de Janeiro, the social housing program in São Paulo and the famous Proyectos Urbanos Integrales Approach in Medellín. The cases show a collaborative and sensitive transformation of landscape and public space, and provide designers and planners with the tools to develop better strategies that can mitigate the volatility that the residents of non-formal neighborhoods are exposed to. The book is a must-read for all who are interested or working in global urbanization as well as social equity.

**Christian Werthmann** is a Professor of Landscape Architecture and Design at the Leibniz University of Hannover, Germany, with extensive professional and academic experience in Europe and the United States. During his time as an Associate Professor at the Harvard Graduate School of Design (2004–2012), he started to investigate informal urbanization and disaster zones with a focus on Latin America. His investigations have led to numerous publications, exhibitions and conferences since. In the past few years, he published, with Jessica Bridger, *Metropolis Nonformal* (2016), curated the "Dangerous Landscapes" conference in Hannover (2017) and co-curated the exhibition "Out There. Landscape Architecture on Global Terrain" at the Architectural Museum Munich (2017). His latest research project, *Inform@Risk*, is concerned with the development of integrative early warning systems in the barrios of Medellín (2020).

"If you are a professional architect or urban planner, a scholar or a student of urban planning and design, or if you work in local or city governments, you will find this book extremely useful. It deals with the biggest challenge for city governments in the twenty-first century: informal urbanization and the appearance of slums, informal settlements and settlements, where nearly 1 billion people live today. The Coronavirus pandemic has exacerbated the problem and showed that we need to change and urgently transform these areas. How to do that? The book provides the reader with real answers and practical examples from Rio de Janeiro, São Paulo, Buenos Aires and Medellín on how to transform slums and informal settlements into livable and safe neighborhoods, integrating them into the urban fabric and planning systems of cities. This is not an easy task and the book is rich in testimonies of those directly involved in real actions that transform ideas into reality."

— **Claudio Acioly**, *urban planner, international housing and development expert*

"Based on long-term research over four case studies, this book investigates the non-formal sector of urban growth in Latin America. Writing from a landscape-architectural perspective, Werthmann puts the geophysical landscape in focus for his in-depth analysis. With its anticipatory and multi-scalar approach, this book is a highly relevant contribution to the debate about improvement of urban ecologies."

— **Andres Lepik**, *Director of the Architekturmuseum, Technical University of Munich*

# Informal Urbanization in Latin America

## Collaborative Transformations of Public Spaces

Christian Werthmann

Routledge
Taylor & Francis Group
NEW YORK AND LONDON

First published 2022
by Routledge
605 Third Avenue, New York, NY 10158

and by Routledge
2 Park Square, Milton Park, Abingdon, Oxon, OX14 4RN

*Routledge is an imprint of the Taylor & Francis Group, an informa business*

© 2022 Christian Werthmann

The right of Christian Werthmann to be identified as author of this work
has been asserted by him in accordance with sections 77 and 78 of the
Copyright, Designs and Patents Act 1988.

All rights reserved. No part of this book may be reprinted or reproduced
or utilised in any form or by any electronic, mechanical, or other means,
now known or hereafter invented, including photocopying and recording,
or in any information storage or retrieval system, without permission in
writing from the publishers.

*Trademark notice*: Product or corporate names may be trademarks
or registered trademarks, and are used only for identification and
explanation without intent to infringe.

*Library of Congress Cataloging-in-Publication Data*
Names: Werthmann, Christian, 1964– author.
Title: Informal urbanization in Latin America : collaborative
transformations of public spaces / Christian Werthmann.
Description: New York, NY : Routledge, 2021. | Includes bibliographical
references and index.
Identifiers: LCCN 2020057868 (print) | LCCN 2020057869 (ebook) |
ISBN 9780367545901 (hardback) | ISBN 9780367545895 (paperback) |
ISBN 9781003089797 (ebook)
Subjects: LCSH: Squatter settlements--Latin America. | Urbanization--
Latin America. | Urban poor--Housing--Latin America.
Classification: LCC HD7287.96.L29 W47 2021 (print) | LCC
HD7287.96.L29 (ebook) | DDC 307.3/3614098--dc23
LC record available at https://lccn.loc.gov/2020057868
LC ebook record available at https://lccn.loc.gov/2020057869

ISBN: 9780367545901 (hbk)
ISBN: 9780367545895 (pbk)
ISBN: 9781003089797 (ebk)

Typeset in Adobe Garamond Pro
by KnowledgeWorks Global Ltd.

*for Marion and Julia*

Figure 1

Figure 2

Figure 3

Figure 4

Figure 5

Figure 6

Figure 7

Figure 8

# Contents

Foreword..................................................................................xiii
*Claudio Acioly Jr*

Preface.................................................................................. xvii

Acknowledgements ............................................................. xxiii

Landscape and the Informal City...........................................1
*John Beardsley*

## PART I INFORMAL NEIGHBORHOODS – AN INCOMPLETE TAXONOMY FOR A DIVERSE UNIVERSE ..................... 5

A Word about Formal and Informal.......................................6
Mapping Informal Urbanization Globally.............................10
Mapping Informal Urbanization in Buenos Aires, Rio de Janeiro,
São Paulo and Medellín......................................................12
Instances ...........................................................................17
Five Modes of Engagement .................................................28
Notes .................................................................................32

## PART II LESSONS FROM LATIN AMERICA ..........................37

**Case Study I: Buenos Aires – Step by Step** .............................39

Villa Tranquila ..................................................................40
Conclusion.........................................................................47
Project Credits ...................................................................49
Notes .................................................................................50

**Interview with Flavio Janches and Max Rohm** .......................51

Note....................................................................................60

**Case Study II: Rio de Janeiro – Equality through Public Space** ...........61

Favela Bairro .....................................................................63
Parque Royal......................................................................67

xi

xii ■ *Contents*

Project Credits ...............................................................................72
Morro da Formiga........................................................................73
Project Credits ...............................................................................79
Reforestation Project Credits ........................................................80
Morro da Providência....................................................................80
Project Credits ...............................................................................86
Conclusion.....................................................................................87
Notes .............................................................................................91

**Interview with Lu Petersen**............................................................**96**

Note................................................................................................98

**Case Study III: São Paulo – Protecting Water**.................................**99**

Guarapiranga Basin Initiative .....................................................100
Project Credits .............................................................................107
Parque Amélia .............................................................................108
Conclusion...................................................................................112
Project Credits .............................................................................115
Notes ...........................................................................................115

**Interview with Elisabete França and Marta Maria Lagreca de Sales** ........**117**

Notes ...........................................................................................122

**Case Study IV: Medellín – Scaling Mountains**................................**123**

PRIMED .....................................................................................124
EDU.............................................................................................126
PUI Nororiental ..........................................................................130
Conclusion...................................................................................134
Notes ...........................................................................................137

**Interview with Alejandro Echeverri** .................................................**139**

Notes ...........................................................................................148

# PART III   AND NOW? ...........................................................149

Choose Carefully Where and with Whom You Work .....................151
Pursue an Integrative Improvement Process...................................156
Use Landscape as Infrastructure ...................................................160
Increase Knowledge of Designers and Planners.............................163
Notes ...........................................................................................165

**Afterword** ........................................................................................ **169**

**List of Figure Credits**....................................................................... **173**

**Index** .............................................................................................. **177**

# Foreword

## The Spatial Dimension of Urban Transformation in Slums and Informal Settlements

Claudio Acioly Jr

A book that draws on research into, and practice of, urban transformations in slums and informal settlements in cities of Latin America is a must for professionals, academics and practitioners who wish to understand the deep-rooted causes of informal urbanization and the different approaches to improve the living conditions of its inhabitants. The goal to integrate these areas into the urban fabric and the systems of urban governance that regulate the territory of cities is a contemporary worldwide challenge. It is part and parcel of the Agenda 2030 and the Sustainable Development Goal 11 that aim to render cities inclusive, resilient, safe and sustainable, and to leave no one behind. This book, *Collaborative Transformations of Public Spaces*, by Christian Werthmann, is one that provides the reader with an exceptional compendium of cases and project experiences that aim to transform the lives of people who face the fate of social and spatial exclusion. It is a contribution to the global effort to change the fate of nearly one billion people living under such conditions.

Werthmann offers us not only a book containing his professional and academic reflections on the theories of informal and non-formal urbanization and on the bulk of knowledge that he has acquired on the subject and that he competently cites throughout the manuscript, he also provides the reader with a deep dive into the processes and rationale of planning and physical interventions where one gets an insight into the hands-on experience of those who were deeply involved in the design, formulation and implementation of settlement upgrading programs and projects in Latin America's biggest metropolises. Participants' observations are one of the added values of this book, and Werthmann makes an effort to interview and hear what key actors and change makers had to say about their experiences in implementing complex projects in Buenos Aires, Rio de Janeiro, São Paulo and Medellín. It is a reality check on what he observed during his visits to the sites. There is a rich amount of testimonies and information derived from one-to-one conversations, seminars and debates that he organized and participated in which make this book extremely valuable for those engaged in the implementation of the SDG (Sustainable Development Goals) 11.

I first met Werthmann in Cambridge, USA, while undertaking a short sabbatical with the Lincoln Institute of Land Policy in 2007. After delivering a public lecture about the work I had been doing with the Rotterdam based Institute for Housing and Urban Development Studies, where I then worked, we engaged in a conversation that led to years of close collaboration after I took over the housing policy, housing rights, slum upgrading and capacity building works at UN-Habitat in 2008. The linking of our work and synergy of our thoughts were triggered by the fact that, together with the Lincoln Institute, I was focusing on the nature, scale, rationale and consolidation of informal settlements and the buoyancy of informal land markets in Latin America, which were central to the annual professional training program conducted for nationals of Latin American countries that I have been running in collaboration with Martim Smolka from 2004 to the present date. Approaches to regularizing and upgrading these settlements were equally important as preventive policies and strategies to provide alternatives to curb the multiplication and persistence of informal urbanization. This twin-track approach has been present in my interactions with Werthmann during the 12 years of my tenure at UN-Habitat.

In our first conversation, Werthmann showed a genuine interest in going further in gaining knowledge about informal urbanization and revealed perspicacity in looking with the eyes of a researcher, a landscape architect and a professional with a profound intellectual curiosity about the bigger picture of the problem of deprived neighborhoods in the cities of the developing world. This book reveals his lens when looking at the reality of these settlements, the institutions behind the programs and projects, the variables and the elements of different dimensions that play a role in their development, stagnation and deterioration that affect people's lives.

Werthmann dared to formulate fundamental questions that drove him to design studios and research at Harvard University and the "Dirty Works" exhibition, and continued when he moved to Leibniz University in Hannover and furthered the collaboration with other universities and scholars from all over the world. I am grateful for Werthmann's decisive leadership in the Hub of Informal Urbanism of the UN-Habitat University Partnership Initiative that I led during my last years with UN-Habitat. He managed to upscale the debate, bringing key universities, PhD researchers and renowned world scholars to a fertile environment of thinking and action. The richness of this journey, the beginning of which coincides with the period that we met, is fully reflected in this book that provides the reader with a wealth of information on, and references to, real projects and programs. The cases depicted in the book illustrate the places and people that make a difference in transformations, big and small, led by individual and institutional efforts to implement ideas, under extremely difficult conditions, that have as their ultimate goal the transformation of slums and informal settlements into livable places where poor people can live in safety and dignity and access the services the city provides to its inhabitants.

The nuances of informal institutions, violence, volatility of different natures and the evolution of approaches influencing policy decisions all fall into place in this book, which will significantly enrich the reader's understanding of the challenges facing city governments and the residents of these settlements alike. This makes the book a valuable asset for those willing to work with urban planning, landscape design and improvement strategies in places where people live under precarious conditions, excluded, and with insecurity of tenure. Places where, very often, the institutions have neither the capacity nor the resources to ensure continuity and long-term engagement that will make possible the integration and transformation of slums and informal settlements into neighborhoods connected to, and integrated with, the rest of the city. The evolutionary character and incremental nature of the development processes triggered by these policy interventions are depicted in various parts of the book. More often than would be desired, Werthmann comes to conclusions that reveal the weakness of these projects in not being able to maintain continuity and consolidation.

What strikes the reader in the narratives and analysis of the cases provided by the book are the spatial and urbanistic dimensions where Werthmann's landscape architecture profession excels. He brings it into his views and subtly presents the reader with the various possibilities that provide good quality spatial planning and meaningful design interventions focusing on the public domain of urban life, and makes a case that it can trigger transformations in the social, economic and environmental dimensions of these areas. The examples of the projects in Rio, São Paulo and Medellín are emblematic in the sense that they elevate the importance of the urban layout and the spatial structure of barrios with the interspersion of public spaces as part and parcel of landscape-driven projects that enable access to services and basic infrastructure. All of this are parts of an effort to (re)connect these areas to the rest of the city. This makes the book extremely useful for students of architecture and urban planning and design, but also for professionals who want to engage in professional practice in cities in the developing world. The unplanned, spontaneous, unauthorized, haphazard and uncontrolled nature of informally developed settlements, be it a favela or a clandestine irregular settlement in Rio de Janeiro or a villa in Buenos Aires, challenges the fundamentals of architecture and urban planning and design education, and presents one of the most challenging and dynamic settings in which to exercise the skills and knowledge learned and developed through traditional university education. It is commendable that Werthmann explores this in his educational role, bringing this reality closer to the academic universe and vice versa, and produces a book that will certainly inspire a new generation of professionals.

The scale of the problem and the severity of the present conditions make informal urbanization, slums and informal settlements the greatest challenges of city governments for the years to come. This publication provides us with an excellent analysis of the metrics available, the challenges of land supply, the poor provision and lack of finance for infrastructure, and it underscores the growth pattern if no concerted and scaled-up actions are carried out by governments. The Coronavirus pandemic has exacerbated the problem, which jeopardizes the future sustainability and social cohesion of cities and, consequently, the fate of future generations. All these factors make Werthmann's book an indispensable publication for city government officials. It is also a key contribution to the bulk of knowledge required for moving forward the Agenda 2030 and the SDG 11. Upgrading of informal settlements is one of the targets of the SDG 11. Werthmann's efforts to unfold the lessons learned from a variety of projects in Latin American cities turn this book into an immeasurable contribution to this global movement towards sustainable and inclusive cities. When releasing the urban data in 2014 and the results of its mandated monitoring of slums in the world, UN-Habitat revealed that one out of every four urban residents in the world live in slum conditions, deprived of adequate sanitation, water, living space, occupying precarious buildings and without security of tenure. In Latin America, this is not so different. Nearly a quarter of the urban population lives in deprived conditions in favelas, barriadas, villas and other local denominations for areas that have been internationally known as slums. This is morally, and from the human rights aspect, unacceptable. I do hope that publications such as this of Werthmann will help to change the trends and provide hope for real and durable transformations in cities in the developing world.

## Notes on contributor

**Claudio Acioly Jr.** is an architect and urban planner, a development practitioner with nearly 40 years of experience in more than 30 countries working as a practicing expert, program manager, resident technical and policy advisor or short-term consultant to governments, bilateral and multilateral organizations, academic institutions, civil society organizations and community-based organizations. For more than a decade, Acioly worked as senior manager of UN-Habitat, the United Nations Human Settlements Program. During the period 2008–2019, Acioly led the Housing Policy and Slum Upgrading, the Capacity Building and the United Nations Housing Rights Programs. During 2020, he was a senior program manager of the German Corporation for International Cooperation (GIZ) and was the Program Director of the European Union's International Urban Cooperation Program for Latin America and the Caribbean (IUC-LAC).

# Preface

## A Simple Question

This book originated from a simple question: What is the role of landscape architecture in informal urbanization?

John Beardsley and I asked ourselves this question in 2007, when we both were still teaching in the Landscape Architecture Department at the Harvard Graduate School of Design. At the time we were still digesting the fact that there was almost one third of the global urban population[i] living in what the UN lists as "slums."[ii] We were wondering if landscape-driven projects existed that would make a positive contribution to these neighborhoods and their residents. If Harvard University was truly a world university (as it claimed), then should not at least a third of its urban teaching and research be dedicated to this phenomenon? At this point in time, this was far from true. In our landscape architecture department, there was little evidence of engagement in the topic besides a recent master studio conducted by John in Buenos Aires (one of the case studies of the book). At the time, most of the studio projects were concerned with urban and landscape issues of highly industrialized countries; topics such as the post-industrial use of brownfield sites were more prevalent.

As we got the chance to curate an exhibition at the school, we jumped on the opportunity to do some background research.[iii] We both had made connections to Latin American cities and knew designers and agencies who worked in self-constructed neighborhoods. We decided to look for traces of landscape-based approaches there. Through an investigative field trip in 2007, I visited several sites of the famous Favela Bairro program in Rio de Janeiro and the Guarapiranga Basin Initiative in São Paulo (both originated in the 1990s). In talking to experts and residents alike, it became clear how much these programs depended on the transformation of landscape and public space. One of the first statements of Elisabete França, the long-time leading urbanist of São Paulo's social housing agency (SABESP), was that public space is the most important issue in the improvement of informal settlements. This was extremely encouraging, but also bewildering, as most of these landscape and public space projects were not developed by landscape architects. This could be partially explained by the fact that landscape architecture in Latin America

**xvii**

is still a young profession with far less influence and less practitioners per capita than in the US or Western Europe. But it was also due to the fact that a project in a crowded informal neighborhood required a holistic approach where architecture, urban design, urban planning and landscape architecture are inextricably linked. In Latin America, where landscape architecture is mostly taught as an appendix to a full architecture education, the upgrading of informal settlements was clearly an architect's game.

Back at Harvard, in 2008 John Beardsley and I mounted a show titled "Dirty Work: Transforming Landscape in the Non-formal City of the Americas." It showcased a wide mix of approaches, including small-scale designer-driven initiatives: Teddy Cruz's cross-border studies of Tijuana and San Diego, Jose Castillo's investigations in Mexico City's drained Texcoco lake, the acupunctural insertions of Alfredo Brillembourg and Hubert Klumpner in Caracas and Flavio Janches and Max Rohm's incremental playground approach in the *Villas de Emergencias* of Buenos Aires. These individual initiatives were contrasted with the large-scale municipal programs of São Paulo with a focus on water issues, of Rio de Janeiro with a concentration on public space, and of Bogotá with an emphasis on public transportation.

Figure 9 View of the exhibition "Dirty Work: Transforming Landscape in the Non-formal City of the Americas" at Gund Hall, Harvard Graduate School of Design (image from 2008)

Together with students, we tried to map the location of informal settlements in these seven cities in relation to topography, water bodies, transportation and overall urbanization. By doing so, we quickly noticed the large differences in the availability of official maps. Whereas the Brazilian cities had excellent data, there was less officially available data, for example, in Buenos Aires and Mexico City. This non-existence of official data also reflected the status of official approaches towards informal urbanization in these cities.

We also were unhappy with global depictions of self-constructed urbanization. The UN had published detailed tabulations of "slum" populations and their growth per country, but no satisfactory maps existed. For the "Dirty Work" show we decided to make our own map, which became the focal point of the show as a large mural.

"Dirty Work" was, in my case, the beginning of a more extensive investigation and laid the groundwork for this book. In the following decade I was conducting studio projects with students and research with professionals on informal conditions in Latin America. Contacts, especially with São Paulo, intensified and a long-term research collaboration with Medellín developed. Overall, there was an urgent need to exchange knowledge with design professionals engaged in the topic. Subsequently, I had the chance to curate and co-curate a series of conferences in Munich, Zurich and Hanover.[iv] With a group of individuals led by Anna Heringer, the *Laufen Manifesto* was issued in 2013 and, in 2015, the book *Metropolis Nonformal* (with Jessica Bridger) was published. It investigated 25 expert approaches voiced at the Munich conferences. In 2017, the exhibition "Out There. Landscape Architecture on Global Terrain" at the Architectural Museum in Munich, curated by Andres Lepik, featured five German landscape architects (myself included), all of whom were dealing with informal conditions in one way or another. Close to 40,000 visitors saw the show, which featured ten research projects.[v] It is evident that, over the years, a certain momentum had been building, and the topic has arrived, at least in the small niche of German landscape architecture.

In the discussion, it became apparent that the engagement with self-constructed neighborhoods went well beyond the reach of landscape architecture; it required a multi-sectorial, multi-scalar and multi-temporal approach that puts the residents at the center of a fair and democratic process. No discipline held sway over another.

But, as for every form of urbanization, the geophysical landscape, where a city is located, whether it is in a river delta or in a mountain valley, must be considered as the base layer of its urban transformation. Especially self-constructed neighborhoods, which often exist on marginal land, the forces of landscape can surface as a source of threat. Flooding and landslides are the most common problems. At the same time, these forces can also offer opportunities (food production, stormwater management, energy production, etc.). Landscape architects are naturally trained to engage landscapes as open-ended systems characterized by myriad human and non-human actors. Death and birth, decay and growth are self-evident parts of a landscape architect's thought process. Unpredictability, uncertainty and change are embraced as characteristics that very much mirror the volatility that self-constructed

**xx** ■ *Preface*

cities have been, and are still, exposed to. Therefore, it was worth a try to study informal urbanization more from a gardener's rather than from a builder's perspective.

From a gardener's perspective, the understanding of the long-term evolution of a place is more important than a snapshot in time. Therefore, it was important for me to revisit, after ten years, many of the places the "Dirty Work" show displayed, to see how they fared, how changes in political and economic context affected them and how the improvement projects (some of them now well over 20 years old) were holding up. Also, many other academics from different sciences have visited, investigated and written about these places in the interim. It seemed prudent to learn about their findings and develop a broader-based understanding. Out of the seven initiatives, I picked the ones to which I had the most exposure over the past ten years: the small-scale playground initiative of Flavio Janches and Max Rohm in Buenos Aires (from 2006), the first city-wide coordinated upgrading program *Favela Bairro* in Rio de Janeiro (from the mid 1990s) and the first large-scale government initiative in the Guarapiranga Basin of São Paulo (from the mid 1990s). As I had the chance to engage in a long-term research collaboration with one of Medellín's premier urban research centers,[vi] I added the more recent and now worldwide known transformation of Medellín's barrios as a fourth case. In sum, this book contains three government-led and one designer-driven initiatives. The government-led initiatives dominate because they deserve the most scrutiny, as they have the most potential to bring widespread improvement, but they also can inflict the most harm when not done well.

The knowledge presented was gained through consecutive site visits, interviews with involved design professionals and community leaders and the study of secondary literature. Some of the interviews were conducted seven to ten years ago and have been updated together with the interviewees wherever possible.[vii] Local experts intimately familiar with the described projects corrected the final version of the texts.

The ten-year observation of the four cases gave a more extended insight into the faring of landscape and public space than would be possible in a single visit. Unfortunately, I must say that the prolonged view revealed a picture of great volatility. Individual progress (when achieved) has been fleeting, or extinguished under a new political leadership with a different set of priorities. In some of the cases, residents have been left to their own devices or, worse, have been evicted (for example, in Rio de Janeiro). During the research it became clear that the improvement of informal urbanization is a fragile undertaking, riddled with setbacks and periods of stagnancy; it is reliant on a continuous and fair democratic process that is hard to build, hard to sustain and that can fall apart at any given moment.

It also became clear that not only a frequently observed lack of good governance and stability can deliver serious setbacks, but also biotic calamities. In 2020, the Coronavirus pandemic has highlighted the increased vulnerability to contagious diseases in dense informal settlements, where social distancing is more or less impossible and a stay-at-home order can mean income loss and hunger.[viii]

Next to pandemics, other kinds of disasters in the form of frequent flooding (São Paulo) or landslides (Medellín, Rio de Janeiro) were striking informal areas especially hard in the showcased cities. It is expected that these events will worsen, as climate change will affect informal settlements disproportionally hard.[ix] When disasters occur more frequently in the future, back-to-back events will reduce recuperation times, potentially leading to a constant recovery mode.

It is not easy to stay optimistic, and one would want to hope that a 50- or 100-year view could produce kinder results. Looking back, overall positive trends in increasing education levels or reducing absolute poverty can, indeed, be observed globally.[x] But the look forward is frightening. With more frequent disasters, further widening income gaps, neoliberal attitudes and rising exclusionary policies, self-constructed neighborhoods will most likely face greater volatility in the future. Designers and professionals who want to make a difference have to learn to negotiate this increased volatility by developing effective tools of engagement. The four investigated cases have shown that it is worthwhile to take a gardener's perspective.

# Acknowledgements

This book was initiated as a result of the exhibition "Dirty Work" at the Harvard Graduate School of Design (GSD) in 2008. Foremost, I would like to thank John Beardsley, with whom I curated "Dirty Work," for his continued support and guidance. I would like to also thank the group of individuals who helped us to develop and mount the show: Chelina Odbert, Jennifer Toy, Melissa Vaughn, Terah Maher, Dan Borelli, Shannon Stecher, Elizabeth Randall, the students of the course GSD 5316 (Fall 2007) and the leadership of the GSD at the time.

In the research period that followed the exhibition, I would like to thank several individuals who helped me with numerous tasks: translating interviews, creating maps, finding data, digging up background information and correcting my English: Peter Christensen, Ryan Madson, Patricia Sakata, Carolina Hidalgo[†], Monica Belen, Fiona Luhrman, Federica Natalia Rosati, Nick Bonard, Hanna Klinger, Leonie Wiemer, Ben Jamin Grau and Julian Lange. I am very grateful to Claudio Acioly for writing a Foreword and giving helpful comments on the Rio chapter. Many thanks also go to Adriana Larangeira, Maria Lúcia Petersen[†] and Claudio Acioly for reviewing the texts about Rio de Janeiro, Elisabete França for correcting the São Paulo texts, Flavio Janches for examining the Buenos Aires texts, Alejandro Echeverri for doing the same on the Medellín writings, and Andres Lepik for reviewing the final chapters and the overall logic of the book. Helpful inputs were provided by David Gouverneur and Undine Giseke on the title of the book.

I would like to thank numerous local designers, public officials, organizations and community residents, who have supported me in my research activities on-site.

Buenos Aires: Flavio Janches, Max Rohm

Rio de Janeiro: Maria Lúcia Petersen[†], Adriana Larangeira, Dietmar Starke, Jorge Mario Jauregui, Gabriel Duarte, Moises Lino e Silva, Bruno Fernandel, Eduardo Rosa Thomé dos Santos, Patrizia Josa Thomé dos Santos, Giselle Dias, Maurício Hora

São Paulo: Fernando de Mello Franco, Elisabete França, Maria Teresa Diniz, Marta Maria Lagreca de Salles, Ciro Biderman, Violêta Saldanha Kubrusly and numerous employees of SEHAB

# xxiv ■ *Acknowledgements*

Medellín: Alejandro Echeverri, Francesco María Orsini, Juan Sebastian Bustamante Fernandéz, Ana Elvira Vélez Villa, Fundación Sumapaz and the whole team of Urbam.

I also would like to thank a group of individuals who influenced the contents of the book by fostering my understanding of informal urbanization through many conversations over the past decade: Claudio Acioly, John Beardsley, Jessica Bridger, Alfredo Brillembourg. David Gouverneur, Alejandro Echeverri, Undine Giseke, Reinhard Goethert, Rainer Hehl, Anna Heringer, Flavio Janches, Regine Keller, Hubert Klumpner, Andres Lepik, Fernando de Mello Franco, Rahul Mehrotra, Janice Perlman, Edgar Pieterse, Jörg Rekittke and Phil Thompson.

I would like to thank the team at Routledge for making this book a reality: Kathryn Schell, Sean Speers, Yvonne Doney and all who were involved.

I also want to express my deep sorrow about the passing of two wonderful persons, who contributed to the book, but did not live long enough to see it: Lu Petersen (†2014), a brave and passionate manager in the Favela Bairro program and Carolina Hidalgo (†2012), a gifted and warm-hearted landscape architecture student at the Harvard Graduate School of Design.

Finally, I want to thank my family, who have had the patience to support me throughout the years.

# Notes

i. United Nations Statistics Division Development Data and Outreach Branch New York, "The proportion of slum "dwellers" decreased from 28% in the year 2000 to 23% in the year 2018, but the absolute numbers went up to over one billion, "SDG 11 Sustainable Cities and Communities" United Nations, https://unstats.un.org/sdgs/report/2019/goal-11/ (accessed September 27, 2020).

ii. Consult Part I for the UN Habitat definition of the term "slum."

iii. The Harvard Graduate School of Design has a long-standing tradition of mounting elaborate exhibitions in its lobby, Gund Hall.

iv. *Metropolis Nonformal,* 2011 and *Metropolis Nonformal – Anticipation*, 2013 at the Technical University in Munich, *Low/No Cost Housing*, 2016 and *Shareland*, 2019 at the ETH in Zurich and *Dangerous Landscapes. Re-Thinking Environmental Risk in Low-Income Communities*, at the VW Foundation in Hanover in 2017. There was also a large conference in Cairo in 2014, "Responsive Urbanism in Informal Areas," organized by Sahar Attia in the series. Since 2013, the capacity building unit of UN-Habitat, under the leadership of Claudio Acioly, was supporting the exchange as part of their UNI Hub initiative.

v. The director of the Architecture Museum in Munich, Andres Lepik visited "Dirty Work" in Harvard in 2008, and was inspired to pursue the topic further in his own curatorial efforts, first at the Modern Museum of Art in New York ("Small Scale, Big Change" in 2010) and then the Munich Architecture Museum ("Afritecture," 2013, "Si/No. The Architecture of Urban Think Tank," 2015, "Francis Kéré. Radically Simple," 2016).

vi. Since 2011 with Alejandro Echeverri, director of Urbam.

vii. Maria Lúcia (Lu) Petersen, one of the passionate founders of the *Favela Bairro* program in Rio de Janeiro unfortunately passed away in 2014.
viii. Aline Gatto Boueri, "Precarious housing a key factor in Covid-19 spread in Latin America," *The Brazilian Report*, August 11, 2020, https://brazilian.report/corona-virus-brazil-live-blog/2020/08/11/precarious-housing-a-key-factor-in-covid-19-spread-in-latin-america/ (accessed September 4, 2020).
ix. Aromar Revi et al., "Urban areas," in *Climate Change 2014: Impacts, Adaptation and Vulnerability, Contribution of Working Group II to the Fifth Assessment Report of the Intergovernmental Panel on Climate Change* (Geneva, IPCC: 2014).
x. United Nations, "Ending Poverty," United Nations, www.un.org/en/sections/issues-depth/poverty/ (accessed September 4, 2020).

# Landscape and the Informal City[1]

## John Beardsley

This book covers new terrain and advances fresh tactics for landscape architecture. It has two subjects. The first of these is physical, dealing with low-income communities – variously called squatter settlements, shantytowns, or slums – that are a dominant feature of the developing world's megacities. The second is professional and pertains to the new activist and entrepreneurial practices that strive to operate in circumstances that are among the most challenging imaginable.

The book presents the various ways in which designers are struggling to upgrade these settlements physically without destroying them socially; saving what they can of their physical structure while alleviating environmental and social problems ranging from inadequate public space and housing to unemployment, insecure land tenure, and unsanitary conditions. It focuses on case studies from four cities in Latin America and uses landscape as the lens through which to examine the selected settlements in terms of (a) their occupation of marginal lands, including floodplains, ravines, and steep slopes; (b) their proximity to damaged or toxic sites, such as sewage canals, industrial facilities, and landfills; (c) their typical separation from urban infrastructure, whether roads, transportation, sewers, water supply, or storm-water management; (d) their severe environmental, public health, and security issues; and (e), their lack of public facilities for economic, cultural, or recreational activities. In this context, landscape is conceived both as the primary problem in these communities and as their main opportunity for intervention and improvement. The book then proceeds to identify the most significant strategies for transforming landscape in the informal neighborhoods of Latin America. Through the critical analysis of these strategies, conclusions can be drawn for future work not only in South America, but also in Africa and Asia, where most of the informal growth will occur in the next decades.

## 2 ■ *John Beardsley*

The United Nations estimates that more than half of the world's population now lives in cities, and that approximately a quarter of these people – close to one billion – do so in *slums* characterized by inadequate housing, insufficient living space, insecure land tenure, and lack of access to basic services, especially clean water and sanitation. Without concerted action, the number of slum dwellers is expected to rise significantly. Categorical and morally fraught terms like *slum*, however, can disguise significant cultural and economic distinctions among low-income settlements. Thus, I opt for more neutral terminology, utilizing the designations *informal* or *non-formal cities*, *squatter settlements*, or *shantytowns*, although these terms also present their problems. The words "non-formal" or "informal" in particular suggest that low-income communities have no form, which could not be farther from the truth: they often display an *ad hoc*, accretive quality that some observers have compared to the morphology of medieval cities. Such flexibility in descriptive terms underlines the fact that these communities differ dramatically in size, character, age, and level of political and social organization; they are found in both rural and urban settings, although they are increasingly associated with the world's largest cities, especially in Latin America, Africa, and Asia.

In recent years, prevailing strategies for addressing informal settlements have moved away from large-scale slum clearance and relocation. The approach favored today involves on-site upgrading and improvement, with the goal of integrating low-income communities into their larger urban contexts. This may prove to have been an inevitable development once we consider the number of informal settlements around the world, many of which are both large and old, making it impractical to think of removing them entirely – all the more so as sufficient vacant land for the creation of replacement communities becomes increasingly scarce. Improving informal settlements has the advantage of leaving relatively intact the economic and social networks that residents have created for themselves over the years. That said, however, there is no clear set of best practices for these upgrades, which span from small, acupunctural insertions to expansive infrastructural improvements; from family-based, government-led programs to designer-supported projects. In the hope of encouraging the emergence of better practices, this study of four distinct cases was made to include both built work and proposed projects by designers both more and less well known.

But why focus on Latin America? Beyond geographical and cultural coherence and shared colonial and post-colonial histories, several reasons make it a compelling area for study. Foremost among them is the fact that some of the world's most interesting efforts to improve conditions in informal cities are taking place there. The restoration of civilian rule in many of these countries, and the rise of populist governments in others, has moved the plight of the poor forward across a range of sometimes very conflicting political agendas. Growing economies have provided sometimes largely improved financial means for the consideration of community-improvement programs, despite significant and sometimes dramatically growing gaps between the rich and poor. Many of Latin America's largest cities, including Mexico City, Buenos Aires, São Paulo and Rio de Janeiro, already rank with some of world's largest urban GDPs when measured in terms of purchasing power parity exchange rates. At the same time, however, Latin America also has some of the world's highest Gini coefficients, which measure disparity in income and wealth distribution. Squatter settlements in Latin America would, thus, seem to be a measure of inequality as much as a standard of absolute poverty. Another outstanding factor is that although the region displays some of the world's highest rates of urbanization, in many parts of the continent, urban growth rates are stabilizing – although informal settlements continue to swell. In other words, cities are consolidating, and many countries are beginning to provide their residents with access to land tenure and services. All in all, Latin America represents a laboratory for slum upgrading that might provide a model for those parts of the world where most of the growth in informal cities will occur in the coming decades.

At the same time, we acknowledge the difficulties and the limitations implicit in these projects. What exactly is so complex about this work? To begin with, it addresses the massive economic, environmental, infrastructural, and social failures of recent urban policies, and it often involves the messy procedures of community design and the compromises of political action. To some degree, it is complicit in neoliberal policies that favor microenterprise and market-based solutions over more ambitious, state-sponsored initiatives that could have a larger impact. Even more, it remains unclear if upgrading can achieve significant permanent improvements or if it will merely perpetuate social and spatial inequalities, with large percentages of the population packed into disproportionately small areas that are still short on basic services.

Improving informal neighborhoods is still an exploratory field, raising questions rather than providing answers. As difficult and complex as conditions are in low-income communities, they do provide us with clues to effecting their improvement. Residents of informal cities, for example, display cultural adaptations and survival strategies that can guide eventual interventions. Designers are beginning to be able to lend spatial form to the environmental, social, and economic ambitions of these communities, helping to marshal the financial and political investment to spearhead their transformations. In brief, this work explores the relationship between creativity and social ethics in design culture. It advances the hopeful thesis that impoverished contexts do not have to result in poverty of imagination. No project is perfect and complete unto itself, of course; many are deeply flawed. Yet the important point is to let the ideas behind them loose, in the hope they may start to define better practices. Climate change aside, few challenges to widespread planetary health and security are greater than the vast proliferation of informal settlements. And, as with climate change, there is no time to waste.

# Note

1. This essay was first published in an extended version in *Harvard Design Magazine*, under the title "Improving Informal Settlements. Ideas from Latin America" (28, 2008). It has been updated, shortened and retitled for the purpose of this publication.

# Notes on contributor

**John Beardsley** is an author, educator, and curator, and currently curator for the Cornelia Hahn Oberlander International Landscape Architecture Prize for The Cultural Landscape Foundation. Trained as an art historian, he earned an A.B. from Harvard University and a Ph.D. from the University of Virginia. He is the author of numerous books on contemporary art and design, including *Earthworks and Beyond: Contemporary Art in the Landscape* (fourth edition, 2006) and *Gardens of Revelation: Environments by Visionary Artists* (1995), as well as many titles on recent landscape architecture. He has taught in the departments of landscape architecture at the University of Virginia, the University of Pennsylvania and extensively at the Harvard Graduate School of Design (1998–2013). From 2008–2019, Beardsley served as Director of Garden and Landscape Studies at the Dumbarton Oaks Research Library and Collection in Washington, DC.

# INFORMAL NEIGHBORHOODS

*An Incomplete Taxonomy for a Diverse Universe*

**6** ◾ *Part I*

Part I is a cursory probe into landscape and urban conditions that can be found in self-constructed neighborhoods of Latin America. Overall, it only can give a very limited glimpse into the diversity one can encounter.

## A Word about Formal and Informal

This book avoids terms like *slum* or *shantytown*, since they incline the reader in an undeserved negative direction.[1] This publication uses the more neutral term *informal* (also *non-formal*). While the term *informal* can be less offensive, it can be less definitive. In contrast, the term *slum* has a clear definition characterized by five deficiencies identified by the UN. The UN definition of slum is arrived at by collating the numbers of people dwelling in such settlements by country, monitoring them over time and putting the topic on the political agenda.[2] There is no comparable data for *informal urbanization*, as the phenomenon has wide overlaps, but cannot be equated with the UN definition of slums. As a working proposition, the term *informal urbanization* in this publication refers only to urbanization that originated outside of official planning efforts (or laws) in approximately the last 100 to 150 years. The term does not give clues to the physical condition, income distribution, current legal status, security situation or social composition of a settlement. It merely indicates that citizens have had to create their own living environments outside of governmental planning (if there was any). A longer time frame of observation than 150 years could be interesting from a historical perspective, but this publication intends to focus on more recently formed informal neighborhoods that tend to have more need for improvement.

Although the term *informal city* has gained wide support due to its non-derogatory nature, the term is less precise, as the development of cities cannot always be neatly separated into informal and formal areas (for example, a legal city expansion can originate through governmental corruption). Beyond disputes of legality, one has to accept that dichotomies such as formal and informal naturally describe only the extremes of a wide spectrum; they are not very descriptive in terms of understanding the more nuanced aspects of a territory, as there are differences of legality and planning history between countries and cities.

Moreover, the term informal urbanization is not descriptive of an area beyond its legal origin. Informal urbanization is extremely diverse. Every informal area has its own history, its own specific physical and ecological conditions and population composition. For example, recently established informal settlements tend to have residents with very low incomes and low education standards, whereas more mature informal settlements that have had the chance to prosper over decades in a more fortuitous context tend to have a more varied income distribution and higher education standards of its young population, although there are still variations in between, which makes it hard to formulate generalizations about informal urbanism.

In light of this, one has to accept the complexity that requires the suspension of certain assumptions that the term *informal urbanization* includes; rather, one has to embrace ambiguities as well as in-between conditions. Therefore, it is necessary to correct a few of the most common misperceptions.

## Formal = Safe, Informal = Unsafe?

In general, there is a strong contrast between how residents of an informal neighborhood perceive their living conditions and how outsiders perceive it. Obviously, a difference of perception between persons with different social backgrounds is a common fact of our lives, but, in the case of informality, it is most strongly pronounced, especially concerning the aspect of safety.[3] There are typically great discrepancies between the problems favela residents themselves cite and the problems the outside world believes a favela might have. While outside viewers generally view, for example, the favelas of Rio as dangerous, overcrowded and insanitary, the favela dweller might see his or her favela as a fairly safe and inexpensive housing alternative with some inconveniences; of course, the police raids and gang wars, ending in deadly shootouts killing innocent bystanders, are feared. Sometimes the outside world seems dangerous, with many favela dwellers actually nervous about becoming victims of crime themselves when leaving the relative safety of their favela and venturing into areas of the so-called formal city, such as the world-famous Copacabana.[4]

There is obviously a culturally driven rift of perception between favela residents and nonresidents. Designers, who, in the majority, belong in the group of nonresidents, have to be very careful that they do not overlay their cultural imprint onto an informal neighborhood, where residents might have different priorities. It is only through effective community participation processes, that these priorities can become visible. No assumptions can be made.

## Formal = Planned, Informal = Unplanned?

Formal urbanism and informal urbanism seem to indicate that the first is a neat structured urbanization process inside the legal municipal framework whereas the second is a random and extralegal activity. However, upon closer inspection, the seemingly random morphology of informal urbanism can be driven by very well-organized processes (e.g., community leaders, organized land invasions), whereas the so-called formal city can be shaped by random and informal processes (e.g., corruption or land speculation). In fact, there are large built portions of Latin American cities that have been planned and built by the private sector outside the legal framework. For example, from the estimated four million favela dwellers living in the São Paulo metropolitan area, approximately two million live within irregular subdivisions (*loteamentos irregulares*, or *clandestinos*). The widespread appearance of these irregular subdivisions has led some researchers to claim that municipalities are quietly complicit in their genesis.[5] In knowing that they cannot provide housing for all low-income citizens, municipalities can see irregular subdivisions as a better alternative to completely unplanned urbanization.

8 ■ *Part I*

Irregular subdivisions have at least some type of urban order that can be more easily retrofitted and integrated than the irregular layout of informal urbanization.[6] Eventually, many Latin American cities consist of a patchwork of legal, semi-legal, semi-illegal and illegal developments. What might look like an informal neighborhood might actually have been planned by developers and tolerated (if not promoted) by cash-strapped municipalities. On the other hand, what might look like a formal urban expansion might be the result of corruption or political favoritism.

## Formal = Legal, Informal = Illegal?

On an ethical scale, the defensibleness of an economic and legal system that forces most of Latin America's low-income citizens into extralegal settling activities should be called into question. Given that, in 2016, around one fifth, or 105 million, of the urban population in Latin America[7] lived in illegal and semi-legal neighborhoods, one could rightfully claim that the legal framework and its executive branch was more than ill-prepared to deal with the massive urban migration of rural populations in the last century, a phenomenon that brought hundreds of thousands of poor people to large cities across Latin America, as well as across the globe.[8] One could rightfully argue that the old formula of formal neighborhoods being legal and informal neighborhoods being illegal cannot any longer be sustained in the face of this human crisis. Similarly, a situation where a minority of landowners hold the majority of constructible land in their hands, whereas a majority of low-income citizens cannot find housing, illuminates the need to invent new forms of land ownership and expropriation. Following the examples of Rio de Janeiro, São Paulo and Medellín, many Latin American cities have renegotiated land property rights and, despite still murky ownership conditions, many informal settlers have now *de facto* security of tenure.[9] New terms and land policies have been developed, readjusting our internal sense of order to enable the legality of squatting in the absence of better solutions. During the improvement of informal areas, Latin American cities have developed processes to give out land titles or long-term leases, transforming illegal squatters into law-abiding citizens. After informal areas have been improved, cities like Medellín or Rio de Janeiro do not list them as informal anymore; they are regarded as regular neighborhoods.[10]

## Are Informal Residents Excluded from the Formal City?

There is the commonly held view that informal city dwellers are treated as second-class citizens, excluded from the services, jobs and education of the formal city. While overwhelmingly true, this characterization does not solely concern residents of informal areas. Most residents of the so-called formal city are afraid of entering low-income neighborhoods, mostly for security reasons (an issue that is heavily promulgated by the media). For example, in some of Rio de Janeiro's favelas, visitors, unless they are in company with somebody well-connected to the favela, will be likely to be expelled. Most residents of Brazilian cities have actually never set foot in a favela. The accessible territory of the city shrinks even more for upper-class

Brazilians. Many high-income Brazilians decide to live in heavily gated communities, drive in armored vehicles and are nervous about entering public space even in the formal parts of the city. Despite their wealth (or just because of it), they are, in fact, excluded from large parts of the city. Obviously, their exclusion from access is much less dramatic than the exclusion of informal city dwellers from education, jobs and medical services, but one has to keep in the back of one's mind that exclusion is not solely a one-way street.

## Informal = Poor?

There is also the common perception that all the poor residents of the city live in the informal sectors of the city and that all residents of informal cities are poor. Both assumptions are wrong. When talking about urban poverty, one actually has to look at the whole city – formal areas as well as informal ones. Not all the residents living in informal settlements are the nation's poorest; often some of the poorest live well within the formal city. For example, there is a large population in São Paulo living as renters in decrepit apartments (*Cortiços*) with severe overcrowding (sometimes 15–20 people within a small apartment). Toilets are broken and running water is dirty, that is if it runs at all. In contrast, the residents of the many favelas in São Paulo mostly own their homes and have basic infrastructure. São Paulo's urban researchers point out that living conditions and poverty in overcrowded tenement housing in the formal city are worse than those of a favela, and get much less attention from the media and academia.[11] Not all residents of informal neighborhoods are poor at all; in older, more established and improved neighborhoods, one can also find lower middle class residents and, in some cases, even very affluent citizens.[12] In some informal neighborhoods that are located in very desirable locations, gentrification processes have already been observed.[13]

## Can Informal Neighborhoods be Easily Recognized?

As the morphological variability of informal cities proves, the physical and social structure of informal settlements is as much varied as in formal settlements. Globally, there are as many commonalities between informal settlements as there are differences. For example, the spectrum of informal dwellings can reach from cardboard shacks to fully finished houses with running water, electricity, internet and TV. Urban layouts can vary from nonlinear systems to urban grids. Infrastructure can vary from dirt paths to paved roads with sidewalks and light poles. Income can vary from extremely poor to middle class. In contrast to popular belief, there is no typical form or face to informal urbanism.

## Formal Urbanism = Superior, Informal Urbanism = Inferior?

The informal urban condition is typically viewed as a condition that needs improvement. However, there are certain attributes of the informal city that are superior to

**10** ◾ *Part I*

many formal neighborhoods. Positive traits such as compactness, pedestrian-friendly accessibility, and vibrancy can be easily overlooked amid the media focus on crime, pollution and poverty.

For example, in the context of highly industrialized countries, compact development is generally seen as a prerequisite for sustainability. In the United States, urban planners often try to reintegrate sprawling suburbs to reduce energy inefficiency and social dysfunction. The informal city is at the other end of the spectrum; typically, it over-develops the available terrain and its density needs to be reduced. Given their high densities, informal cities can be served effectively by public transportation (such as the cable cars in Medellín, Caracas and Rio de Janeiro). Its morphology, often not unlike medieval towns, is shaped by the small movements of pedestrians, resulting in narrow alleyways, stairs and footpaths. The pedestrian-friendly streets make car use unattractive, since there is not much space to drive or to park, an attribute very much desired and hardly achieved by modern transit-oriented development. Actually, rising car ownership creates problems of parking and congestion in dense informal neighborhoods.

The informal city's few public spaces are typically vibrant, full of people and children who use the small amount of open space intensively (unless in positions where heavy crime and gang activity rule). Neighbors typically know each other very well; there is no anonymity. Contemporary urban planners in highly industrialized countries actually try to bring back exactly these qualities for their cities. They seek to reinvent the street as a social space and foster informal exchanges in public spaces. They want to build resilient neighborhoods where people know each other well. These inherent qualities of many informal neighborhoods are actually diametrically opposed to the rising and disturbing phenomenon of shopping malls as exclusive places for the socializing of the middle class.[14]

Another positive characteristic is the flexibility of informal cities in build-out and use. Contemporary urban planning seeks to bring back mixed zoning, where working, living and shopping are closer together in order to cut travel distances. Informal urbanization often entails its own economy in "mixed zones" where living and working can occur in the same building. This flexibility can also be noticed in the internal build-out: informal cities grow vertically by adding living space on top of the original house.

Idiosyncrasies of informal urbanism such as density, vibrancy, flexibility, mixed use, entrepreneurship, pedestrian friendliness and social cohesion are the less reported upsides of informal urbanization.

# Mapping Informal Urbanization Globally

Mapping informal urbanization on a global scale is a complicated task. The closest approximation is the world maps displaying slum shares and numbers by country;[15] their basic data source stems mostly from the UN or the World Bank. As

Informal Neighborhoods ■ 11

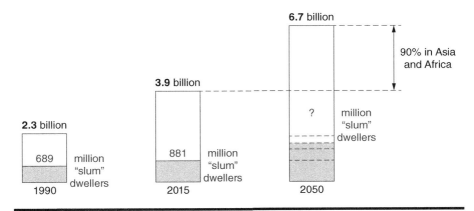

Figure 10 Slum numbers from UN-Habitat's *Slum Almanac 2015–2016*. Urbanization numbers and projections are from UN *World Urbanization Prospects* (2018) and *The Millennium Development Goals Report* (2015). There are no projections available for the number of slum dwellers in 2050

explained above, informal urbanization is not congruent with slums as defined by the UN, but there are many overlaps. In lieu of global numbers of residents in informal neighborhoods, the UN numbers of slum households are a helpful indicator. But one has still to be careful with these numbers, as the accuracy of information on countries can vary greatly. UN-Habitat's Millennium Development Goals Report (2015) features a whole section about data gaps, especially when it comes to reporting poverty. The described gaps can literally obliterate the visibility of low-income citizens.[16] Therefore, data on "slums" have to be understood as vague approximations:

The United Nations calculated in 2015 that there are close to 881 million people on the planet who qualify as living in slum households. This was, in 2015, close to a quarter of the global urban population. The numbers also showed some positive trends; the overall share of slum dwellers in developing world cities has declined from 46% to 29% in the period from 1990 to 2015. However, the absolute numbers had increased by 200 million in that same time period, due to continued urban growth.[17] Consequently, the message conveys mixed results. While overall percentages have plummeted, there was still a gain in absolute numbers.

But, what will the future bring? The global urban population is to swell from over four billion in 2018 to almost seven billion in 2050. 90% of this increase is supposed to take place in Asia and Africa.[18] How many of the 2.5 additional billion urban dwellers will fall under UN-Habitat's definition of slums remains unclear. At the beginning of the millennium, the UN issued alarming slum projections up to the year 2050, but since then the UN has not provided any new projections; the latest reports vaguely stated that slum numbers will increase worldwide without giving estimates.[19]

12 ■ *Part I*

---

**Box 1**

UN-HABITAT defines
*a slum household as a group of individuals living under the same roof in an urban area who lack one or more of the following:*

1. *Durable housing of a permanent nature that protects against extreme climate conditions.*
2. *Sufficient living space, which means not more than three people sharing the same room.*
3. *Easy access to safe water in sufficient amounts at an affordable price.*
4. *Access to adequate sanitation in the form of a private or public toilet shared by a reasonable number of people.*
5. *Security of tenure that prevents forced evictions.*

Un-Habitat's definition of "Slum household" does not differentiate if it is in the informal or formal part of the city; it just centers on deprivations:

> *Not all slums are homogeneous and not all slum dwellers suffer from the same degree of deprivation. The degree of deprivation depends on how many of the five conditions that define slums are prevalent within a slum household.*

Residents of self-constructed neighborhoods easily fulfill in most cases one of the five deprivations.

Source: "Slums: some definitions," UN-Habitat, http://mirror.unhabitat.org/documents/media_centre/sowcr2006/SOWCR%205.pdf (accessed August 25, 2020).

---

# Mapping Informal Urbanization in Buenos Aires, Rio de Janeiro, São Paulo and Medellín

Mapping of informal neighborhoods at the city level can be tedious, as data are not always homogenous, sometimes outdated, not easily accessible, not tracked well or simply not tracked at all. Definitions of informal areas vary from case to case. Sometimes conditions on the ground change so fast that registration lags behind.

The maps of informal neighborhoods of each of the four cities featured in the case studies presented in this book have been started as part of a student exercise in 2008 and subsequently updated with the latest information in 2014 and 2020.[20] Various data sets have been combined to display roads, rivers and topography. While Rio de Janeiro, São Paulo and Medellín have official maps of their informal areas available to be downloaded, the informal areas of Buenos Aires could only be retrieved via the mapping of an NGO (TECHO).

All four cities are rendered similarly, in an effort to make them comparable. Light gray lines represent principal roads and rail lines, but also rivers. Administrational boundaries are shown as white lines. The dark shaded areas indicate topography, large water bodies are in dark grey. Informal settlements are shown in white.

As the definition of informal urbanization varies from city to city, the white areas shown in the maps are not directly comparable, as they are derived from a heterogeneous data set. Overall, the four maps just give a rough snapshot in time of the lie of the land and the very approximate allocation of informal neighborhoods in relation to topography, water bodies and major infrastructure in these cities. It is a natural characteristic of these maps that they are already outdated at their point of publication, as informal neighborhoods and administrational classifications are highly dynamic.

## *Buenos Aires*

Buenos Aires and its greater metropolitan area house some 15 million people (2020) and is the political, economic, and cultural capital of Argentina. Occupying an area of about 3,800 square kilometers along the Rio de la Plata, greater Buenos Aires is almost

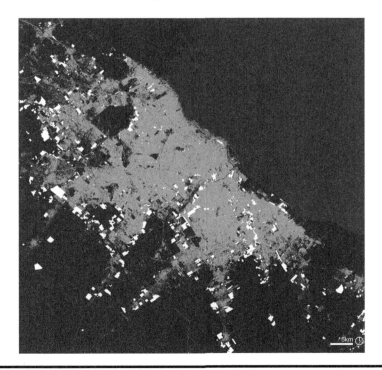

Figure 11  Buenos Aires: the white patches constitute informal areas defined and mapped by the NGO TECHO. The patches combine three typologies listed by TECHO: *asentamiento* (settlement), *villa* (the colloquial term for a low-income area) and *barrio popular informal* (informal neighborhood); they all display urban areas without property titles and/or without access to services (survey from 2016)

uniformly flat. The city proper is comparably small, with roughly three million inhabitants on around 200 square kilometers.[21] With a few notable exceptions, including one near the main train station, informal settlements, known also as *villas*, are located on the urban peripheries or along the Riachuelo River, the historic axis of industrial development in the city. According to the census of 2010, one fifth of the population of the Greater Buenos Aires Area live in inadequate housing conditions.[22] In the absence of official maps, NGOs such as TECHO (or UTMP) have started to map and count informal neighborhoods. TECHO's survey used in the map (seen as the white patches) defines an informal settlement as a group of a minimum of eight families, where more than half of the population does not have land title, or regular access to at least two of the basic services: running water, electrical energy with a household meter and/or a sewage disposal system through the formal sewage network.[23]

## *Medellín*

Medellín is the second largest city of Columbia, located in the Aburrá Valley in the foothills of the Andes and housing 2.5 million within its city boundaries and four million residents in its metropolitan region (2020).[24] Its location is fairly dramatic, as it is confined in a scenic valley whose steep sides reach up to 2,300 meters above

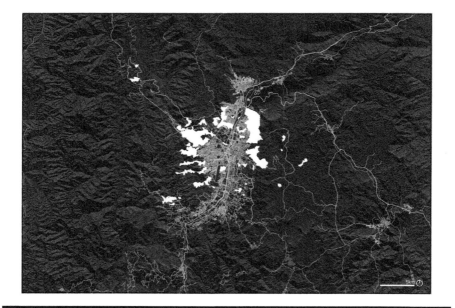

Figure 12 Medellín: the white patches shown in the Masterplan of Medellín (POT 2014, DAP, Municipality of Medellín) combine the areas listed as *mejoramiento integral* (defined as areas of incomplete and inadequate development) and *consolidación nivel 3* (defined as areas that present a precarious support capacity)

sea level. The first Spanish explorers who came to the Aburrá Valley compared it to paradise, based on its lush vegetation and perfect climate.

The municipality of Medellín keeps detailed track of the conditions of its neighborhoods and has developed its own classifications. A 2018 estimate by the city lists over 900,000 residents who live in areas in need of urban upgrading.[25] Its *Plan de Ordenamiento Territorial del municipio de Medellín* (territorial planning plan) from 2014 makes a point of not using the term *informal settlements*, but offers two classifications: areas of *mejoramiento integral* and *consolidación nivel 3*. Areas of *mejoramiento integral* are typically located higher up the mountain on the fringes of the city and tend to be younger. They are the least developed areas in the city with serious deficiencies. Areas of *consolidación nivel 3* are typically further down the mountain and have certain critical deficits of public space and other facilities. They tend to be older and more consolidated.[26]

## Rio de Janeiro

Rio de Janeiro, Brazil's second-largest city, is renowned as much for its astonishing topography as for its exuberant cultural life. Spread over some 1,200 square kilometers along Guanabara Bay and the Atlantic Ocean, it encompasses extensive beaches and the mountainous Tijuca National Park, a restored rainforest that is among the largest urban parks in the world. More than six million people live in the city, in its

**Figure 13** Rio de Janeiro: the white patches show favelas as listed by the Instituto Pereira Passos (2016 outlines)

metropolitan region around 13 million (2020).[27] The city keeps a detailed record of its favelas, with official maps of location and sizes of favelas publicly available. Official numbers list about 1.4 million residents in 763 favelas inside Rio's city limits.[28] A 2010 census established that, for the metropolitan region, 1.7 million, or about 14%, of the residents live in informal neighborhoods.[29] In size, favelas can range from 500 to 70,000 residents. Some of these settlements are on the urban peripheries; others occupy prime sites near the city's landmarks – a number of them have colonized the national park and overlook the ocean at Copacabana and Ipanema. Like many cities, Rio experienced rapid informal development after the Second World War.

## São Paulo

São Paulo is one of the most populous cities in the southern hemisphere. Inside its city limits live around 12 million residents; its metropolitan area is home to about 22 million people (2020) and covers an area of roughly 8,500 square kilometers.[30] Located at an average elevation of around 800 meters (2,625 ft) – though at a distance of only about 70 kilometers (43 miles) from the Atlantic Ocean – the urbanized area ranges from floodplains to mountainsides. As always, numbers vary by source, but, according to an official 2010 census, 1.3 million out of São Paulo's 11 million residents lived in 1,020 favelas.[31] In the whole metropolitan region, an

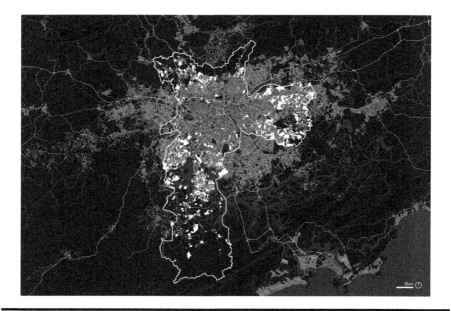

Figure 14 São Paulo: the white patches combine three classifications created by the municipality of São Paulo: favela, *loteamento irregular* (irregular settlement) and *núcleo* (favelas with water/sewerage/lighting infrastructure) from 2017

estimated 2.1 million residents, or about 10%, lived in *setores subnormais* (subnormal clusters).[32] Per its definition, a subnormal cluster in São Paulo consists of 51 or more housing units characterized by the absence of title deeds and at least one of these characteristics: irregularity of pathways and the size and shape of lots and/or lack of essential public services.[33]

Some favelas are dispersed throughout the city, but most of them are at the fringes of the metropolis. They can be found especially on steep slopes, around reservoirs and along rivers. The city keeps good records of its urban conditions; official maps of size and locations of its *setores subnormais* are publicly available.

## Instances

The following series of graphics highlights some aspects of informal neighborhoods in Latin America.

### Settlement Process

In the formal city, development typically follows a pattern in which land title is secured, services are installed, construction occurs, and occupation is finally achieved. Development in the informal city reverses this pattern: land is occupied, sometimes

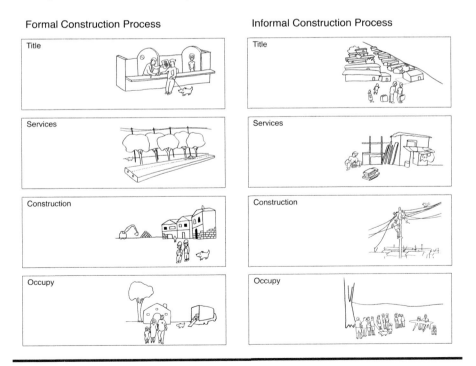

**Figure 15** Divergent settlement processes

even before any building occurs; when construction happens, it is often incremental and prolonged; services – if they ever arrive – are later negotiated and retrofitted; and land titles – if they are ever secured – come last.

## *Occupation Types*

### *Informal Occupation*

Informal occupation can occur through individual or organized groups. Individual squatting is an incremental process and often occurs in close proximity to existing informal neighborhoods. Group invasions are typically planned and can occupy larger tracts of land. The upper image in Figure 16 shows public land invaded in 2013 by a group of 3,000 residents in the hills of Medellín.

### *Informal Subdivision*

Informal subdivisions occur when developers informally occupy land, divide it into parcels and sell it to families who cannot afford to buy a house or rent a decent apartment in the formal real estate market. Once families have built their own houses, they still lack basic services as they find themselves in an official "no build" zone.

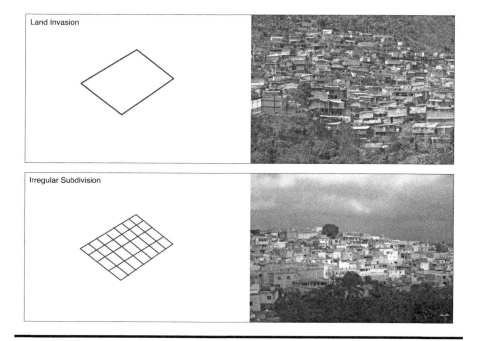

**Figure 16 Types of informal occupation**

Informal Neighborhoods ■ 19

After making themselves heard to the authorities, these areas are sometimes retrofitted with electricity, water, sewerage and roads by the municipality (something that the developers and residents actually count on). The lower image in Figure 16 shows Canthino do Céu, an irregular subdivision of 30,000 located in the sensitive watershed of the Billings reservoir of São Paulo.

## *Size*

Informal settlements can vary from small neighborhoods to sizable cities. Population numbers are fairly dynamic; exact census numbers are hard to come by, sometimes politically motivated and are often quickly superseded by developments on the ground. In general, it makes sense to speak only in round numbers.

Smaller, often recently established, informal neighborhoods can be regularly found on the outskirts of larger, more consolidated agglomerations. Once these neighborhoods grow and become more established, they can number into the thousands. If this growth continues for a longer period of time, these neighborhoods can grow into urban districts with over tens of thousands of residents.

For example, in the north eastern hills of Medellín, one can find all stages and sizes of informal urbanization depending on their location in height. High up in the hills, one can observe the establishment of small new neighborhoods mostly

Figure 17 Varying population sizes of informal settlements

comprising civil war refugees. A little bit lower than these new formations, one can find older neighborhoods that are already in a process of urban consolidation with a mix of unpaved and paved streets. If one ventures even lower down, closer to the bottom of the valley, one enters the well-established communities of NorOriental. It comprises many neighborhoods that grew over half a century and is now one large agglomeration with tens of thousands of citizens.

In Latin America's biggest cities, one can even find informal agglomerations that reach into the hundreds of thousands. Probably the largest one, Ciudad Nezahualcóyotl, or, more commonly, Ciudad Neza, in Mexico City, is estimated to have over one million residents.[34] Neza was semi-legally founded in the drained lakebed of Texcoco.

## Growth

Once an informal settlement is established, it grows either vertically or horizontally, or by crowding more families into the same space. Following the same principles as the formal city, informal areas in desirable, mostly inner-city locations, close to jobs and services, fill up pretty fast and then grow vertically; areas on the periphery tend to grow horizontally first, based on the greater availability of land. In most Latin American cities, available land has grown scarce, even on their peripheries, and there

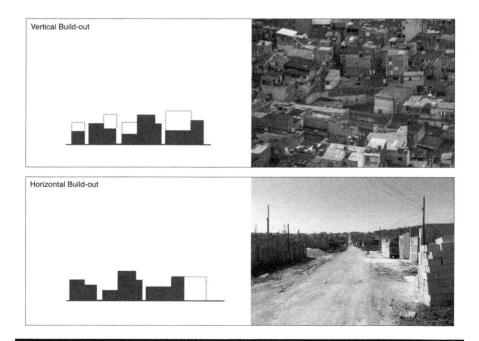

**Figure 18 Illustrating vertical and horizontal build-outs**

is a general tendency towards verticality. In some very desirable locations, such as Rocinha in Rio de Janeiro, building owners sell air rights on top of their buildings as a form of income generation.

## *Density*

The densities listed are rounded figures. Population densities for São Paulo and Manhattan were sourced from World Population Review. The density for Paraisopolis was calculated with data from *Grade Estatística e Atlas Digital do Brasil*, published by the Brazilian Institute of Geography and Statistics (IBGE, 2010).

Most informal settlements in central locations of large urban agglomerations are very dense. Highly established favelas in central locations, such as Rocinha in Rio de Janeiro or Paraisopolis in São Paulo, tend to have population densities beyond 400 inhabitants per hectare, substantially higher than, for example, Manhattan Island with roughly 270 persons per hectare. The difference in space availability becomes even larger when one considers that Brazil's favela residents live in three- to four-storey buildings compared to the high rises of Manhattan. Even peripheral favelas, such as Canthino do Céu in São Paulo, feature 190 persons per hectare, a density that is still substantially higher compared with the average density of São Paulo. However,

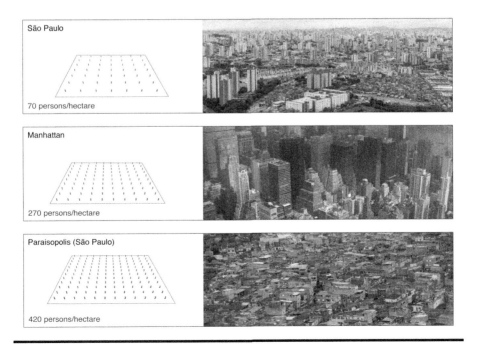

**Figure 19 Informal and formal population densities**

Latin American cities are still modestly dense compared to India's informal cities, such as the now famous Dharavi in Mumbai, with an estimated population density of over 3,000 residents per hectare.[35]

## *Landscapes*

Low-income populations are often forced to settle in areas that have been protected from formal urbanization. Most of these areas are considered unfit for development or are protected for ecological and infrastructural reasons. A majority of the settlements are in ecologically sensitive areas – floodplains and riparian areas, low ground, coastlines and marshes, steep hills and ravines. Many settlements can be in protected watersheds of reservoirs or be built on valuable farmland. Some settlements are in post-industrial landscapes, such as closed (but also open) landfills and former factories. Informal urbanization can increase the environmental risk of the terrain. For example, urbanization on steep hills increases erosion and landslide frequency, or settling in flood plains increases impermeability and, subsequently, the frequency of floods. It is the tremendous and often catastrophic force of the underlying terrain that makes informal settlements especially suitable for study and improvement from a landscape perspective.

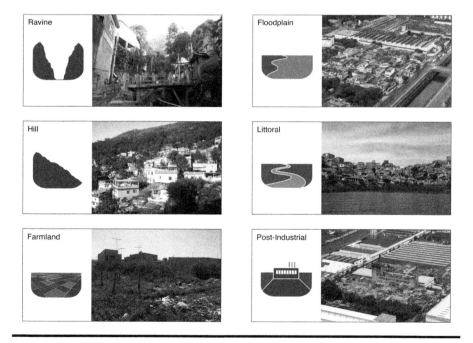

**Figure 20 Types of landscapes occupied by informal neighborhoods**

## Water

Open water is, in most informal neighborhoods, an unattractive, even threatening element. Informal urbanization typically faces away from creeks and rivers for good reasons. Many informal neighborhoods of Latin America are located in tropical and subtropical climates characterized by periods of heavy rainfall. Many settlements are prone to flooding, since the impermeability of previously open terrain can reach up to 90% and has increased runoff tremendously. In a neighborhood connected to water mains, and where residents have installed flush toilets, there is also an additional flow of untreated sewer water into the drainage basins of the watershed. Flooding problems can be exacerbated when informal housing is located at low points, flood plains of rivers or drainage basins of cities. Accordingly, the poorest settlers can be found in the low-lying parts of the terrain or along (or over) water bodies, which is very pronounced, for example, in the low-lying areas of Rocinha in Rio de Janeiro or the valleys of Paraisopolis in São Paulo. In general, there is an overabundance of polluted water, whereas clean water can be scarce. Even an irregular subdivision such as Canthino do Céu, which has been built next to one of São Paulo's largest water reservoirs, had no easy access to clean water for the greater part of its existence.

**Figure 21 Examples of drainage in informal neighborhoods**

## Streets, Alleyways, Unbuilt Public Spaces, Exteriors, Floors, Roofs, Fruits and Vegetables

Derogatory terms like "slum" do disguise valuable cultural and economic activities in informal settlements; moreover, they tend to obscure patterns of smart adaptation that make life manageable for residents of the informal city. These collected impressions hint at both the considerable variation among such communities and the many survival strategies at work within them. They reveal the provisional nature of services and economies, as well as the links between them; obtaining basic necessities is often the foundation of the informal economy. Many informal settlements begin with pirated electricity and rudimentary water and sewage connections; drinking water is typically bottled and very expensive. Transportation is improvised, often taking the form of bicycle and motorcycle taxis. Limited trash collection gives rise to informal recycling, and safety concerns generate private security operations. Heterogeneity is the norm.

Figure 22 Varying street dimensions in informal neighborhoods

## Informal Neighborhoods ■ 25

**Figure 23** Alleyways typical of informal neighborhoods

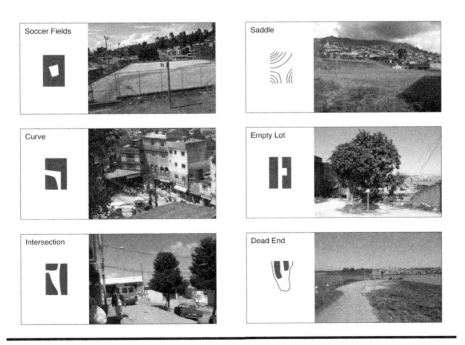

**Figure 24** Examples of unbuilt public spaces in informal neighborhoods

Figure 25 Different build-out levels of houses in informal neighborhoods

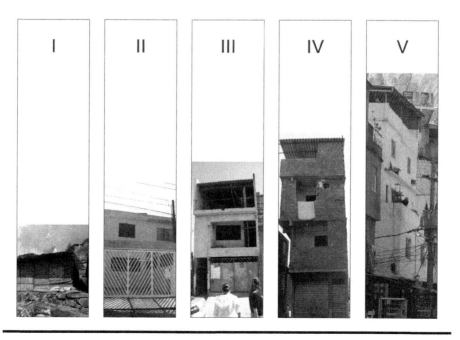

Figure 26 Number of floors of buildings in informal neighborhoods

Informal Neighborhoods ■ 27

Figure 27 Different roof types on informal neighborhood buildings

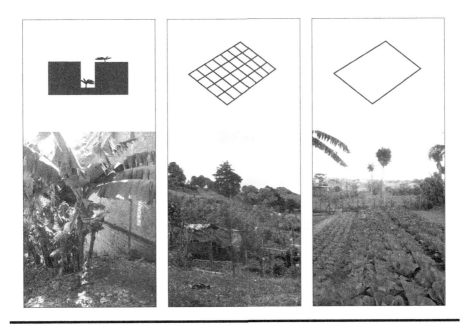

Figure 28 Examples of fruit and vegetable plots in informal neighborhoods

## Five Modes of Engagement

Throughout the last century and up to today, one can observe various modes of how governments have dealt with informal urbanization. Modes of engagement reach from denial and clearance to tolerance, improvement and anticipation. Not necessarily all cities go through all five modes, and sometimes several modes of engagement can be found in a single city.

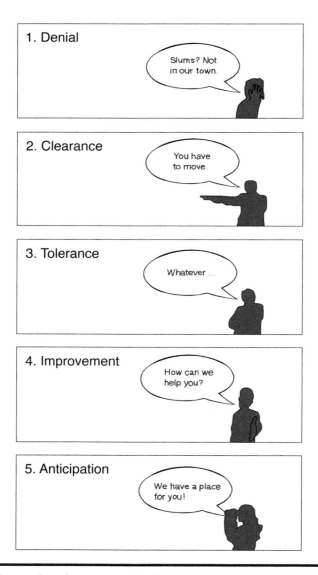

Figure 29 Five modes of engagement with informal neighborhoods

## 1. Denial

There are still many cities in the world that have enduring informal settlements that are not officially recognized. Sometimes, informal neighborhoods are not even shown on city maps (occasionally as green areas). This denial can stem from various reasons. In general, no city is proud to have informal settlements and city officials in general prefer not to highlight the fact. An official acknowledgement of informal settlements might have legal repercussions. The specific circumstance that land was invaded illegally provides an easy justification for not acknowledging it as a part of the city. In cities where denial prevails, the only official policy for informal settlements might be clearance. Some politicians are afraid that more tolerant policies will attract more informal dwellers and believe that the threat of clearance serves as the best deterrent. Every informal settlement is then seen as a temporary phenomenon that the government is obliged to eliminate at the earliest possible opportunity. In cities where denial reigns, no improvement measures are taken by the government, leaving it mostly to NGOs and religious organization to fill the gap. In the absence of funds and other interests, clearance might never happen and the settlements can go unassisted for decades. The biggest fight for informal dwellers in cities of denial is to get official acknowledgement and the right to remain.

## 2. Clearance

There can be numerous reasons for the clearance of an informal neighborhood. One very common reason is that informal neighborhoods are located in desirable locations in the city and city officials want to replace them with more profitable developments.[36]

In other cases, the municipality plans large infrastructural projects in informal areas and clears them out. When settlers build on private land, it often happens that the owner of the land forces the government to evict the settlers from the land. In other cases, authoritarian governments decide to "clean up" the city and evict illegal settlers from the land. And then there is the situation where a government has to relocate settlers who live in life-threatening areas while they are improving the area.

There is obviously a big difference between forced evictions and voluntary relocations. The worst case, where informal areas are cleared out without notice overnight and settlers are left stranded on the street are not common anymore in the democratically governed countries of Latin America, but still exist in other parts of the world. The somewhat more benign version, where informal areas are evacuated with proper notice and then relocated into government housing on the outskirts of the city (as was done in Rio de Janeiro in the 1960s), is not considered best practice anymore in Latin America. Clearance and relocation was a common practice in the 1950s, but has been largely abandoned because of the insoluble social hardship that the government housing creates for its inhabitants. When settlers were stranded far away from the city, removed from their economic and social networks of work, friends and relatives, the new housing areas deteriorated very fast into crime-infested neighborhoods.[37] Established informal settlements have today a de facto right to remain in Latin America.[38]

As a best practice, housing agencies try to avoid clearances and only undertake small-scale relocations as a last resort today.[39] They mostly occur when residents live in life-threatening areas (such as floodplains or landslides zones) or are in the way of strategically inserted infrastructure that should benefit the whole community (such as the widening of a street for emergency access or sewerage infrastructure). These relocations are only carried out with the voluntary agreement of the residents. In that case, agencies try to relocate settlers as close as possible to their former neighborhood, or provide them with funds to find housing elsewhere if the residents want to leave the neighborhood. In general, best practices for relocations are still a hotly debated topic in planning and design circles, and many different models exist.[40]

## 3. Tolerance

In the end, forced evictions of informal areas reduced due to the proliferation of self-constructed urbanization at the end of the last century. From 1950 onwards, many cities in Latin America experienced tremendous growth rates and it became clear that the governments did not have the resources to provide social housing for all the poor migrants that would eventually enter the city. Especially with regard to the strategically less important outskirts of cities, governments grew more complacent about, and sometimes complicit in, land invasions and pirate development.[41] At some point, these agglomerations were so large that plans to move them into government housing were abandoned. An attitude of sometimes grudging, sometimes benign tolerance ensued, especially for informal neighborhoods in less strategic locations or on the periphery. Some Latin American governments would make modest attempts at improving informal neighborhoods, some were just silently complicit with the informal construction activities as they knew that they could not finance proper housing anyway. This phase of tolerance was also fostered by an academic movement in the 1960s towards a respect and admiration for the capacity of the settlers to build large cities in difficult terrain in the absence of planners, engineers and government or large machinery. Urban planners such as John Turner postulated, in the late 1960s, that "slums are not the problem, but the solution"[42]. And, in 1964, the architect Bernard Rudofsky opened his highly influential exhibition, "Architecture without Architects," in New York's Museum of Modern Art, illustrating the intelligence, inventiveness and resourcefulness of self-construction.[43]

## 4. Improvement

The practice of *in situ* improvement gained traction in Latin America in the beginning of the 1980s, although the concept of it is much older; the Scottish urban planner Patrick Geddes was the first to survey informal areas in India in the 1920s and then to propose small corrections to the urban fabric for their improvement.

Up to this point, it had been the practice of British engineers to clear informal areas and overlay them with a grid of regular streets. In contrast, Geddes introduced the principle of "Conservative Surgery," eliminating a building here and there to improve mobility in tight quarters while strengthening cultural and social spaces.[44] It took almost half a century for sensitive *in situ* upgrading ideas to find more widespread application in Latin America. In the 1980s many of the governments in Latin America changed from dictatorships to democratic systems; large-scale neighborhood clearances were no longer acceptable by the residents. At that point, the first tentative attempts at improving informal areas were made on a community self-help basis. Eventually, larger programs, such as the way-finding Favela Bairro program in Rio de Janeiro, were developed in the 1990s. In these government-led projects, city officials develop a municipal framework to address citywide problems and develop potential solutions. With support from large aid agencies, such as the Inter-American Development Bank or the World Bank, governments identified project sites and affected communities. In these programs, the government is responsible for all stages of implementation, from development of support programs and hiring of consultants to financing and long-term maintenance.

In the absence of large government programs, there is *in situ* improvement carried out by many bottom-up projects on a more limited scale, initiated by designers, NGOs or the communities themselves.

In designer-driven initiatives, projects originate from research instigated by a designer or firm working with a community-based organization. Together, they identify problems, needs, and potential solutions. The designer seeks funding from aid organizations, as well as approval and implementation support from local authorities. Sometimes, a community-based organization has an idea about how to deal with a building or infrastructure problem facing the neighborhood. Recognizing that the remedy will involve outside expertise, they seek the participation of a professional designer. Together, they find the human and financial resources to develop and implement the idea.

## 5. Anticipation

It is rare to find governments that display effective strategies for responding to the likelihood of future informal settlements. The problem of providing housing for the poor is typically delegated to the housing sector; however, the original goal of the housing agencies to provide dwellings for poor migrants has not been successful in most developing countries. In the past, municipal governments which experienced a large influx of low-income dwellers simply did not have the financial means to build fully finished houses for all.

In the past, alternative models to the provision of fully finished housing have been tested. *Sites and Services* projects were introduced in the 1960s and heavily favored by the World Bank in the 1970s. Sites and services (today called owner-driven or incremental housing) was based on the idea that if a site is given and basic infrastructure is built, a guided self-construction process for the houses could stretch the funds of the city to house many more of its low-income migrants. Unfortunately, the promising sites and services approach did not easily proliferate, since buildable land was hard to come by and could often be found only at quite a distance from city centers and jobs. Municipalities also had a hard time providing and maintaining basic services, such as potable water, sewerage, electricity and waste management to the low-income settlements. The idea of sites and services defines a process and not a product and relies on a decade-long improvement process by the individual families, characterized by growth spurts but also periods of stasis. Unfortunately, too, the long time spans needed to assess success run contrary to the short time vision of funding agencies, and the sites and services approach eventually fell out of favor in the late 1970s. However, many of the sites and services projects of the 1970s have matured in the past 40 years and now display signs of success.[45] Today, sites and services thinking is experiencing a renaissance with projects such as Alejandro Aravena's much acclaimed Elemental housing proposal in Chile, or new approaches favored by the World Bank's Cities Alliance group. Urbanists such as David Gouverneur put forward urban landscape strategies that allow the managed growth of informal neighborhoods.[46]

Whether they are twenty-first-century variations of sites and services or other urban housing strategies, new approaches for ameliorating the lot of poor urban settlers are in high demand. It is obvious that better solutions have to be found that enable sustainable living standards for future urban populations that do not have the means to afford a dwelling in the formal housing sector.

## Notes

1. The discussion around the usage of the term *slum* remains controversial. Claudio Acioly, a former representative of UN-Habitat, points out that UN-Habitat defends the continued use of the word "slum" despite all the controversies and pejorative attributes it brings from Victorian London times. The term is based on the operational definition internationally agreed upon by experts, governments and representatives of NGOs in expert group meetings when defining the metrics to monitor the Millennium Development Goals. Besides, the word brought a political and morally explosive issue to the international development agenda. This definition led the data collection and has influenced the statistical basis of multiple censuses carried out by national governments. Acioly rightly points out that even an important association that safeguards the interest of residents of informal neighborhoods like SDI (Slum Dwellers International) prominently features the term in its name and policy documents.
2. UN-Habitat, "State of the Worlds Cities 2006/7, Slums: some definitions," http://mirror.unhabitat.org/documents/media_centre/sowcr2006/SOWCR%205.pdf (accessed August 25, 2020).
3. To give a specific example, in 2010 I asked a mother of two from Rocinha, one of the largest favelas of Rio de Janeiro, what her biggest problems were. It was not finances, nor the violence of drug gangs or frequent flooding of the favela. It was noise; the

constant din from neighboring houses and apartments, young people partying well into the night, couples arguing, or teenagers having their stereos on full blast. Given the levels of violence and crime in Rio's favelas, it seemed to me at first like an unusual answer.

4. Conversation with Moises Lino da Silva, anthropologist who had lived in Rocinha as part of his doctoral field work, 2010.

5. Eckhart Ribbeck and Sergio Padilla, *Die informelle Moderne: Spontanes Bauen in Mexico-City* (Heidelberg: awf-Verlag, 2002).

6. It is ironic that irregular subdivisions do have similarities to the way-finding *Sites and Services* approach promulgated by John Turner and the World Bank in the 1960s. There the strategy was to provide settlers with properties and basic infrastructure to enable them to build their own houses as part of the legal framework of city planning.

7. UN-Habitat, *World Cities Report 2016: Urbanization and Development – Emerging Futures* (Nairobi: UN-Habitat, 2016)

8. And they are still coming. While the proportion of slum dwellers has gone down from 33% to 24% between 1990 and 2010 in Latin America, the absolute numbers have increased by five million, due to urban growth. UN-Habitat, *State of Latin American and Caribbean Cities 2012: Towards A New Urban Transition* (Nairobi: UN-Habitat, 2012), 65.

9. Ibid., 12.

10. For example, Colombia, Nicaragua and Peru have reduced the number of people without adequate housing by a quarter from 1990 to 2007. Ibid., 65.

11. Personal conversation with Regina Meyer, University of São Paulo, 2007.

12. The journalist Robert Neuwirth describes the experience of meeting a millionaire who lives in Rocinha, one of the largest favelas in Rio de Janeiro. Robert Neuwirth, *Shadow Cities: A Billion Squatters, A New Urban World* (New York: Routledge, 2016)

13. For example, gentrification processes have been observed in the centrally located neighborhood of Morro da Prôvidencia, the oldest favela in Rio de Janeiro. Einar Braathen et al., "Rio de Janeiro: favela policies and recent social mobilizations," Norwegian Institute for Urban and Regional Research, 2013, www.hioa.no/content/download/130716/3566290/file/2013-110.pdf (accessed August 25, 2020).

14. The UN-Habitat report "State of Latin American and Caribbean Cities 2012" states that "Shopping malls are becoming the main public spaces for socializing." In UN-Habitat, *State of Latin American and Caribbean Cities*, 59.

15. For example, Global Change Data Lab, "Our World in Data – Urban population living in slums, 2014," https://ourworldindata.org/grapher/urban-slums-total (accessed August 25, 2020).

16. UN-Habitat, *The Millennium Development Goals Report* (Nairobi: UN-Habitat, 2015), 11.

17. UN-Habitat, *Slum Almanac 2015–16: Tracking Improvement in the Lives of Slum Dwellers* (Nairobi: UN-Habitat, 2016). United Nations (2015), see also *The Millennium Development Goals Report* (Nairobi: UN-Habitat, 2015), 61.

18. United Nations, "2018 revision of world urbanization prospects," 2018.

19. UN-Habitat, *Slum Almanac*, 2.

20. The maps originated in a Master course led by John Beardsley at the Harvard Graduate School of Design in 2008 and were updated and reworked at the Institute of Landscape Architecture at Leibniz University Hannover by Nick Bonard in 2014 and Leonie Wiemer in 2020.

21. World Population Review, "Buenos Aires Population 2020," https://worldpopulationreview.com/world-cities/buenos-aires-population (accessed August 25, 2020).

22. Instituto Nacional de Estadística y Censos (INDEC), *Censo Nacional de Población y Viviendas 2010*, Ministerio de Economía, República Argentina, Buenos Aires.
23. Metodología TECHO, "Unidad de análisis," http://relevamiento.techo.org.ar/metodologia.html (accessed September 29, 2020).
24. World Population Review, "Medellin Population 2020," https://worldpopulationreview.com/world-cities/medellin-population (accessed April 23, 2021).
25. Number was calculated by cross-referencing information between treatment areas according to Agreement 48 of 2014 (Concejo de Medellín, 2014) and the population data in the Sisben registry (Sisben, 2018).
26. Alcaldia de Medellín, *Acuerdo 46 de 2006*, Articles 242 and 243.
27. World Population Review, "Rio de Janeiro Population 2020," https://worldpopulationreview.com/world-cities/rio-de-janeiro-population
28. Instituto Brasileiro de Geografia e Estatistica, *Censo Demográfico 2010: "Aglomerados subnormais: Informações territoriais,"* 2010.
29. Ibid.
30. World Population Review, "São Paulo Population 2020," https://worldpopulationreview.com/world-cities/sao-paulo-population (accessed April 23, 2021).
31. Elisabete França, "Slum upgrading: a challenge as big as the city of São Paulo," *Focus* 10(1): Article 20, 75.
32. Instituto Brasileiro de Geografia e Estatistica, *Censo Demográfico*, 2010.
33. Ibid.
34. City Population, "Nezahualcóyotl," www.citypopulation.de/php/mexico-admin.php?adm2id=15058 (accessed August 25, 2020).
35. MIT, "Density Atlas," www.densityatlas.org/casestudies/profile.php?id=120 (accessed September 29, 2020).
36. For example, in 2011 there was strong pressure to relocate residents of the massive informal settlement Dhavari in Mumbai to make way for high-rise development. Dhavari is centrally located in the city and a hot object for real estate speculation.
37. The famous Cidade de Deus (City of God) is one of these examples of a government housing project far away from the center of Rio. Without access to jobs, City of God was notorious for gang activity and made famous by the film of the same name.
38. UN-Habitat, *State of Latin American and Caribbean Cities*, 2012, 10.
39. Elisabete França, former leader of the Social Housing Unit in São Paulo, made the argument that not more than 6% of a neighborhood should be relocated in order to avoid deep disturbance (personal communication, 2008).
40. For example, the residents of Morro da Providência in Rio de Janeiro did not trust a municipal study that declared a large proportion of the houses at geological risk and up for relocation. The residents hired their own engineers, who made a counter assessment. For more information see Einar Braathen, "Ups and downs in Rio de Janeiro: the changing phases of mobilisation in Morro da Providência," in *The Politics of Slums in the Global South Urban Informality in Brazil, India, South Africa and Peru*, ed. Véronique Dupont, David Jordhus-Lier, Catherine Sutherland and Einar Braathen (Abingdon: Routledge, 2015).
41. The history of Medellín is an example of this phase of tolerance where, in the 1960s, strategically located small non-formal neighborhoods in the center of the city were evicted, while large informal settlements on the periphery of the city were grudgingly tolerated.
42. Michael Cohen, "John F. C. Turner and 'Housing as a verb'." *Built Environment* 41(3) (2015), 412–418.

43. Bernard Rudofsky, *Architecture Without Architects: A Short Introduction to Non-pedigreed Architecture* (Albuquerque: UNM Press, 1987).
44. Jaqueline Tyrwhitt, *Patrick Geddes in India* (London: Lund Humphries, 1947).
45. MIT Professor Reinhard Goethert has systematically revisited some of these settlements in Latin America with his research group, SIGUS. http://web.mit.edu/incrementalhousing/articlesPhotographs/laPresitaSurveys.html (accessed August 25, 2020).
46. David Gouverneur, *Planning and Design for Future Informal Settlements* (New York: Routledge, 2015).

# LESSONS FROM LATIN AMERICA

# Case Study I

## Buenos Aires – Step by Step

Argentine designers Flavio Janches and Max Rohm have been working in the informal settlements, or *villas de emergencia*, of Buenos Aires since 2000. They have focused on the potential of public space to improve the social, environmental and economic operations of the informal city. Public space, they insist, is crucial to rituals of citizenship in the polis as a locus of cultural, political, economic and recreational

Figure 30 Opening day of the playground in Villa Tranquila (image from 2010)

life. Readily accessible public space is not, however, available to *villa* residents (*villa* is the Argentinian term for low-income neighborhood). By addressing the interstitial areas within and around informal settlements, they hope to generate new forms of public space that serve as starting points for the revitalization of the villas and their integration with the rest of the city.

## Villa Tranquila

### Situation

Around 2004, Janches and Rohm focused their attention on Villa Tranquila, a 25-hectare settlement of about 7,000 people in the municipality of Avellaneda, just south of downtown Buenos Aires.[1] The settlement sprang up in the mid 1940s and increased in size because of the successive economic crises experienced by Argentina during the past 60 years.

Prior to the implementation of the municipal government's urbanization plan, Villa Tranquila was one of the most dangerous areas of Buenos Aires, with staggering violence and crime indexes. Though the situation has since improved considerably, it is still the largest emergency settlement in Avellaneda, and, consequently, a center for the production and dealing of drugs.

Cut off from the capital by the Riachuelo River (also known as the Matanza River), and further isolated from downtown Avellaneda by a district of abandoned

**Figure 31 Villa Tranquila (image from 2008)**

**Figure 32 Villa Tranquila (image from 2008)**

warehouses, the villa is characterized by the unusual extent of both its social and spatial isolation. Being flood-prone and punctuated by wetlands, its marginalization is only compounded by the flat topography and proximity to the river. Geographer David Keeling described his visit in 1996 to a typical villa along the Reconquista River, similarly polluted to the Riachuelo River, in no uncertain terms: "Stagnant water and untreated sewage created an overpowering stench, and the entire area was overrun with rats, mosquitos, flies and other insects."[2] The villa also had the more typical problems of inadequate housing, sanitation, and underemployment. A plant formerly operated by Unilever stands idle at the heart of the neighborhood, and unemployment hovered at about 50%.

The city had begun construction of new housing in the settlement; it had also proposed redeveloping the redundant Unilever facility as a community center and reopening a rail line to link the villa directly with downtown Buenos Aires. Other than the opening of a few dead-end streets, it had not, until then, addressed the role of landscape or public space in considering the community's improvement.

## *Intervention*

With the help of residents, students and municipal officers, the designers developed a network of open spaces that strategically redistributed playgrounds and social spaces within abandoned properties. With children and young adults comprising more than half of Villa Tranquila's current population, Janches and Rohm's strategy was based on a socio-spatial conversion predicated on the transformative energies of the settlement's youth. The designers believe that the act of playing in its various forms (whether recreational, cultural or competitive) and at different ages (from toddler to young adult) in the context of public space is a major catalyst for peaceful coexistence in fragmented and marginalized communities. Janches and Rohm cite Dutch architect Aldo van Eyck, who built a network of 700 playgrounds in Amsterdam following the Second World War as a triage to re-civilize a devastated city, as a precedent.

Accordingly, the duo strategically located new public spaces along major travel routes adjacent to commercial or cultural buildings or other places with pre-existing programs. They designed the spaces so as to have them relate to existing community groups and neighborhood institutions in the vicinity, such as churches and sport clubs. They describe this network not as being fixed, but, rather, as an open framework for dynamic locations and programs, subject to development and change through time. Thus, theirs is not a prescriptive strategy, but a descriptive one that indicates possible locations for public spaces that might be utilized on the basis of community interest and funding. In this process, they expected that the first of these built public spaces would trigger a transformation process by gradually altering the population's social habits in the realm of public space. Their aspiration was (and still is) that this ever-so-slightly tweaked society would set in motion new social demands to activate the program, its frequency and locations, on a subsequent generation of public spaces within this very network. The dynamic would then continue, so that the latest generation of projects would set the new conditions for the next one. In this manner, later public spaces will differ from the public spaces built today in ways as yet unforeseeable, dependent on the current context of their time and their spatial conditions. The final shape, exact location and specific programs of the future spaces are unknown, but ripe with possibility through the creation of a network of opportunistic adaptation, as opposed to the how-to of authoritarian determinism and speculation. In the absence of integrative government programs, Janches and Rohm's strategy relied on incremental implementation by employing a modular kit that can be adapted in size, materials and programs according to the socio-territorial conditions of the chosen place. The designers hoped that the synergy produced by the overlap of new and existing uses would reverse the process of decay, neglect and social fragmentation, and help to build a new identity for the community.[3]

In 2009, Janches and Rohm built the first of these playgrounds on a derelict 2,500 square meter parcel of land. The new playground offers a picnic and seating area, a soccer field and play equipment.

## Process

Flavio Janches and Max Rohm began the project in 2006 as an academic exercise with students from Buenos Aires, the Harvard Graduate School of Design, and the Amsterdam Architecture Academy. In addition to creating a detailed physical analysis of the area, the students conducted a series of interviews with villa residents that helped to identify the many social networks that were already operating in the villa:

community kitchens, sports facilities, educational and cultural organizations, after-school and elder care, employment cooperatives, and so on and so forth. Among other findings, they learned that children, who make up a majority of the villa's population, were especially underserved, and so those very children were given cameras and asked to document where and how they played. They were also asked about their ambitions for improving the community. Extensive site analysis and mapping of social and spatial conditions led to long-term proposals for the improvement of water quality, drainage, and transportation connectivity.

Mindful of raising expectations, and aware that it might take years to secure public funding for some of their more ambitious projects, Janches and Rohm sought to give proof of their commitment to improving the community by devising a network of public spaces – plazas, playgrounds, and connecting pathways – that could be quickly and stealthily inserted into interstitial areas throughout the settlement. Their aim was to provide cultural and market facilities together with recreational opportunities; the spaces would create links within the community and to the surrounding city. Community input was requested on decisions regarding where to locate the new spaces, and which of the available places should be selected for intervention.

Janches and Rohm sought sponsors for the funds with which to build the network, and they were ultimately able to identify a private foundation in the Netherlands dedicated expressly to the funding of playgrounds in poor areas.[4] When it became clear that the funds would be insufficient to build all of the dedicated spaces, the designers decided to concentrate the investment on one site, rather than spread it less effectively to more locations.

Figure 33 Site of envisioned playground before construction (image from 2008)

In trying to identify the optimal location for the first intervention, it became quite clear that the 7,000 inhabitants of the villa were not a homogeneous group, and that any given location would have to contend with the attendant particularities of the people and place it was set to engage. Cultural and social differences existed between sometimes opposing factions, so that some children were not allowed to play in certain areas. The designers were often caught in the middle of discussions among residents, who found themselves debating the various merits and pitfalls of the areas that could potentially receive the first playground. Finally, a site adjacent to the recently opened continuation of Vicente Lopez Street, a derelict space at the edge of the villa once used to burn stolen cars, was selected. The privately owned land was bought by the municipality and officially designated as a recreational public space. Preliminary plans were then reviewed by community and recreational groups in weekly sessions. Meetings for the younger residents became particularly important. Being the first project, the final program for the small parcel of land was intensely discussed by the population in a process that, among other things, revealed its gender-specific needs. The community's soccer enthusiasts vied for a new playing field, while the female population of the villa wanted more public spaces for girls to play in, with a special emphasis on young mothers wanting areas for toddlers to safely enjoy under their supervision. The final design was a reflection of diverse desires accommodated in a fairly small space.

**Figure 34 Playground shortly before completion (image from 2010)**

The next challenge was to find a contractor who was willing to work in Villa Tranquila. Many refused: the area was perceived as being too dangerous. Eventually, a local cooperative that screened and hired construction workers from the community itself was initiated. Accepting the challenge of identifying appropriate contractors as an important lesson for the future, the designers ultimately found that the obstinacy of the large construction firms worked in their favor, as direct involvement of the local workforce helped to better root the project within its own community. Supervised by the public works department of Avellaneda, the cooperative built the basic structures of the space, such as the substructure, foundations and concrete work. The designers reached out to members of the community, people from neighboring dwellings who were sometimes seconded by their children, and asked for their help on some of the work that did not demand skilled labor, such as the installation of the playground equipment, the planting of trees and painting. This proved to be yet another strategic action that brought the community into closer alignment with the project. Throughout the process, the key to success for Janches and Rohm was to stay in close contact with the community and to react and adapt quickly to the changing circumstances: this alone brought up myriad unexpected alternatives that ultimately served the project. They cite, as an example of this, a group of teenagers who approached the designers with the proposal to paint a mural on a large wall beside the playground: the mural was the first element to actually appear on the site, and in the eyes of the general population, it came to symbolize the transformation of the hitherto abandoned land into a civic space before anything else was completed.

## Post-intervention

Within the time that has elapsed since its completion (2009), the designers report that the new playground has gained very fast acceptance by the residents. It has been widely perceived not as something novel, but rather like something that has always been there. In a survey conducted a couple of months after the inauguration of the playground, a full 90% of the interviewed residents said they believed the plaza had promoted greater interaction amongst neighbors and that people from other parts of Villa Tranquila were visiting the area. The new public space was populated by people of all ages, and it has given the children of the area a relatively secure space in which to play. A group of neighbors that helped throughout the process were paid a basic salary by the municipality to work part-time cleaning, conducting repairs and preventing vandalism on the site. The new public space has already created synergy with the surrounding buildings: adjacent to the playground, a small children's library has been opened for working parents to drop off their children.

Daniel O. is one of the residents responsible for the maintenance of the playground in Plaza Vicente Lopez. He observed that on most afternoons one could easily find 150 children from all over the neighborhood, not just the areas immediately

Figure 35 Playground shortly after completion (image from 2010)

adjacent to the park. Seeing how the plaza helped transform the neighborhood into a safer place led Daniel to initiate the creation of a smaller gated plaza in the neighborhood – one that could be used by younger children (ages one to six) who did not have a place to play in Plaza Vicente Lopez. In both cases, the plazas' success is owed not only to what they add to the neighborhood in the form of gathering and play spaces, but what they subtract. Prior to becoming a playground, Plaza Vicente Lopez was a derelict vacant lot where stolen cars were burned and residents disposed of their trash.[5]

Since the construction of the first Plaza (Plaza Vincente Lopez) in Villa Tranquila, the Playspace Foundation (formed by Janches and Rohm to support the first project), has completed another plaza in Villa Tranquila (Plaza Daniel), together with a third, Plaza Pinzón. The foundation has also expanded its sphere of influence to other areas of Buenos Aires, and is now involved in the process of bringing public spaces to Villa Independencia in the district of San Fernando, and Barrio Pinazo in the district of Pilar, both in the metropolitan area of the city of Buenos Aires, with the help of the local municipal governments and academic research from Carleton University and the Berlage Institute.[6] The steady increase of public space and community interaction bodes well for Janches and Rohm's vision to transform the region through small-scale interventions.

**Figure 36 Playground on opening day (image from 2010)**

## Conclusion

The Janches–Rohm approach is simultaneously a pragmatic and spirited reaction to adverse circumstances. What can designers do in the face of scant government oversight, uncoordinated municipal agencies, next to zero budget, fractured factions of clients and no salary? Janches and Rohm found their particular way into solving the problem by reaching out to a variety of groups and entities to their strategic advantage. They used academia to analyze the situation and develop critical ideas; they built upon the basic public works of the city and their own experience; they used the various community groups to define and build the project; they found money from outside sources. The two had to play many roles: besides being designers, they also had to play the parts of social workers, fundraisers and community organizers in such a way that they were ultimately able to develop an operational approach that reflected the means of solving the problems inherent to the situation. Their strategy of additive implementation of small-scale projects over large periods of time is not unique to the Villa Tranquila project, but is used by many activist practices and small nongovernmental organizations.[7] Its advantages are obvious: smaller projects are easier to fund in the absence of big donors; mistakes remain limited in scope and amenable to correction at a later point. Construction phases tend to be quick, with less disruption to the daily lives of the inhabitants. Small projects discourage preconceived and generic designs in favor of uniquely tailored solutions that are anchored to the needs of the community. A manageable project size further allows that same group of designers to become deeply involved in every aspect of the process. The incremental implementation of small projects over long periods of time allows for the organic induction of new projects into the daily life of the community. In the long term, the designers can become intimately familiar with the community and increasingly capable of addressing its changing needs and situations as they arise. When firmly grounded in the reality of a population's requirements, small-scale operations also tend to favor decentralized solutions that can be more effectively maintained than large-scale systems. Given the volatile conditions of the informal city, whether one pursues the creation of public space, urban agriculture or youth education, small-scale decentralized projects offer many substantial advantages.

**Figure 37  Envisioned network of playgrounds in Villa Tranquila, by Flavio Janches and Max Rohm (drawing from 2008)**

One must also ask if the work of Janches–Rohm will have an impact beyond the 7,000 residents of Villa Tranquila who already enjoy it. The admirable work of a small design practice in the absence of a coordinated government approach clearly fills a gap in Buenos Aires, but can it address larger environmental or infrastructural problems? In the case of Villa Tranquila, the small project was not able to mitigate the problems of flooding and water pollution that plague the area. One can rightfully question the limited impact of small-scale incremental approaches in comparison to broader government initiatives such as *Favela Bairro* in Rio or *Social Urbanism* in Medellín, both of which affect hundreds of thousands of people. In each of these sites, veritable armies of social workers, engineers, administrators and designers coordinate the construction of public spaces, attack larger systemic environmental problems of drainage, sewage and erosion; build large-scale transportation infrastructure, and run governmental programs in education, recreation and culture. They build hundreds of playgrounds per year, so how do a few playgrounds in Buenos Aires compare?

Clearly, a well-run government initiative can have an impact on a larger scale and at many levels, but, unfortunately, these initiatives are quite rare to find. Essential qualities that make large municipal programs beneficial, such as long-term political will, a capable administration, independent funding and strong planning and design capacities, rarely align. Instead of waiting for the perfect set-up, the design profession is required to act under less-than-perfect conditions in order to set the stage for more coordinated efforts.[8] Indeed, most large integrative initiatives, such as Rio's Favela Bairro or Medellín's PUI programs, began as small-scale projects led by pioneering groups of designers, whose methods were then tested in larger agglomerations and further refined. In the end, each government program developed the methods with which it would address the various types of informal city in its area: once a successful mode of operation was found, it was mostly a matter of organizing, refining and reproducing it. Informal city projects cannot be fairly measured by the quality and quantity of built products, but, rather, in terms of how they operate; that is, how well they were implemented, how they improved community life (which, because hard to measure, is rarely done) as well as the whole city and its environment. In the absence of an integrative government approach, Janches and Rohm developed their particular method for informal city upgrading in Buenos Aires, with Villa Tranquila as their prototype. Its particular merit is based on taking on the informal city's youth as the vehicle for the entire settlement's improvement.

## Project Credits

Designers: Blinder Janches & Co., architects
Architect: Max Rohm
Construction and management: Municipality of Avellanda
Sponsorship: Playspace Foundation, Rotterdam, the Netherlands

# Notes

1. Statistics are from a municipality report in 2004, as cited in Janches, 2012. Municipality of Avellaneda, *Villa Tranquila. Programa de urbanizacion de la Municipalidad de Avellaneda*, Decreto Municipal N. 565-04 del 23-08-04 y ratificado por ordenanza N. 17705 del 10-09-04, 2004.
2. David J. Keeling, *Buenos Aires: Global Dreams, Local Crises*, World Cities Series (New York: Wiley, Vol. 49, 1996), 102–105.
3. Flavio Janches, "Significance of public space in the fragmented city: designing strategies for urban opportunities in informal settlements of Buenos Aires City," *Working Paper 2011/13* (World Institute for Development Economics Research, 2011), 12.
4. PlaySpace Foundation, "Tranquila," www.youtube.com/watch?v=6ybJ8sCiV2Y (accessed August 25, 2020).
5. Flavio Janches, *Public Space in the Fragmented City: Strategy for Socio-physical Urban Intervention in Marginalized Communities* (Buenos Aires: Nobuko, 2012).
6. PlaySpace Foundation, "Tranquila," www.youtube.com/watch?v=6ybJ8sCiV2Y (accessed August 25, 2020).
7. See also the incremental work of the Konkuey Initiative in Kibera, Nairobi, www.kounkuey.org/projects/kibera,_public_space_project_network (accessed August 25, 2020).
8. Actually, small-scale, step by step initiatives are most likely to be the dominant improvement model of the developing world.

# Interview with Flavio Janches (FJ) and Max Rohm (MR)

## Interviewer: John Beardsley (JB)[1]

**JB:** When did you start working in *villas* [Argentinian term for low-income neighborhood], and why?

**FJ:** We started trying to understand slums after the Argentine economic crisis of 2001. We researched the issues: their urban condition; how settlements originated; how they survived the economic crisis; what the opportunities for urban transformation were; what similar experiments had been undertaken elsewhere, etc.

**JB:** Was your involvement a matter of architects – that is, of you as designers – trying to find meaningful work for yourselves, or was it a response to the conditions of the slums themselves?

**FJ:** I think it was not just "we" as designers, but also as teachers and researchers who were trying to articulate questions and answers for pressing contemporary questions.

**JB:** Was it apparent to everyone that the slums were growing; or were the conditions the same and slums merely a new research interest?

**FJ:** It was not just that the slums were growing. One of the main problems at that time was that lower middle-class people began to lose their jobs and, because of this, their homes. In some cases the slum was the only alternative for them to find a place in which to live.

**JB:** So the economic crisis made the presence of slums and the life conditions in them more vivid in everyone's mind?

**FJ:** Yes. It was possible to understand the conflict because informality started to find its way into the city: the *cartoneros* [discarded cardboard and other recyclable trash collectors] are the best example of how informality and formality began to be socially and physically interdependent.

**52** ■ *Part II*

**JB:** How did you find your way to the Villa Tranquila, or why did you pick that particular settlement?

**FJ:** The first criterion for us to pick a site was related to the necessity of having a connection with its community. The second condition was the status of land-ownership, because it was essential for us to work in a place that was not in a legal conflict; the third was to have access to information about the site from the municipality. We started our research in a slum north of the metropolitan area of Buenos Aires, in Villa Las Flores.

**JB:** Near the university?

**FJ:** It is not far. We started to work in this location because it was a small settlement and, as such, its physical and social conditions were easier for us to understand. We also had the contacts that allowed us to get into the place and access information. Our second case study was Villa Tranquila in the municipality of Avellaneda, south of the city of Buenos Aires. We chose to work in this settlement because a colleague introduced us to the mayor and this allowed us to have access to a great deal of information, already developed by the municipality, not just in terms of numbers or physical conditions, but also regarding people and the social dimension of the place. Through the municipality's social workers, we were able to interact with and meet many neighborhood residents.

**JB:** So the municipality had already done a census and a map of the settlement?

**FJ:** Yes, because at that time – and today still – it was working on an infrastructure and housing project for the area, and of course, this produced a lot of data. Another important condition in choosing a site was its possibilities for transformation because first, as we said, most of the land belonged to the municipality and so there would be no legal conflicts; second, the place could withstand transformation without moving people; and third, it had a manageable scale, in terms of population and of surface area.

**MR:** We sought out places that opened up the possibility of working with the academic realm before any actual interventions were made. So, these studies were planned as academic experiments and then, over time, the possibility of realizing the project began to surface.

**JB:** Speaking of your relationships with people, how did you manage your contacts in the community? Who were your leads into Villa Tranquila?

**FJ:** Our first contact was, of course, was the municipality. The social workers, planners, and other experts who were working there introduced us to the settlement community. From that point on, we started to meet a lot of people from the villa and from NGOs who supplied us with new information more related to the everyday activities through which the inhabitants experience their urban environment.

**JB:** What sort of organizations were your contacts in the community?

**FJ:** Community leaders, religious groups, sports clubs, dining rooms, etc.

**MR:** These programs, like dining rooms for children, attend to some of the most urgent needs of the poorest members of the community, and they are fully or

## Interview with Flavio Janchez & Max Rohm ■ 53

partly funded by the municipality. They are managed by organizations that oftentimes consist of just two or three very proactive neighbors.

**JB:** Is there anything like a formal or informal network of community leaders or neighborhood captains?

**MR:** There are, of course, leaders of the institutions that organize activities in the neighborhoods, and often they become the automatic representatives of the community, the ones who have a relationship with the municipal government. The municipality contacts them, for example, when it wants to bring visitors to the settlement or when it wants to organize any kind of a special event.

**FJ:** There are two types of institution in the *barrio* [neighborhood]; the formal and the informal ones. The formal institutions belong to the government and are therefore "external," coming from the government to work in the slum. An example of this is *envión* – the word means to give someone a friendly push to get them to start something – a program that focuses on teenagers by helping them finish their school studies and giving them diverse technical training, as well as sport and social recreation. Then you have the informal instances that relate directly to residents who create social institutions tailored to attend to the most urgent and tangible needs of the settlement.

**JB:** And those are sports clubs and kitchens, and so forth?

**FJ:** Yes, and there are also many small churches, like Evangelist ones, that not only serve the purpose of worship but also provide places for social exchange and activism.

**JB:** Are the Evangelists involved in pushing the government for improvements?

**FJ:** Yes, they serve as a means of social demand to ask the government for help.

**JB:** What were the particular urban and environmental challenges you met in the villa?

**MR:** Environmentally, there was the matter concerning the flooding of the site, which sits on low land, with some areas in it even being former wetlands. You also have sewage and stormwater management problems that are actually very difficult to address because the villa is below the annual flood line. The urban challenges are mainly related to the social fragmentation that more generally affects these settlements.

**JB:** Was your intention to generate a whole range of large-scale urban design strategies, or was it to focus on public space? Was it both?

**FJ:** The integration of the people of the settlement with the rest of the city is a key issue we want to work with.

**JB:** Do you refer to physical and social integration?

**FJ:** Both.

**JB:** Was your goal, then, to work at a sort of large-scale environmental design level, or more at the level of public space?

**MR:** We are working at a smaller scale in different spaces, and the idea is to eventually generate a series of small public spaces that can become interconnected. So, in a sense, it's working with small spaces that would, in conjunction, generate larger change as time goes by. It is a kind of mix of small-scale intervention embed-

**54** ■ *Part II*

ded in a broader strategy that eventually grows into a large-scale intervention. Though maybe it would not be regarded as large-scale in relation to surface area, but more in terms of the social effect that it could have. We think, or we hope, that it could really help in regard to what Flavio was saying about integration, and not just with the formal city, but also within the villa itself.

**JB:** There's fragmentation within the villa?

**FJ:** Yes, a lot.

**MR:** From one street to the other you actually have residents who are fighting with one another because they think that some people are more fortunate and connected and therefore more privileged, and no small part of the violence that transpires in the Villa is related to this sort of struggle. The kids that are honored in the mural that you saw lost their lives in incidents related to different forms of violence within the settlement.

**JB:** So the public space truly becomes emblematic of an effort to integrate groups within the community, but also to integrate the community with the surrounding city?

**FJ:** We have a general strategy to dig deeply into three levels of social relations. The first is that between the formal city and the informal city, so we find places and programs at the edge of the slum that can break the barriers between both. The second involves distributing places and programs within the settlement, to help reverse the internal fragmentation that plagues Villa Tranquila. The third component that we wanted to develop was a network of very small public spaces relating to groups or families, so as to help them build their own communal environment.

**MR:** That's very important; the project needs to accommodate the possibility of many types of social spaces. It is an additive process: the network is generated over time, as spaces become available for intervention.

**JB:** You actually involved community members in identifying the spaces, but also in preliminary design work?

**FJ:** We did. To choose a space for intervention we first analyzed the possibility of incorporating it into the greater urban strategy. Then we worked with the people who lived near and next to the future public space, not just because they will be its main users, but also because they will ultimately become its managers and keepers. So we showed them drawings with different ideas, and they gave us their feedback, changing our proposal in terms of adapting, adding or abandoning those first inputs.

**MR:** We identified a series of places that we thought were open or available for interventions, and then went back and talked to the neighbors, who said things like "this place may not be so good. We'd rather move it to this other place, here." A lot of compromises had to be made. With that in hand, we returned to the residents, presented the work again and they indicated further changes, so we adapted the project once more and then started working on the specific design of the spaces as we continued these exchanges with the neighbors. We also thought it would be useful for children to take photographs of themselves and their friends at play, and eventually this told us a great deal about how they used recreation sites and how they played. Basing the designs on this data, we developed sports areas and safe rest spaces for the parents or grandparents who wished to be with the children, to sit and watch them play. It was ultimately very important for us have this direct communication, to be allowed to connect with people and to make them a part of our project.

**JB:** So, you gave the children cameras and asked them to photograph where and how they played? And that helped generate the design?

**FJ:** Yes. At the time we were trying to find economic support for the project with Henk Doll, from Rotterdam. They proposed this as a participatory project. Alijd van Doorn, who organized the objectives of this activity, had developed a similar program in a Rotterdam neighborhood.

**JB:** And the particular kinds of play equipment, too?

**FJ:** Well, it's not that simple; but sometimes, yes.

**JB:** And how are you hoping to finance the construction of these spaces?

**FJ:** After many years of looking, we found a possibility – also in the Netherlands – with a group of people who were interested in finding international support for this project. We met them through Liane Lefaivre, who had researched Aldo van Eyck's playgrounds project, and Henk Doll, a Dutch architect who was working with Liane in a playground project for Rotterdam. Through my PhD adviser, Jurgen Rosemann, I met Liane and Henk and together we started to look for help to build at least part of the playground and the wider public space project. Henk in turn introduced me to a group of Dutch people who were interested in supporting the project, and so the *Playspace Foundation* was born. This gave us a platform from which to find further financial support, in the form of individuals or of other foundations from many different places: the United States, Brazil and Argentina.

**JB:** What's the relevance of Van Eyck for your work?

**FJ:** I think he's very relevant. Van Eyck was able to isolate a relatively small element of urban fabric – the playground – and transform it into a tool capable of setting into motion the recovery of a traumatized city. Because the city was not only completely destroyed but also empty, no one was using it as a public space; the war obliterated most of the social relations within it. But the project was not only Van Eyck's, it was developed by the municipality of Amsterdam beginning in 1947, and was able to create a network of more than 700 playgrounds in the city. Through kids and play, here was a way to bring the people back into the streets, so the creation of a huge network of places for city life re-established the relationship between the people and their public space. The project was also very important not just in terms of the activities it fostered, but also in terms of its methodological approach to city recovery and transformation. According to Liane, the playground network was defined by principles she has designated as participatory, interstitial and polycentric. Our project takes cues from these principles because they allow it to be flexible, adaptable and, hence, recognizable as something that may just always have been there.

**MR:** It also emphasizes the fact that you don't need large-scale projects or a master plan to generate change in the city, that you can work on a smaller scale that brings significant change over time.

**JB:** So, playgrounds can be the seed for larger redevelopment or for the humanization of the city?

**FJ:** Yes, but the playground is not the final aim of the project: the community improvements we believe can be produced through the improvement of the quality of life of the children are our main objective.

**JB:** You say upgrading projects are done differently in Brazil? Is that because the Argentine municipalities are not involved in the production of public space like they are in Brazil?

**MR:** I think one of the answers to this question is that people, for the most part, don't expressly ask for public space. They ask for housing and then they ask for infrastructure. They ask for the things that are really urgent and, in a way, public space is not; when you think about it, it does not function as a basic need. But we think that the generative process of improvement for these places has to include public space. And so, we work with municipalities that are themselves already working on basic steps like housing or infrastructure, and complement that work with public space projects.

**FJ:** For many years, Brazil has had integrative slum upgrading programs. Rio de Janeiro and São Paulo are the most well-known ones, but what made them different is that they were projects not only aimed at covering the need for housing and infrastructure, but meant to include integral strategies to improve, through public space and public facility projects, the neighborhoods' overall urban conditions. At the time, this kind of program did not exist in Buenos Aires, where we have several separate programs, some in the physical sphere, like housing and infrastructure, others in the social realm, like envión. Since then the situation has improved in Argentina, there are more official municipal, provincial and national programs for slum upgrading strategies that have been developed in the last five years. Of course, there is also a vast difference in the investment that each country is making to improve informal settlement conditions, and the difference can be seen in the results.

**JB:** Let's try to imagine the social dynamics of these play spaces themselves. Is there any danger that they'll be used by, for example, only boys and not girls, or only older children and not younger ones? How do you try to ensure that the spaces will be suitable for all children?

**FJ:** There are many types of play spaces; of course they can be defined according to age, but it is also possible to understand them with regard to the existing and proposed urban structure. After several meetings that taught us how our projects and programs were going to be used, many of our proposals were changed because we realized that we had tried to understand the area in a way that didn't account for a lot of variables. For example, in one of the meetings,

## Interview with Flavio Janchez & Max Rohm ■ 57

a group of mothers helped us understand that most of our designs were more apt for boys than for girls.

**JB:** And what was it that the mothers wanted for the girls?

**FJ:** They wanted places where the girls could meet boys but always under the mothers' watchful eyes. *[Laughter]* They also asked for games and sports that could be played together by both sexes.

**JB:** So, there are specific games that are more oriented towards girls?

**FJ:** Or mixed. The spaces should be open for everybody and should be able to be used in ways unforeseen during the design process.

**JB:** And what about getting things built in the villa? Is that a challenge?

**FJ:** That's a big challenge, and for us, a big conflict, because public space should always be built by the government. It is not possible to build public space without official agreement. If a public space is not recognized by institutions, it will not be maintained, controlled, or supported by municipal activities. So the first step was to have the project approved by the mayor and the City Council. This approval gave the project a sort of special status that made the new space legally and officially recognized. It took us a lot of time to understand the conflict, and to complete all the bureaucratic processes that we had to go through, but now we know the way to do it and the steps that need be covered to get things going. The other conflict was how to pay for the construction of the project, which is not only a financial conflict but a legal one as well, especially in terms of responsibilities assumed during and after the construction process. In order to solve this, we decided to develop only the design and to give financial support, but not to be involved directly in the construction process.

**JB:** So there's an elaborate process of negotiation with the government to secure approvals. The money basically goes to the government to pay for the building and for the construction?

**FJ:** Yes.

**JB:** And as for the contractor who builds it, are you using construction workers from within the villa, or is it an outside contractor?

**MR:** It is a mix. The contractor came with some of his own workers and also hired people from Villa Tranquila who did part of the work. We were planning to have residents build the actual play equipment, but this turned out to be too complex, so ultimately the neighbors collaborated in different tasks like the improvement of houses around the plaza, the planting of trees, simple masonry work, and the final cleaning of the site.

**JB:** So, the sense of ownership comes in part from involving community people in the construction process.

**FJ:** Yes. The construction process involved two steps. The first was the main construction and site work conducted by a construction company that agreed to hire a few residents with previous building experience. This helped develop the relationship between the company and the community. The second had the community helping in many different ways like painting, installing the play

## 58 ■ *Part II*

elements, and planting trees. Most of this work was organized by cooperatives formed by neighborhood residents.

**JB:** And how else do you guarantee a sense of ownership, or that people will protect the space?

**MR:** An important factor in that regard was the mural. A small group of artists had been working in the Villa for some time; they contacted us and proposed to paint the mural on the large empty wall at the edge of the plaza. They presented the idea to the community, and gathered a group of teenagers to design and execute the mural. These kids are from one of the most violent areas in Villa Tranquila, but they were able to generate a positive group dynamic and an outstanding work of art. The mural is an homage to the people who died in or around the plaza's site because of violence in Villa Tranquila. It provoked revalorization of the space: people started taking care of it, cleaning the future plaza site and preventing vandalism. It became a respected place, and that was really good for us because it served as a first step towards its transformation into a public space.

**JB:** It's taken you four years to research and establish connections with the community, as well as with the city; four years to raise money and to find contractors. In fact, you are still in the middle of it (2009). How do you sustain your energy, enthusiasm and commitment?

**MR:** We acknowledge it took a very long time, but it was a first attempt. We will work from this experience knowing all that we know now. We have learnt from our mistakes, especially when it came to managing funds, negotiating domain issues and interacting with the municipality, all of which are things we didn't know before. This is a one-space-at-a-time process that could eventually develop a real system of networked space. To generate something like that from scratch is impossible unless you have the full approval for both location and program from government and neighbors alike, and the money to cover the construction costs. Both of these are very difficult to obtain in contemporary Argentina. Regrettably, there was no advance of the project after the Vicente Lopez plaza was built, only a second plaza in Tranquila also supported by Playspace.

**FJ:** We never thought that we would be involved in the project for so long. When we began work here, we didn't think this project would be built at all. It started as an academic research exercise and now it has not only been developed, it has actually spawned an urban design methodology that is allowing us to open new programs and projects in different environments. Like you say, things happened very slowly, but they kept growing all the time.

**JB:** Would you recommend this idea of working through a university, starting with an academic project and trying to move it further along, to other designers?

**MR:** Yes. We actually consider this a methodology that could be taken elsewhere with the necessary site-specific adjustments. The way in which we have been working until now, starting with an academic exercise for the production of new data and proposals which are then developed in our offices, and eventually taken to the people to gauge how they react, while staying amenable to their suggestions for the improvement of our plans, makes the realization of this kind of project much more feasible.

**FJ:** I think that academic input is very important because it generates a lot of information that is more difficult to grasp if it is coming only from the government or private designers. In my view, what the students from Harvard, the University of Buenos Aires and the Architecture Academy of Amsterdam did was to open new ways of understanding the site's reality.

**MR:** Yes, and it's also interesting to see that the relationship between the residents of the villa and the students is completely different from the one they have with municipal workers, because the residents have a preconceived notion of municipal workers as people with power who are giving, or not giving, them things. They are under the impression that municipal workers are always doing them favors. With the students, it was different. The connection – the way in which people actually debated questions, and how they spoke to the students about problems – was different. I think this goes to show how vital it is to go into a place and foster lasting relationships that allow for the possibility of realizing projects and maintaining them.

**JB:** What do you imagine your next steps to be?

**FJ:** To begin with, we are trying to generate continuity in the building process. In Villa Tranquila we built two play space plazas, but we never managed to build a proposed youth center in an abandoned factory there. Through an academic project with Berlage University, we developed a project for a kilometer of linear public space in the district of San Martin. The municipality is now trying to build it and parts of it have been already built.

**MR:** We applied a basic work methodology here, and we are thinking that what's successful in Villa Tranquila could be applied to other places. At the same time, we also think that it is really important to consider that each place in which we may work will conform to a different experience, where we may only roughly have to retread some of the same big steps. Considering it took us about three years to develop the relationship with Villa Tranquila, and because of what we learned, we think it will take at least one year to generate similar relationships with other municipal governments that would ultimately allow us to build something.

**JB:** So, your goal is to take this basic framework and apply it to the other villas around Buenos Aires, but also to other cities around the country?

**FJ:** Yes.

**MR:** Exactly. I would say it is our hope that other people can apply similar methodologies elsewhere.

**JB:** It also seems as if you were interested in initiating other kinds of projects besides play spaces: what different kinds of public space would you be interested in?

**FJ:** We could be dealing with a public space or other public facilities, as long as we always focus on improvements for the youngest people in these settlements.

**MR:** So maybe libraries, educational spaces, or community spaces that help bring people together.

**60** ■ *Part II*

**JB:** So, you started with the smaller-scale projects to establish a kind of beachhead within the community, though your goal may ultimately be to address some of these larger environmental problems?

**MR:** Indeed, we are interested in the possibility of developing projects that somehow generate a relationship between design and the environment, investigating how design can actually be part of environmental improvements. The slum creates more opportunities for that than the formal city.

**JB:** So, the informal city provides a little more flexibility to address environmental problems than the formal city?

**MR:** Yes, because in the informal city, environmental problems affect people every day. For example, in Villa Tranquila and a lot of other slums near the contaminated Riachuelo River, children are starting to get sick in connection to the environmental conditions of this river.

**JB:** But at the same time managing flood control and cleaning up the Riachuelo is well beyond what you can raise money for. Do you imagine that you can, through the example of your work, pressure public agencies to make the sort of investment that is needed to address these larger environmental issues?

**MR:** I believe there will be more pressure for municipal governments to start working on larger issues. By this I am referring to the entire plan for Villa Tranquila, which includes the urbanization/housing/infrastructure project of the municipal government that we complemented with our public space project. As informal settlements become more integrated, formal city governments will be pressured to resolve the environmental issues that affect them. For example, in recent years there have been advances in plans and improvements for some of the settlements in the city, including Villa 31 in the center of the city, which has a project for major upgrading work that includes public space, infrastructure, the insertion of institutional buildings in the site, etc.

**FJ:** To clean the Riachuelo River requires not just a huge amount of money but also a joint effort between different districts, governmental institutions, communities, NGOs, private companies, communities, etc., and I think it is very difficult to influence any decisions from the vantage point of an organization that builds public spaces for kids in a slum. I don't really think that is our goal. What we are trying to do is to integrate the youth of these urban settlements through sports, games or cultural activities, in order to improve their possibilities of making the most of city life. I'm also sure that our work is not the solution to the informal settlement issue, though it certainly can be part of it.

# Note

1. Interview conducted in January 2009, revised in August 2017 and July 2020. A 2009 version of the interview was published in Flavio Janches, *Public Space in the Fragmented City: Strategy for Socio-Physical Urban Intervention in Marginalized Communities* (Buenos Aires: Nobuko, 2012).

# Case Study II

## Rio de Janeiro – Equality through Public Space

Rio de Janeiro is an excellent showcase for varying governmental approaches to informal settlements in the past century, going through phases of indifference, removal and relocation, up to slum upgrading, integration and pacification efforts.

Figure 38 Waterfront Parque Royal (image from 2010)

**62** ■ *Part II*

In the 1920s, the rise of Rio de Janeiro as an industrial city started to attract immigrants from the countryside and from abroad. As a consequence, the city began to grow very fast over the next 80 years. Although the earliest favelas date back to the mid-nineteenth century, their growth accelerated in the 1940s as low-income citizens, who were excluded from the formal housing market, started to build their own neighborhoods in left-over land, mostly unsuitable for urbanization, such as steep slopes and wetlands. In the early 1950s, the authorities began to react to these self-built neighborhoods, widely known under the term *favela*. The federal government began to relocate these citizens into public housing built on the periphery of the city. Far removed from any work opportunities, the peripheral neighborhoods rapidly deteriorated into extra-legal zones. During the dictatorship (1964 to 1985) favela removal continued as the dominant practice. Still, there were modest attempts at *in situ* upgrading. Small programs of the 1970s, such as *Mutirão Remunerado*, administered by the Municipal Social Development Secretariat *Companhia de Desenvolvimento de Comunidades* (CODESCO), assisted favela residents in building basic infrastructure. After the dictatorship, these modest efforts were the prototypes for the first large scale and widely copied program, called *Favela Bairro*, that improved favelas in the 1990s. At this point, favelas in Rio had grown massively, sometimes into agglomerations of more than 100,000 people. Removal was not a feasible (or desirable) option, due to the destruction of social networks, the widespread resistance among favela dwellers and the high relocation costs. In addition, the majority of the favelas were taken over by extra-legal forces as part of the rising international drug trade, making them virtually off-limits for outsiders, including the police. In 1995, then Mayor Maia was able to solicit a large contract with the Inter-American Development Bank, which provided US$180 million, as well as pledging US$120 million from the Rio de Janeiro government to fund a city-wide neighborhood upgrading program: Favela Bairro.[1]

By juxtaposing the terms *Favela* and *Bairro*, which mean slum and neighborhood, respectively, the program attempted to transform favelas into formal neighborhoods within the city. The program took the novel approach of accepting favelas as a new urban morphology that should not be destroyed but, rather, changed, improved, converted into a modest but livable neighborhood.[2] It aimed to integrate slums through the provision of improved infrastructure, services, housing, and public facilities, including plazas, parks, schools, sport fields, and employment and health centers. Public space especially was seen as the basis and symbol of citizenship proper, and was meant to invigorate the self-esteem of the favela residents. By retrofitting favelas with adequate streets, plazas, and public buildings, the excluded areas were prepared to become a more integral part of the surrounding city.[3]

Favela Bairro was one component of a larger urban renewal strategy that meant to address the whole city through land tenure regularization, resettlement of unsafe housing, renovation of tenement houses and new housing.[4] The program originally started with pilot projects in 16 small and mid-sized settlements of between 500 and 2,500 dwellings. It was soon expanded to more than 40 settlements, and paved the way for a second phase.[5]

Inspired by the approach, several new government-led programs were initiated in 1997. The *Bairrhino* program was started, which addressed smaller settlements with fewer than 500 dwellings and *Grandes Favelas*, which targeted larger and more complex communities with populations of up to 70,000 people.[6] Post intervention programs called POUSOs (*Postos de Orientacao Urbanistica e Social*, or Posts for Social and Urban Orientation) were created in 1996 to manage the maintenance of the various Favela Bairro projects in each favela and to monitor and consult favelas up to five years after construction work was finished. In 1999, *Célula Urbana* (Urban Cell), was founded by the municipal architects Lu Petersen and Dietmar Starke, with a focus on small-scale catalytic interventions.[7] In 2007, the federal government created yet another program (Urban PAC – *Programa de Aceleração do Crescimento*, or Acceleration Development Program) to target large favelas all throughout Brazil. In 2010, 22% of Rio de Janeiro's population still lived in *subnormal settlements*.[8] Driven by the large redevelopment plans of Rio for the World soccer Cup in 2014 and the Olympics in 2016, Favela Bairro, including the other municipal programs listed above, were phased out and replaced by another large-scale program titled *Morar Carioca* ("living as a Rio resident") in 2010. It had the ambitious goal of upgrading all of Rio's favelas by 2020 and promised to exceed Favela Bairro by better including cultural, educational and medical services together with improved participation procedures.[9] Early Morar Carioca projects went hand in hand with a federal pacification effort by the Unidade de Polícia Pacificadora (UPP) in 2008 in the build-up for the Olympic Games.[10] Despite official claims to have reached half a million people from 2010 to 2016,[11] critics assert that the hopeful Morar Carioca program never fully took off and was prematurely downsized by 2014.[12]

## Favela Bairro

Given the unsuccessful nature of the Morar Carioca program, it is more fruitful to study its predecessor program, Favela Bairro, in more detail. Its projects have now weathered more than 20 years (2020) and its long-term effects can be better observed. Moreover, Favela Bairro is frequently credited with being the first systematic favela upgrading project in Brazil that reached a citywide scale,[13] and one of the first government programs that introduced a spatially critical practice of urbanism to the issue of informal urbanization that has been followed worldwide.[14] Five years after its start in 1995, the Favela Bairro program claimed to have directly affected around 105 favelas, roughly 10% of all of Rio's favelas at the time. At its ten-year mark, 556,000 residents in 143 favelas were affected, 550 kilometers of sewerage lines, 170 hectares of streets and 60 hectares of parks and plazas, including 80 new soccer fields, were supposedly built.[15] Lessons were learnt and deficiencies identified, most notably the exaggerated focus on construction while social aspects such as community participation, education and job creation seemed to fall behind.[16]

After the first phase of projects was completed in 1999, the Development Planning Unit of University College London performed an outside evaluation of the

64 ■ *Part II*

Favela Bairro program by holding 39 interviews with residents, architects and Favela Bairro managers.[17] One of their key findings was that Favela Bairro's community participation methods left room for improvement. The report paints a portrait of good intentions not always realized by the projects.

In the beginning, the program put the onus of community participation on architects who, despite their finest efforts, were not trained for – but were rather frequently overwhelmed by – the complex task at hand. Residents were often under the impression that community participation in Favela Bairro happened mostly during construction with the aim of rendering the construction process smooth, instead of involving the residents in the design phase of the project itself. In some projects, people felt their voices were only heard when they were raised in protest. Complaints were also made to the effect that outreach was insufficient and that frequently the poorest members of the community were not included.

On the other hand, architects sometimes complained that favela dwellers did not understand the plans set before them and demanded changes in the middle of construction, making alterations difficult and delaying the project's timely conclusion. They also felt it was often impossible to keep the project on schedule while attending to the multiple, conflicting voices in the community. In some favelas, the high turnover of residential leadership made community participation difficult and incoherent. In other cases, Favela Bairro managers were under the impression that some community leaders pursued personal interests or were directed by the ruling drug traffickers. In all of the projects, participants thought that the drug traffickers distorted community outcome when residents were too afraid to speak against their interests. In sum, the researchers concluded that:

> The strong culture of authoritarianism in Rio, the infiltration of favela residents' associations by the drug trade, and the political manipulation and co-optation of community organizations, have not favored the emergence of any trend towards democratization and the devolution of power to civil society.[18]

On the whole, the program still needs to involve its residents more as equal partners and less as subjects of study. Despite these shortcomings, the report also acknowledged that Favela Bairro was still an improvement over previous government-run interventions, handled in a top-down authoritarian manner.

As a response to the criticism, Favela Bairro changed its community practices after 2000, placing a stronger emphasis on outreach through community assistants, thematic workshops during the design phase and a more equalized representation through block leaders to best circumvent the negative influence of drug traffickers.

When the second phase of Favela Bairro was launched in 2000, the city tried to correct the social weakness of the program by augmenting the urbanization projects with programs catering for children, adolescents, the disabled and the elderly. A program for the generation of labor and income was incorporated for adults, and partnerships were established with nongovernmental agencies to align social initiatives. A new regimen of community participation was launched with greater outreach and more citizen involvement in the planning phase. According to the IADB, Favela Bairro Phase 1 and Phase 2 and their numerous subprograms have brought change to about 570,000 residents.[19] However, critics note that the Favela Bairro project unfortunately started to level off after 2000, due to political and institutional discontinuities. Especially, the implementation of the social programs was not up to the promised level.[20]

## *The Idealized Process of a Favela Bairro Project*

When the Favela Bairro program was launched, an open competition took place (organized by the Brazilian Architect's Institute, IAB). Besides being a legal instrument for selecting architectural practices, the competition reignited the public discussion of how to deal with informal settlements in the city. It was the start of a diverse multi-year search for a proper implementation process of a medium-sized Favela Bairro project. It had been developed, altered and refined over the span of the program. It had to be adjusted from one situation to another in consideration of the particular favela's size, location and social conditions. The following is a rough summary of an idealized process in five steps.

### *1. Identification*

Social workers typically established first contacts with the residents of a community and began to gauge the favela's social structure and physical needs. They further engaged with the community to assess its level of acceptance for a government-led project. A requisite

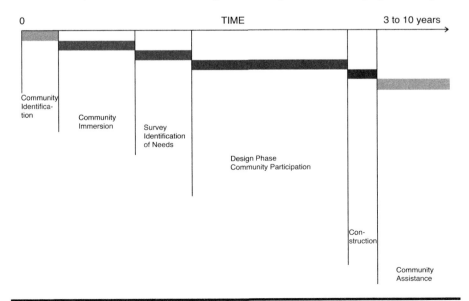

**Figure 39  Sequence of a Favela Bairro project**

## 66 ■ *Part II*

for the inclusion of a favela in the program involved the pre-existence of a functioning resident organization. Over the years, the municipality of Rio has gained some familiarity with the informal leaders of the respective communities through resident associations.

## 2. Survey

Once an upgrading project was determined to be feasible, Favela Bairro started to make a physical and social survey of the favela. Individual dwellings were measured; property boundaries recorded; extant infrastructure (water, sewerage, electricity) was mapped and hazardous conditions, such as unstable buildings or areas prone to erosion, were identified. Social data (size of households, income structures, employment status and expressed needs) were collected through questionnaires. Community meetings were held so that the residents and leaders of residential organizations could express their opinions and needs on specific topics such as sanitation, access, recreation, health, education and the economy. Four to six residents were chosen as "community assistants": they accompanied the upgrading project until its conclusion, were in permanent close contact with Favela Bairro managers, distributed information from house to house, gave updates on the progress of projects, answered questions and related concerns. The community was divided into multiple blocks and block leaders were identified in an effort to distribute community representation evenly throughout the favela.

## 3. Design

Based on the survey results, designers, together with civil and sanitation engineers, proceeded to develop first concepts for implementation. These plans were repeatedly discussed in the context of community meetings, subcommittees and individual conversations, and further refined until a common consensus was reached. The community officially voted on the plan's final version. This phase can last several months, or even years, depending on the individual circumstances of the community, such as the site or the size of the settlement.[21]

## 4. Construction

The next stage of construction was frequently handled in a couple of years or might be divided into two or three phases lasting several years. Favela Bairro asked contractors to hire local workers to foster income generation, build consensus and enhance security. In many cases, houses located on unstable ground, flood zones or in emergency access areas were removed. The owners of these houses received either a settlement in cash or were given the option to move into nearby government-sponsored public housing. During the construction phase, these families sometimes moved to interim housing until the on-site public housing facilities were built. Along with civil works like the installment of electrification, sewerage and potable water lines, Favela Bairro had to orchestrate construction sequencing between several agencies.

## 5. Monitoring

Once construction was finished and the inhabitants regained secure use of their houses,[22] official street addresses were assigned and the favela was considered a regular part of the city. It was at this point that the post-intervention program POUSO began. In its initial phase, designers and social workers (often from the community) were available at an on-site office. They initiated and oversaw maintenance, and consulted on new construction projects. POUSO architects and social workers mediated between the build-out plans of individual home owners and the newly established public open space.[23]

From a landscape architect's perspective, the most interesting interventions in the context of the hundreds of the Favela Bairro projects involve the improvement of public space and the treatment of landscape conditions. Over the years, literally hundreds of plazas, streets, alleyways and sports grounds were inserted into the dense favela fabric of Rio. The favelas themselves can be found in a wide range of landscape conditions, from Guanabara Bay to the Atlantic rainforest, from plains to extremely steep terrain. The selection of the following three examples is intended to illuminate three very specific landscape conditions and the impact of Favela Bairro: the first case, Parque Royal, sits on a flat island in the Guanabara Bay; the second, Morro da Formiga, is located on a steep slope surrounded by Atlantic rainforest; and the third, Morro da Providência, rests on top of a mountain close to the old port.

# Parque Royal

## Situation

Favela Parque Royal is located on Governor's Island, east of the runways at Rio's international airport. It was first settled by fishermen in 1973, and then by immigrants from the Northeast, lured by the airport's construction. It gradually grew into a community of 5,000 inhabitants by expanding into the Guanabara Bay. The neighborhood is tightly populated with 714 persons per hectare, a density two and a half times higher than that of Manhattan. Favela Parque Royal is bounded by a highway to the south and two canals to the east and west, respectively. Sewage and storm water flowed freely into these canals and into the already heavily polluted Guanabara Bay. In the early 1990s, 150 of the poorest families lived in housing precariously perched on stilts over the bay or along the contaminated canals. Public access to the open waters of the bay was very limited, and adjacent neighborhoods had raised a wall against the favela.

## Intervention

The Favela Parque Royal was among the first communities targeted in 1994 by the Favela Bairro program over a seven-year period. All houses were connected to water and electricity, including public lighting, as well as to a pump system to get the

**Figure 40 Alleyway in Parque Royal (image from 2007)**

sewage out of the low-lying favela. Streets and access ways were paved. The center of the town integrated a plaza with a multi-use sport fields, a job-training center, a day-care center for 140 children, and new housing and shops. A post office was opened, garbage began to be collected and a telephone company began to wire the city.[24]

The most important improvement, from a public space perception, was made along the water's edge. The architectural firm ARQUI 5 turned the most undesirable building locations into the most prominent of public spaces, commanding magnificent views of the bay and the surrounding mountains through the building of a new waterfront. A 500-meter long promenade was built by resettling 28 families into new housing inside the favela; dead-end streets were opened and the interior of the favela was reconnected with the ocean. The promenade has two sections: the narrow,

**Figure 41  Waterfront of Parque Royal 13 years after completion (image from 2010)**

southernmost one accommodates a two and a half meter one-way driving lane for local use and services, next to a promenade with a meter and a half-wide bike lane and pedestrian sidewalk with a planting strip alongside the water. A slender sidewalk that varies in width to accommodate the irregular layout of the individual residences lies beside the houses. The north section begins at the point where the village fishermen accessed the water: it has been improved by a new concrete stairway, a small plaza and a quay. From there on, the profile broadens with a two-way five-meter wide driving lane for public use, connecting the dead-end streets of yore to the Bay. The ARQUI 5 designers stress that connection to the formal city's traffic was meant to increase security and a sense of belonging to the informal one: an original goal of Favela Bairro.

The edge of the promenade was built with a wall of gabions at the limit of where the stilt houses were removed. Water was pumped from behind the seawall and the space filled with soil. The sewerage and water mains were then inserted in the fill, making for the first seawall constructed with gabions in Rio de Janeiro. In terms of its layout, choice of materials and plant selection, it follows the classical ocean promenades of Copacabana or Ipanema Beach at the heart of the city. The three share the carefully placed cobblestone paving, the alternation of two or three types of trees along a strip and the intermediate street furniture of concrete benches and bollards. The planting choices are of tried and true species that are proven, tough survivors in urban environments and commonly found throughout Rio.

## Process

ARQUI 5 divided the community into various sectors based on common interests or problems, and on the location of residents. A special group was formed with the residents who lived in the stilt houses, for example; another one comprised residents who lived around the football field. On weekends, the architects held special meetings in which they would present their proposals to these subgroups and solicit opinions. In addition to this, social workers trained by the architects would go from house to house and explain the proposals to the dwellers. ARQUI 5 notes:

> that the difference in our approach [...] is that we used participating tools to know the desires of the people and to explain our design to them, but not to substitute our role as architects, our responsibility as "form givers". In a word, we did not act with them differently than we act with our institutional, or corporate or private clients. Because of that, we think we made better designs, more efficient, and faster, not getting lost in the process of 'participation'.[25]

The architects also discovered that the ruling drug gang's influence on the project could be felt: the only two, large open spaces in the community were soccer fields owned by the drug traffickers. In the construction phase, the architects could only commence the conversion of one of these spaces into a new plaza with smaller playing fields, new residences and a community center.

## Post-intervention

The promenade was finished in 1997 and its effects and its treatment over the years can be studied. As expected, the promenade had a stimulating effect on the houses directly adjacent. The owners built out and improved their dwellings; some of them took advantage of the scenic landscape and increased traffic by opening small shops on the first floors of their homes. Ten years after the intervention, one could find small bars and convenience and hardware stores along the promenade. The surface

Figure 42 **Small businesses take advantage of the waterfront location (images from 2007, 2010)**

**Figure 43 Remnants of mangrove forest (image from 2010)**

materials of the promenade had experienced some heavy wear and tear. Paving was broken in various spots; bollards had been painted, or hit by cars. The planted trees had fared well: they started to form a dependable canopy. One could experience how the daily life of Parque Royal's residents spilled over onto the promenade and gave it an intimate touch: clothes were hung to dry between light poles and the formal trees of the promenade; washing troughs, potted plants or construction material were stored on sidewalks. The opening up of the waterfront also caused some unintended negative consequences, since it made the dumping of construction waste into the ocean easier. In addition, lots of trash that spilled in from the sewage canals could be found in the waters of the bay and between vegetaion of the mangrove forest.

## Conclusion

As one of the first Favela Bairro projects, Parque Royal has been promoted as one of its flagships and has been extensively reported on by countless government publications. The waterfront promenade of Parque Royal is a good example of the effect of new public space spurring business opportunities and the increased extending of private residences. Despite signs of wear and tear, the ocean promenade of Parque Royal has weathered fairly well (2010). The observed private encroachments into the public space are modest and should be valued as a genuine part of the neighborhood character. The trash and pollution levels of the bay are an issue that transcends the scale of this particular neighborhood and the reach of the Favela Bairro project.

**Figure 44** Unintended consequences: easier waste dumping into the bay (image from 2010)

Unfortunately, Parque Royal is not exempt from the complex dynamics of violence and power struggles that play out in Rio's favelas for some decades now. When the author tried to assess the condition of the promenade in 2017, one year after the Olympics, access was impossible due to an ongoing conflict of an unspecified nature.[26]

## Project Credits

### First Phase

Favela Bairro Program: SMH
Program manager: Lu Petersen, architect
Project/works coordinator: Wilson Luiz Queiroz Correia, architect

### Urban Project

Firm: ARQUI 5 Arquitetos
Project term: September 1994–March 1996

### Works

*Urban Infrastructure*

Firm: Companhia de Engenharia Anil
Project term: November 1995–March 1997

*Visibility*

Firm: Jovenel
Project term: April 1999 -September 1999

## *PROAP II*

*Second Phase*

Sector II – Urban infrastructure

Firm: Ses – Construção e Saneamento Ltda
Works coordinator: Alberto Mendes da Silva, engineer
Project term: August 2000–April 2001

# Morro da Formiga

## *Situation*

Morro da Formiga was initially settled in 1911 and went through several phases of informal and formal settling activity; by 2007, some 8,200 inhabitants dwelled on this steep slope of the Tijuca Mountain range in northern Rio. The location is a dramatic one, with an altitude difference of more than 200 meters from top to bottom, and an average gradient of more than 30%. Besides its notoriously difficult access, Morro da Formiga has been plagued by landslides as a result of deforestation. Since colonial times, Rio's Atlantic rainforest has been reduced to 10% of its original size through farming and uncontrolled urban expansion. The loss of vegetation increased erosion in the hills, causing frequent mudslides during heavy rains. In the past 40 years ten people have been killed and 230 houses damaged or destroyed by soil, rock, and garbage slides. Erosion issues aside, the favela also caused serious water pollution. Several springs surface in the hills and converge in the Cascata River, which eventually flows into Guanabara Bay. Before the clean-up, the river was an open sewer and a dumping ground, with the areas next to the river being the least desired locations in the favela.[27]

**Figure 45 Morro da Formiga surrounded by restored Atlantic rainforest that was planted in the early 1990s (image from 2007)**

## Interventions

Morro da Formiga has seen many phases of municipal upgrading efforts, starting in 1984 with the installation of sewers, storm drains, streets, alleys, stairways and bridges through the Mutirão program. In 1986, Rio's municipal government initiated a community preservation and reforestation project for low-income areas. Morro da Formiga was among the 57 communities chosen to take part in it. In a ten-year period, thousands of trees were planted and grown by community members in the hills above the settlement. In 1995, Formiga's resident association successfully applied to be included in the Favela Bairro program. In a halting and often contentious process, garbage collection with micro-tractors was implemented, a community center (CEMASI) that included a day-care center and elementary school was built, 220 families in risk locations were resettled, reforestation efforts continued, and the Cascata River was cleared of debris. The favela dwellings were connected to a sewerage system that greatly reduced the eutrophication of the river. Numerous bridges and simple concrete

**Figure 46 The steep terrain of Morro da Formiga (image from 2007)**

**Figure 47** The Cascata River roughly ten years after construction work (image from 2007)

pathways were built to connect both sides of the river and provide better access to individual homes. After the cleanup, the municipality enrolled Morro da Formiga as part of the Guardiões dos Rios program, where trained community workers regularly cleaned the river and posted reminders of proper stewardship along its banks.[28]

## *Process*

The residents of Morro da Formiga experienced various types of approaches, from early top-down interventions to the improved Favela Bairro approach. It is a noticeable fact that the community had, throughout the years, a very active and vocal residents association. Not only did it accommodate the many government interventions undertaken there in the past 40 years, but it also initiated, steered and sometimes vetoed them.

The Favela Bairro program in Formiga was not flawless. In the year 2000, a review of the project by University College London revealed that the then five-year-old Favela Bairro project in Formiga had suffered from communication problems.[29] It was found that the poorest families, living in the most precarious conditions, had not been reached by the community participation program. Some of the upgrading work did not match the original plans approved by the community. There was also disagreement on some major interventions: for example, the community was against the construction of costly new roads inside the favela, and would have preferred to see the funds used for the improvement of pedestrian access instead. Drug traffickers had even built roadblocks to halt construction. But there were also successes: the phasing of the project was better defined together with the community groups, resulting in the immediate resettlement of families living in dangerous areas; 22 residents were employed in the reforestation project and 15 as community cleaners. Despite the disagreements on road construction, the community acknowledged the overall improvement in how communication was conducted, compared to earlier government interventions.

## Post-intervention

In a 2017 visit roughly 30 years after the first reforestation attempts, it was evident that Morro da Formiga was fully surrounded by rainforest. Community representatives confirmed that the reforestation efforts are still continuing, with about 12 community workers who focus on planting fruit trees.[30] In addition, a community garden was installed halfway up the hillside. In 2015, horticulture lessons were given and a beekeeping program run.[31]

In an earlier 2007 visit, there was little to no trash in the Cascata River, thanks to the municipal Guardiões dos Rios program. In 2016, this program had been terminated and replaced by a training program targeting children and young adolescents to keep their neighborhood clean. It is too early to judge the consequences for the Cascata River; however, more trash was already visible in the river in 2017 than had been in 2007.

According to representatives of the residents' association, the community has been shrinking from 2007 to 2017, from 7,000 to roughly 5,000 residents, which was attributed to relocations of families in landslide prone areas. For the remaining

**Figure 48** Impressions of the Cascata River in 2007 (left) and 2017 (right)

families in risky locations, a warning and evacuation system has been successfully installed. It seems to be effective and accepted by the population, since it already has been proven to save lives in several instances.

An earlier 2007 proposal by former Favela Bairro architect Dietmar Starke, with the New York-based firm XPEKT, to build a multifunctional community theater and a tourist path did not find the required support of the municipality. This might be attributed to the general slowing down of Favela Bairro after 2000 and the rise in drug violence in Rio's favelas thereafter.

The biggest change for Morro da Formiga in this context was the occupation by UPP (Unidade de Polícia Pacificadora) in 2010. According to community representatives, the occupation yielded positive results with a significant reduction in drug-related violence. This was mostly attributed to the smart leadership of a female commander at the time. Unfortunately, this changed in 2015 when a new commander took over, whose authoritarian management style is generally disliked by the community.[32]

A PhD thesis in 2015 by Joseph Michael Marriott investigated how the UPP occupation changed the use of public spaces in Formiga. He found that some groups gained, while others lost some of their freedom. Some users experienced public spaces to be safer, more secure and more accessible (i.e., playgrounds), while others lamented that UPP introduced rules that made social and cultural events more difficult to organize. For example, regulations imposed by UPP rendered the organization of popular *baile funk* dance parties impossible, much to the chagrin of the young population. Most importantly, Marriott found that informal socializing in the streets was reduced after UPP occupation. Marriott perceived this tendency as potentially troubling, because such a transformation touches the core of Favela life, where the frequent informal socializing in the streets is the basis of community cohesiveness. Marriott therefore concludes: "it [the transition to a more regulatory structure of public space] has the potential to significantly and permanently alter the favelas' distinct qualities that are essential to the social life of these communities."[33] His conclusion is key for future improvements of public spaces in Favelas, especially in light of the fact that Marriott found that the plazas built by Favela Bairro were not working as intended: "the formally conceived public space types were not integrated with patterns of everyday movement and activity, and were neglected by residents."[34] In his detailed examination of Morro da Formiga's public space, he found that the strongest public use was in the streets (pre-existing Favela Bairro) and not the formal plazas. Marriott attributes the lack of use of the plazas to a lack of understanding of public space behavior by the designers. But he also deduces a more general observation that

> the use of formal public spaces for activities in line with broader social norms and values of the formal city has not developed as a core part of the practices of favela residents. Rather, residents of favela communities have developed their own distinct ways of both using and conceiving public space.[35]

Figure 49 Public spaces created by the Favela Bairro Program roughly ten years after installation (image from 2007)

## Conclusion

Morro da Formiga is a prime example of how effective community leadership and internal organization is a key driver for community development. Had there not been a very strong residents association since the 1960s, Morro da Formiga would have failed to receive government assistance in the 1980s and not been included in the Favela Bairro program of the 1990s. Morro da Formiga's upgrading history confirms Fiori, Riley and Ramirez' proposition to treat Favela communities not as recipients, but as equal partners in the upgrading process.[36] It also underlines

Figure 50 Public spaces created by the Favela Bairro Program roughly 20 years after installation (image from 2017)

how important it is to offer "soft" programs for community development and maintenance next to the "hard" programs of built work.

Marriott's finding of underused and neglected new plazas built by the Favela Bairro program highlight the well-known fact that a user-appropriate improvement of public spaces is key for their success. The belief that the transfer of public space typologies and symbols of the formal areas of Rio (*asfalto*) into favelas presents a general improvement appears naïve, misplaced and does not necessarily advance the particular community life in favelas. The critical examination of the public spaces of the Favela Bairro experiment require us to re-think the true meaning of integration and improvement in the context of favelas. Is favela upgrading an exercise aimed at equalization with the "formal" city (which is as diverse as the "informal" city)? Is there a danger that "integration" by classical urban development standards threatens the particular qualities of community cohesiveness? Should, then, upgrading be independent of classical urban development standards and just foster the particular life qualities found within the favelas? The answers are obvious.

## Project Credits

### First Phase

Projeto de urbanização Comunitária/Mutirão remunerado: SMDS
Community Participation Project implemented by the Municipal Social Development

### Secretariat Team

Project manager: Lu Petersen, architect
Execution coordinator: Ronaldo Toledo
Urban infrastructure works.: Jose Stelberto, engineer
Nursery: Carlos da Silveira, architect
Project term: 1986–1992

### Second Phase – PROAP I – Programa Favela Bairro

SMH program manager: Lu Petersen, architect
Urban projects: Empresa Plan-Planejamento
Project term: December 1995–December 1996

### Phase 1 – Urban Infrastructure Works

Firm: Construtora Junqueira
Project term: April 1997–February 1998

### Phase 2 – Urban Infrastructure Works

Firm: Dratec
Project term: May 1998–October 1999

80 ■ *Part II*

*Phase 3 – Emergency Services*

Firm: Topázio
Project term: April–September 1998

*Phase 4 – Physical Limits*

Firm: Soloteste Engenharia Ltda
Conclusion: December 2000

# Reforestation Project Credits

Projeto Mutirão de Reflorestamento/SMDS
Project coordinator: Márcia Garrido, forest engineer
Works coordinator: Celso Junius, forest engineer
Project term: 1986–1992

# Morro da Providência
## *Situation*

Providência Hill is Rio's oldest favela. Freed slaves, soldiers and refugees from the *Canudos* war (1896–1897) began to settle there over 100 years ago. They named their community after a hill called *Morro da Favela* where they were stationed during the war. The hill was overgrown with *favela* (*Cnidosculus phyllacanthus*), a tough thorny shrub. Later, the term became synonymous with spontaneous settlements throughout Brazil.

Morro da Providência is prominently located on a very steep hill overlooking the old port area of Rio de Janeiro, which had been a source of employment until its reconfiguration. A 2010 census reported roughly 3,800 residents living on the hill. Morro da Providência has a rich cultural history as the home of famous samba dancers and musicians. A decline in employment opportunities since the 1970s fostered an increase in extra-legal activities, especially the drug trade, which remains a strong force in the favela despite ongoing attempts at suppression. Because of its prominent location and cultural importance, Morro da Providência attracted various municipal and federal upgrading efforts, most notably the Favela Bairro and Célula Urbana interventions in 1994 and 2000, the Cimento Social Program in 2007 and the Morar Carioca Program in 2010.

## *Interventions of Favela Bairro and Célula Urbana*

Similar to Morro da Formiga, Morro da Providência underwent various stages of upgrading phases before Favela Bairro. Most of it was done by the community through its neighborhood association (*associação de moradores*, established in 1968). Built infrastructure included better access to the steep hill and better water connections in the 1970s, and more paved pathways and stairs (partially helped by religious organizations). When a Favela Bairro project was proposed for the hill in 1994, Lu Petersen, former

**Figure 51** The chapel of Morro da Providência at the top of the hill with a 12-year-old playground constructed by Favela Bairro (image from 2007)

director of the Favela Bairro program and founder of Rio's Célula Urbana program, proposed revealing its historical significance by restoring some of its landmark buildings and adding interpretative interventions to them.[37] The hope was to attract tourism and generate income for the favela dwellers. The plan was enacted and historical structures, including a massive granite stairway built by slaves, a church, a chapel, a water tank, and the home of a Brazilian carnival legend, were restored. Interpretative elements—such as three scenic viewpoints—were built along a special path marked by a continuous aluminum plate that leads potential visitors through the maze of the favela.

As one of the two built examples,[38] the experimental Célula Urbana project in Providência suffered from a deteriorating security situation in the favelas, as well as from decreased support because of the changed political leadership after 2000. In 2007, Lu Petersen made several attempts to bring official tours into the favela, but fragile security conditions forced the project to stop. Morro da Providência has been exposed to sporadic but deadly police raids, which rendered regular safe entry for tourists impossible.[39] Lu Petersen retired from public service in 2009 and the program ended.

## Interventions of Cimento Social

At the end of 2007, a program titled *Cimento Social* was started by a Brazilian senator as a federal initiative.[40] Cimento Social focused on the renovation of private homes, complemented by public infrastructure (sewerage network, nurseries and

Figure 52 A stainless-steel band installed by Célula Urbana in around 2003 was meant to guide visitors to historic features inside the favela (image from 2007)

Figure 53 Several scenic viewpoints were constructed by Célula Urbana in around 2003 (left image from 2017, right image from 2007)

community centers), with the involvement of the federal Housing Ministry and Defense Ministry. Eventually the program was halted one year later due to charges of unlawful political promotion, and continued with private funding. Only a small fraction of the 800 designated houses in Providência were improved. The program has been criticized for its murky beneficiary selection process, for its weak technical execution and for its narrow focus on housing, but mostly for the heavy-handed involvement of the Brazilian army, which eventually resulted in tragedy.[41] In 2017, one could observe a group of yellow-colored houses on the west slopes of the hill. For prominent community activists such as Maurício Hora, the program was lopsided:

> Living in the favela is not limited to housing. One of the biggest challenges is the public space. In several places in the favela there is no street, only narrow alleys without accessibility. There is no yard, no places for children to play. Interventions should be more concerned with creating streets than with aesthetics.[42]

## Interventions of Morar Carioca

A bigger influence than Cimento Social on Morro da Providência was the events in the build-up to the Olympic Games. Shortly after Rio won its bids in 2007 and in 2009 for, respectively, the 2014 World Soccer Cup and the 2016 Olympics, it began frantically to prepare for the two mega-events. In respect of security, the city started a "pacification" campaign with the goal of freeing an estimated 210,000 favela residents from the rule of Rio's gangs. Morro da Providência was among the 40 selected, and had been occupied by police forces in the spring of 2010. While the occupation was only partially successful,[43] it was still the basis for an ambitious intervention of the Morar Carioca program.

Morro da Providência was a prime target for program, since the favela is close by the largest urban renewal project of Rio, "Porto Maravilha" ("Marvel Port"). It was one of Rio's signature projects for the Olympics and its first public–private partnership that would attract national and international capital. The 30-year project comprises an area of 500 hectares and a projected investment volume of R\$8 billion. The first phase had been concluded in 2017 with the demolition of a highway, the construction of new transport infrastructure, public spaces, a few office towers and two new museums, most prominently the *Museu do Amanhã* ("Museum of Tomorrow") jutting out into the bay. Critics of the mega project are quick to point out the non-inclusion of urgently needed social housing and the authoritarian treatment of neighboring low-income quarters.[44]

In the case of Morro da Providência, it meant that the residents had to mount a fight against the authoritarian removal of all houses initially (later 800 houses, nearly half of the neighborhood) for public works that they were not consulted on. Morar Carioca planned to build a cable car, a funicular, a "Knowledge Square" (multi-purpose IT center), an amphitheater and a kindergarten. Against the stated principles of the Morar Carioca program, there was no public participation in the first two years of these interventions (2010–2012). For the residents, it felt as if the municipality wanted to rid the hill of its inhabitants in order to make it palatable for

**Figure 54** Cable car stations were constructed as part of the Morar Carioca program in 2012, sitting idle in 2017 during the economic crisis (both images from 2017)

the Olympics.[45] As a counter-reaction, Providência's citizens mounted several waves of resistance against the evictions and formed alliances with other afflicted groups in the port area.[46] Especially infuriating to the residents was the cable car construction that obliterated their main gathering place at Praça Américo Brun. They were less interested in a fancy public transport system halfway up the hill than in better infrastructure and schools. They also were fighting the removal of houses that were deemed to be in "risky areas" by the city and hired their own experts to carry out a counter-assessment. Eventually, a court order in 2012 stopped the work because of a lack of public hearings. At this point, the construction of the cable car had progressed to a point of no return and was allowed to continue. In the end, around 200 houses were removed. The cable car was the only project that was finished as part of Morar Carioca (using up half of the allocated funds). The promised upgrading of public spaces, basic infrastructure and educational facilities did not occur. The cable car operated through the Olympics, but its service was discontinued in the financial crisis of 2017.

In 2013, the obvious failure and the negative effects of Morar Carioca in Providência were already evident and were summarized as three main issues in a detailed investigation by the political scientist Einar Braathen: "Relocations, inflated house prices, and degradation of the public spaces."[47] He came to the bleak assessment that Providência's residents had been exposed to three distinct forms of oppression: "the tyranny of time," "the tyranny of science" and "the tyranny of force."[48] Time constraints were used as the main excuse to push through unsolicited improvements, the misuse of scientific arguments were employed to relocate residents at will, and brute force, either by gangs or corrupt policemen, was used to subdue citizens.

## Post-interventions

A visit in 2017 revealed the ongoing discontent of its citizens. Giselle Dias, a community leader and Maurício Hora, a community activist, confirmed the overall resentment of the cable car, the removals, the incomplete pacification efforts and the lost opportunities to improve education and infrastructure. Hora continues to work on

**Figure 55** A small bar at one of the scenic viewpoints in 2007 (left) and 2017 (right)

state-independent educational projects such as the *Casa Amarela* (the Yellow House).[49] According to them, the revitalization of the port has not yielded new employment opportunities for the community. In considering the question of what the last positive change for Providência had been, they both independently named the Favela Bairro intervention of the 1990s, with its improvements to pathways and sanitation.

On closer inspection, it was found that at least one of the three scenic viewpoints of Célula Urbana still existed, though the bar next to it had been closed. No other commercial activity in the form of bars or restaurants could be found next to the decks. A robust steel structure erected from Célula Urbana 20 years ago for providing shade to prospective bar customers was turned into a house. The hope of the designers that the great views of the amenity would attract service businesses had not been realized. Security constraints prevented visiting the other two decks. On a calm and sunny weekday morning, most of Providência's public life was being conducted in the cool shade of its narrow alleyways.

## Conclusion

Morro da Providência underwent several phases of municipal interventions, many of them unfinished, some of them misguided. The hopeful Morar Carioca program in Providência is actually a textbook case of a failed municipal intervention. The stated goal to make Providência, as Rio's oldest favela, a natural and valued part of the city and its history did not materialize.[50] On the contrary, its citizens have endured many hardships through oppression by the drug dealers or through authoritarian state interventions. It is understandable that there is an engrained mistrust of official improvement attempts among the Providência's residents.

In 2017, the interventions of Favela Bairro and Célula Urbana from 20 years ago seemed to be the only municipal acts that engendered appreciation. This confirms the notion that simple infrastructure improvements in public spaces (pathways and sanitation), carried out in a respectful and collaborative process, is a basic condition of upgrading. The ambitious goal of Célula Urbana to transcend the provision of infrastructure and include cultural aspects was rendered non-functional by political decisions and the overall deterioration in security. The notion of increasing tourist access to the oldest favela in Rio is still a moot point (2017), but was originally meant to create income opportunities, and to preserve and raise awareness of local history. The historical and educational concept behind the project was not, however, universally applauded at the time; it also attracted critics who warned that the project might be misinterpreted as a "romanticization of poverty."[51]

Indeed, the topic of favela tourism is highly controversial. The past decades have seen a surge in private favela tours that, at its worst, caters to voyeurism and threatens the dignity of favela residents, but at its best can generate income and reduce stigmatization.[52] Out of all the favelas in Rio, if not Brazil, Morro da Providência is the most historically significant and warrants recognition as a historic site. The problem is that poverty and disadvantage are still prevalent in Morro da Providência: many of Providência's residents continue to live in substandard conditions, belong to the most undereducated *favelados* (Brazilian term for a favela resident) in Rio and are, despite the police occupation, under the influence of gangs. Exclusion, violence and urban poverty were still very much alive in 2017. The tourist enterprise only makes sense once other, more important, goals are reached, most importantly by treating Providência's residents as partners and not as recipients of projects. Ultimately, the future decision on the question of tourist access should be in the hands of Providência's residents. In the end, the small viewpoint decks of Célula Urbana are just a blip on the radar of Providência's long history and dynamic development. With up to four-storey homes, it belongs to the more built-out favelas in Rio. As housing prices and rents have already gone up, questions about the danger of gentrification are becoming more prevalent than those about the negative influences of potential tourism.[53]

The most important lesson of the upgrading attempts in Providência concerns the outsized influence of governance. As a designer, one can have the best intentions and ideals of collaboration and co-creation, but once the project is caught in the current of larger events and political decisions, the project might be doomed to fail. Einar Braathen posited that Rio, at the beginning of the twentieth century, tried to make itself attractive to investors.[54] As it gained two major sporting events and as clientelism started to dominate politics, a neo-liberal sell-out occurred and the most fundamental principles of participation and collaboration were thrown out of the window.

## Prohect Credits

### *Favela Bairro Program and Open-Air Museum*

Special advisory, urban infrastructure and building restoration: SMH and Célula Urbana
Project manager: Jozé Candido Sampaio de Lacerda Jr., architect
Célula Urbana Special Advisory Manager: Lu Petersen

**Figure 56 One of the scenic viewpoints in 2007**

Project development: Dietmar Starke, architect UCSA
Project coordinator: Wilson Luiz Queiroz Correia and Amarílio S. Gastal, architects, SMH; Carlos Eduardo Petersen, architect, UCSA
Works manager: Sebastião Bruno
Fiscal works: Alberto Mendes da Silva

## *Favela Bairro Project*

Firm: Consórcio BCM/Fernanda Salles, architect
Project term: November 2001–January 2003

*Works*

Firm: Hécio Gomes Ltda
Project term: April 2004–March 2005

# Conclusion

Rio de Janeiro's efforts to upgrade favelas went through many phases with mixed results. Favela Bairro was a groundbreaking program, the first of its kind to engage informal settlements at the urban scale. In comparison to other programs, such as

**88** ■ *Part II*

Morar Carioca, the now historic Favela Bairro program of the 1990s still holds up as a pioneering experiment with successes and failures, as noted by various critics. A closer look at the three cases of Parque Royal, Morro da Formiga and Morro da Providência confirmed some of the strengths and weaknesses of the whole program.

First, it ranked among the great merits of Favela Bairro that it recognized urban environment instead of income as the first line of attack by which to achieve greater equality and integration. Favela Bairro's faith in the effectiveness of physical interventions was its most important contribution to the 1990s discussion around urban poverty, the recent understanding of which has widened to acknowledge that "the concept of poverty signifies much more than just a lack of income, also embracing factors such as ill health, poor access to essential services, vulnerability and insecurity."[55] In Favela Bairro's efforts to improve urban conditions, it became clear that the provision of infrastructure and public space (not the construction of housing) plays a major role. Indeed, the most apparent indicators of an upgraded favela are its new outdoor spaces: plazas, parks, sporting fields, playgrounds, streets, stairways and alleys.[56] After almost 20 years, the public spaces of Favela Bairro are a great repository for learning. Not all new public spaces created under Favela Bairro were equally successful (see Morro da Formiga), and designers who work today in Rio's favelas should take those lessons to heart.

On the flipside, Favela Bairro showed us the limits and downright weaknesses of an approach that focuses too strongly on built improvements. Any upgrading project is bound to fail when it does not place equal importance on social programs such as job creation, education, health care, child care and more (something Favela Bairro promised to correct later). The Favela Bairro experience teaches us that a holistic all-encompassing approach where no profession is dominant is needed.[57]

As a third key lesson, Favela Bairro teaches us that a proper community participation and co-creation is the most basic ingredient for the success of a municipal favela intervention. How this process should actually look will be subject to ongoing discussion; it might be different for each favela and will be subject to further investigation.

When it comes to the improvement and creation of public spaces in favelas, seven aspects can be deducted from the Favela Bairro experience:

## 1. Eye-to-eye Collaboration

Community collaboration and participation on an eye-to-eye level in all project phases is key to the development of public space in a favela. It is only with community input that an adequate program for the right location can be determined, and acceptance and a sense of ownership of the new space be gained. Every inhabitant has to be reached in the process, especially the poorest families. A process that allows all residents to be recognized as partners and not as objects of investigation must be devised. A co-creation process is desired. When the partnership principle cannot be fulfilled, a designer should pull out of the project.

## 2. Usability of Public Spaces

Public spaces must respond to a basic community need in order not to deteriorate and be subject to invasion once again. The programs can cover recreational (soccer fields), economic (market plazas, urban farming) or basic needs (stabilizing slopes, cleaning water, access). Areas designed for passive recreation are seldom respected and tend to be misused.

## 3. Public Space Connectivity

Public spaces must be strategically inserted into the dense fabric of a favela with a minimum amount of resettlement. Their placement and form have to be derived from the public space behavior of the residents and cannot be based on extraneous principles. Much more concentration has to be placed on the formation of streets and alleyways that are the traditional spaces of informal socializing in favelas. New public spaces can either upgrade existing informal uses in the same location or be implemented in resettlement areas over subsurface infrastructural work or marginal unused spaces. Plazas or recreational areas are preferably connected to new public infrastructure such as schools, community centers and transportation nodes and corridors, or near extant institutions such as churches, NGOs and residential organizations.

## 4. Durability of Materials

The materials used in Favela Bairro are typically durable and inexpensive. Were this not the case, there is a possibility that materials would be dismantled and reused for private construction projects. For this reason, paving in Favela Bairro consists mainly of materials that are not easy to remove, such as concrete or asphalt, rather than joint-based systems. Handrails are welded, rather than screwed; playground equipment should be very sturdy.

## 5. Continuity of Maintenance

The community's desire for, and acceptance of, the public space is fundamental for its continued existence. It is, therefore, easier to establish maintenance for a public space that responds to a vital community need. Obviously, the degree of maintenance required is subject to the choice of materials and their layout; for example, the painted bleachers in the plazas of many Favela Bairro initiatives can rapidly seem decrepit, with peeling colors and broken edges, when no one in the favela can be found to renew the color. Generally, maintenance is the weakest aspect of Favela Bairro interventions, notably when it comes to planting.

## 6. Open-ended Planning

Designing in a favela means embracing change in ways that cannot be entirely foreseen. The inevitability of alteration demands designs that will anticipate and survive

**90** ■ *Part II*

change. The best designs actually resort to the self-constructing and entrepreneurial dynamics typical to the favela. That means a project is never finished.

## 7. Valorization of Existing Public Space Culture

The notion of Favela Bairro to introduce public space elements of the formal city into the informal city in order to achieve equality needs to be challenged. Instead of introducing symbols of the formal city into the favelas as an external symbol of integration, spatial strategies that do not override, but rather register, sensibly change and complement the distinct spatial structure, qualities and history of the informal ones need to be developed. Most of Rio's favelas established, over their lifetime, a strong identity and a particular use of public space. Designers have to recognize, respect and foster the special identity of a particular place instead of introducing preconceived notions of what a proper public space has to look like.

Overall Rio de Janeiro's 50-year-long efforts to improve favelas have shown that large-scale programs are highly dependent on the unpredictable currents of political decision-making and macro-economic events. Broken promises (like Morar Carioca), autocratic interventions (as in Morro da Providência) and changing priorities pending on the whims of the respective political leaders and their constituencies, have eroded the little trust that favelados have had in public institutions. The big hopes of improvement because of the Olympics evaporated. In 2017, one year after the Olympics, the living conditions in the over 1000 favelas of Rio still remain unduly harsh.[58] It was not supposed to be like that. Back in 2004, Spanish architect Oriol Bohigas had an overly optimistic vision for Favela Bairro:

> It is very clear that if all goes well, in a few years the old slums will become the most attractive neighborhoods in Rio. Clean areas preserving an upgraded local architecture, located on privileged sites – the best slopes along this lovely coastline – complete with a cultural and social identity [...].[59]

This vision clearly did not come to fruition, and neither did the promise of Favela Bairro's successor, Morar Carioca, to improve all of Rio's favelas by the year 2020. In 2017, one year after the Olympics, just the opposite seemed to be the case.

The ongoing economic stagnation (since the 1970s) made more favelados jobless. Diminished prospects of employment pushed many young people into the hands of criminal gangs. After 2000, an increase in unemployment further amplified violence. Only a small fraction of Rio's favelas was pacified, with mixed results,[60] while the large remainder is still run by drug lords, subject to deadly police raids and basically inaccessible to outsiders. In the eyes of the public, the surge in favela violence discredited the overall achievements of the Favela Bairro program. As a population, favelados continue to suffer; they are still stigmatized and have a harder time finding jobs in the formal labor market.[61]

On the other hand, critics are worried that upgrading efforts will accelerate the ongoing gentrification of the favelas, expelling the poorest by making them more attractive to the lower-middle class.[62] In centrally located favelas such as Morro da Providência, this trend has already been observed. This leads to the general worry that the peculiarity of these neighborhoods, their history and distinct qualities, are in danger of being eradicated by gentrification or by over-regularization through insensitive upgrading efforts.[63]

This mix of problems maybe symptomatic for a continuing neo-liberalization of the city. According to the political scientist Einar Braathen, Rio's slow withdrawal from the public good has been long in the making.[64] He pointed out that Rio de Janeiro already tried, at the end of the twentieth century, to turn into a global city through private–public partnerships. Political leaders made efforts to make the city attractive for foreign investment (which critics refer to as a general sell-out of the city).[65] Favelas clearly stood in the way. Since critics already took notice of the fact that most of the favelas targeted by Favela Bairro were situated in prominent locations, Braathen suspected ulterior motives for the program and gave a bleak assessment: "The underlying logic driving the whole project [of Favela Bairro] was to improve favelas closer to richer neighbourhoods and touristic areas in order to improve the attractiveness of Rio de Janeiro to the private capital."[66] How much the selection of Favelas into the Favela Bairro program had to do with free market forces, or with convenience or pure happenstance, is still a point of contention.[67]

Nevertheless, in 2017, these tendencies were compounded by the most serious political and economic crisis the country has seen for a long time; the prime minster was ousted, the State of Rio went bankrupt (with its former governor in prison), and the Favela residents in the City of Rio were disaffected from the unfulfilled promises of the Olympics. Morar Carioca had fizzled out under the old mayor and the new mayor began to withdraw from public space by favoring indoor improvements of Favela homes. Improvement efforts were at a low point.

# Notes

1. IDB, "Brazil Favelas: Inter-American Development Bank," www.iadb.org/en/news/idb-brazil-sign-180-million-improving-infrastructure-services-rio-de-janeiro-favelas (last accessed April 23, 2021).
2. Luiz Paulo Conde, *Favela-Bairro: Uma Outra História Da Cidade Do Rio de Janeiro: 1993–2000 Uma Ação Urbanizadora Para O Rio de Janeiro* (Rio de Janeiro: ViverCidades, 2004).
3. Prefeitura do Rio, Inter-American Development Bank, *Favela Bairro: Ten Years Integrating the City*, Rio de Janeiro, 2003.
4. Unfortunately, the outsized success of Favela Bairro had the negative side effect of eroding the other programs. They had less traction and fizzled out (conversation with Adriana Larangeira, long-term Favela Bairro manager, March 16, 2017).
5. Jorge Fiori, Liz Riley and Ronaldo Ramirez, "Urban Poverty Alleviation through Environmental Upgrading in Rio de Janeiro: Favela Bairro," Draft Research Report,

## 92 ■ Part II

Development Planning Unit, University College London, 2000, 59–62, http://share. nanjing-school.com/dpgeography/files/2014/05/Favela-Bairro-Report-1f64qi1.pdf (accessed August 25, 2020).

6. Conde, *Favela-Bairro*, 88–91.
7. Rio Prefeitura, *From Removal to the Urban Cell. The Urban-Social Development of Rio de Janeiro Slums*, Rio de Janeiro, 2003.
8. 2010 Census conducted by the Brazilian Institute of Geography and Statistics (IBGE).
9. Prefeitura do Rio de Janeiro, "Conheça o Programa: Morar Carioca," www.rio.rj.gov.br/web/smhc/conheca-o-programa (accessed September 28, 2020).
10. Thirty-nine of the 1,040 favelas in Rio experienced a UPP occupation with over 2,000 police officers involved (2014). The program had a decisive influence on the daily life of the residents. Its overall results were mixed, ranging from satisfaction to dissatisfaction. Critics claim that the selection of favelas was based more on their proximity to prominent urban areas than on their levels of crime. Overall, there seems to be a decline in trust of the police over the course of the program. For a detailed account from a residents' perspective, read the five-part "UPP: series," *Rio on Watch*, 2015, www.rioonwatch.org/?tag=series-upp (accessed August 25, 2020). For an academic evaluation, see Sarah Oosterbaan and Joris van Wijk "Pacifying and integrating the favelas of Rio de Janeiro: an evaluation of the impact of the UPP program on favela residents," in *International Journal of Comparative and Applied Criminal Justice* 39(3) (2015).
11. Prefeitura do Rio de Janeiro, "Conheça o Programa: Morar Carioca."
12. Luisa Fenizola: "Políticas em Favelas na Era Crivella: Cartão Reforma, Cimento Social e o Desaparecimento do Morar Carioca," *Rio on Watch*, 2017, http://rioonwatch.org. br/?p=24587 (accessed August 25, 2020).
13. Although one could say that the $262 million Guarapiranga Basin Initiative that was started in 1992 in São Paulo comes close in ambition and scope, it just concentrated on one large watershed and not the whole city.
14. Jorge Fiori and Zeca Brandão, "Spatial Strategies and social urban policy: urbanism and poverty reduction in the Favelas of Rio de Janeiro," in *Rethinking the Informal City: Critical Perspectives from Latin America*, ed. Felipe Hernández, Peter William Kellett and Lea K. Allen (New York: Berghahn Books, 2010), 182.
15. Prefeitura do Rio, Inter-American Development Bank, *Favela Bairro: Ten Years Integrating the City*, Rio de Janeiro, 2003.
16. Edesio Fernandes and Márcio Moraes Valença, *Brasil Urbano* (Rio de Janeiro: MAUAD, 2004). Fabio Soares and Yuri Soares, *The Socio-Economic Impact of Favela-Bairro: What do the Data Say?* (Washington, DC: IADB, 2005), 14.
    Jorge Fiori, Liz Riley and Ronaldo Ramirez, "Urban poverty alleviation through environmental upgrading in Rio de Janeiro: Favela Bairro," 108–117.
17. Jorge Fiori, Liz Riley and Ronaldo Ramirez, "Urban poverty alleviation through environmental upgrading in Rio de Janeiro: Favela Bairro."
18. Elizabeth Riley, Jorge Fiori and Ronaldo Ramirez, "Favela Bairro and a new generation of housing programmes for the urban poor," *Geoforum* 32(4) (2001): 521–531.
19. Inter-American Development Bank, "BR0182 : Rio de Janeiro Urban Upgrading Program," www.iadb.org/en/projects/project-description-title,1303.html?id=br0182 (accessed August 25, 2020).
    Inter-American Development Bank, "BR0250 : urban improvement Rio de Janeiro II," www.iadb.org/en/projects/project-description-title,1303.html?id=br0250 (accessed August 25, 2020).

20. Jorge Fiori and Zeca Brandao, "Spatial strategies and urban social policy. Urbanism and poverty reduction in the favelas of Rio de Janeiro," in *Rethinking the Informal City. Critical Perspectives from Latino America* (New York: Berghahn Books, Vol. 11, 2010), 181–205.

21. As has been noted before, the first wave of Favela Bairro lacked proper participation procedures. The description here describes an ideal process that, in practice, was not that often accomplished.

22. Land ownership is a complicated issue, not only in Brazil, but in most parts of the world. During the Favela Bairro program, residents rarely gained formal land titles to their house. The municipality rather gave out grants for land use (Concessão do Direito Real de Uso – CDRU). The concession allows the secure tenure for 99 years (it is inheritable and without cost). Critics pointed out that the concession does not give the residents access to the financial market by selling their houses or getting loans. Proponents pointed out that the CDRU protects the residents from real estate speculation and potentially losing their homes (communication with Adriana Larangeira, 2017).

23. POUSO was, in general, well received. Critics point out that it was unfortunately understaffed and underfunded. The program ended in 2008. See also Caitlin Dixon, "POUSOs: urbanistic and social orientation posts in Rio's favelas from 1996 to 2008," *Rio on Watch*, April 27, 2014, www.rioonwatch.org/?p=14641 (accessed August 25, 2020).

24. Prefeitura do Rio, Inter-American Development Bank, *Favela Bairro: Ten Years Integrating the City*, Rio de Janeiro, 2003, 50–58. La Biennale di Venezia, *Brasil Favelas Upgrading*, 2002.

25. Bruno Fernandel, ARQUI 5, correspondence, August 17, 2007.

26. According to Rio's housing authority; conversation with Adriana Larangeira, March 16, 2017.

27. Conde, *Favela-Bairro*, 130–132.

28. Fiori et al., "Urban poverty alleviation," 59–62.

29. Ibid.

30. Conversation with Eduardo Rosa Thomé dos Santos and Patrizia Josa Thomé dos Santos, March 18, 2017.

31. Claire Lepercq, "Living with nature in Morro da Formiga: an interview with Amadeu Palmares da Silveira," *Rio on Watch*, 2015, www.rioonwatch.org/?p=25137 (accessed August 25, 2020).

32. Conversation with Eduardo Rosa Thomé dos Santos and Patrizia Josa Thomé dos Santos, March 18, 2017.

33. Michael Joseph Marriott, "Territoriality and the regulation of public space in Favela Morro da Formiga, Rio de Janeiro," PhD Thesis (Queensland: School of Design, Creative Industries Faculty, Queensland University of Technology, 2015), 316.

34. Ibid., 267.

35. Ibid.

36. Fiori et al., "Urban poverty alleviation," 59–62.

37. Rio Prefeitura, *From Removal to the Urban Cell*, 38–45.

38. Its other built project was in the 60,000-person Favela Jacarezinho, developed in collaboration with the University Bauhaus Dessau. The project consisted of several strategic events culminating in the design and construction of a cultural cell, namely, a building that houses an Internet café, a computer center, a media school and spaces for dance and music, including a small plaza.

39. Conversation with Lu Petersen, 2008.

# 94 ■ Part II

40. Marcelo Crivella, a former bishop of the Universal Church of Kingdom of God (Pentecostal Church), who eventually would become mayor of Rio de Janeiro in 2017.

41. In 2008, an insubordinate act by an army soldier led to the execution of three young adolescents by a rival drug gang. See detailed story described by Cristina Tardáguila, "O Exército, o Político, Omorro e a Morte," *Folha de São Paulo*, 2010, http://piaui.folha.uol.com.br/materia/o-exercito-o-politico-o-morro-e-a-morte/ (accessed August 25, 2020).

42. Louisa Fenizola, "Políticas em Favelas na Era Crivella."

43. In 2013, 21 policemen were arrested for having connections with the drug trade in Morro da Providência.

44. Aercio de Oliveira, "Porto Maravilha: Verführungskraft der schönen Bilder," Heinrich Böll Foundation, 2016, www.boell.de/de/2016/05/27/porto-maravilha-verfueh rungskraft-der-schoenen-bilder (accessed August 25, 2020).

45. A more detailed account of the events has been prepared by Einar Braathen et al., "Rio de Janeiro: favela policies and recent social mobilizations," Norwegian Institute for Urban and Regional Research, 2013, www.hioa.no/content/download/130716/3566290/file/2013-110.pdf (accessed August 25, 2020).

46. For more information, see Einar Braathen et al., "Ups and downs in Rio de Janeiro: the changing phases of mobilisation in Morro da Providência," in *The Politics of Slums in the Global South Urban informality in Brazil, India, South Africa and Peru*, ed. Véronique Dupont, E. Braathen, David Jordhus-Lier and Catherine Sutherland (Abingdon: Routledge, 2017).

47. Ibid., 26.

48. Ibid., 30.

49. The Yellow House came out of a subsequent engagement of Mauricio with the photo artist JR, who prominently installed in 2008 large-scale photographs of eyes and faces of female residents on Providência's house walls. See Phaidon, "The house that JR built (and then rebuilt!)," www.phaidon.com/agenda/art/articles/2016/january/28/the-house-that-jr-built-and-then-rebuilt/ (accessed August 25, 2020).

50. Providência clearly did not become "a second Sugarloaf Mountain" as Mayor Eduardo Paes promised at the opening of the cable car. Waleska Borges, "Teleférico do Morro da Providência passa pelo primeiro teste," *O Globo*, http://oglobo.globo.com/rio/teleferico-do-morro-da-providencia-passa-peloprimeiro-teste-7115734 (accessed August 25, 2020)

51. Daniela Fabricius, "Resisting representation," *Harvard Design Magazine* 28 (2008): 4–17.

52. Kennedy Odede, "Slumdog tourism," *New York Times*, Opinion, August 9, 2010, www.nytimes.com/2010/08/10/opinion/10odede.html (accessed August 25, 2020).

53. Einar Braathen et al., "Rio de Janeiro: favela policies and recent social mobilizations," Norwegian Institute for Urban and Regional Research, 2013, 29, www.hioa.no/content/download/130716/3566290/file/2013-110.pdf (accessed August 25, 2020).

54. Ibid.

55. Riley, Fiori and Ramirez, "Favela Bairro and a new generation of housing programmes for the urban poor," *Geoforum* 32 (2001).

56. This achievement should not be underestimated, since the overall trend of favela upgrading in Rio goes towards the individual house (2017). The new mayor, Crivella, thinks about individual subsidies (*Cartão Reforma*) that provide federal payments for low-income households to fix up the interior of their houses or get assistance by specialists. The apparent criticism: (1) with the proposed budget, only 3% of

Case Study II: Rio de Janeiro ■ 95

3.5 million low-income citizens can be reached, (2) a refurbished bathroom is insufficient if the house is not connected to water and sewer, or is structurally unsound. Conversation with Adriana Larangeira, former program manager in the Favela Bairro Program, March 16, 2017.

57. An aspect that was soon recognized after the first phase of Favela Bairro in 2000 and promised to be improved in the second phase (which, unfortunately, leveled off).

58. For an account of on the ground conditions, see Janice Perlman's anthropological study ranging over 40 years: Janice Perlman, *Favela: Four Decades of Living on the Edge in Rio de Janeiro* (New York: Oxford University Press, 2010).

59. Luiz Paulo Conde, *Favela-Bairro: Rewriting the history of Rio* (São Paulo: ViverCidades, 2004).

60. In 2015 a five-part "UPP: series" by the news organization *Rio on Watch* attempted a ground-level perspective of the gains and losses of the 39 pacified favelas. Initially some positive results in favelas were reported. Residents felt safer on streets, less weapons were visible, drug dealing was more covert. Still, a feeling of being occupied, watched and controlled remained. Later in the program, more untrained policemen were used, more police violence occurred, extrajudicial killings eroded the trust of the population. Over the years, violence and misbehavior against policemen increased, drug bosses partially returned and incidents of police corruption were reported. In 2015, both sides were unhappy. Favelados still felt treated as secondary citizens and victimized for the sake of the Olympic games. Inside the police force, unhappiness increased over the years with complaints about mistrust of population and internal funding problems. In: www.rioonwatch.org/?tag=series-upp (accessed August 25, 2020).

61. Janice Perlman, *Favela: Four Decades of Living on the Edge.*

62. Ney dos Santos Oliveira, "Favelas and ghettos: race and class in Rio de Janeiro and New York City," *Latin American Perspectives* (23) (1996): 71–89.

63. Riley, Fiori and Ramirez, "Favela Bairro and a new generation of housing programmes for the urban poor."

64. Einar Braathen et al., "Rio de Janeiro: favela policies and recent social mobilizations."

65. Carlos Vainer, "Cidade de Exceção: reflexões a partir do Rio de Janeiro," *XIV Encontro Nacional da ANPUR*, 2011, http://memoriadasolimpiadas.rb.gov.br/jspui/handle/123456789/193 (accessed September 28, 2020).

66. Einar Braathen et al., "Rio de Janeiro: favela policies and recent social mobilizations."

67. Adriana Larangeira, long-term manager at Favela Bairro, rather critiques the lack of a clear strategy of Favela selection in the Favela Bairro Program (conversation with Adriana Larangeira, July 17, 2017).

# Interview with Lu Petersen (LP)

## Interviewer: Christian Werthmann (CW)[1]

From 1994 to 2000, Maria Lúcia Petersen, more commonly known as Lu Petersen, was an architect and project manager for the Favela Bairro program. In 2001 she founded Célula Urbana, implementing projects in Jacarezinho and Morro da Providência. Lu Petersen retired from public service in 2009.

**CW:** Lu, you worked with the poor for more than 20 years. You have seen each and every phase of community work. Together with Dietmar Starke, you established the Célula Urbana program as an improvement over Favela Bairro. Can you tell us how Célula Urbana is different from its predecessor?

**LP:** The primary distinction between Célula Urbana and Favela Bairro is that Célula Urbana is not just about the construction of public spaces but about social implementation. It wasn't just concerned with the built environment within of the favela, but with trying to integrate the favela into the city as well. Looking at the Jacarezinho favela, which, at nearly 70,000 inhabitants, is almost as large as a medium-size city, it became clear to me that greater impact had to be directed to the functions of the city. This is the main conceptual difference between ourselves and Favela Bairro. Célula Urbana is committed to bringing urban economic, social and cultural components – and not just urban space, as with Favela Bairro – into the favela.

**CW:** Can you give us more examples of this? What sort of programs are we speaking of?

**LP:** The first project we created in Jacarezinho was the first broadband internet cybercafé in the favela. It hosts between 5,000 to 6,000 people per month, and was established in direct dialogue between the favela and the city. We also implemented dance and music programs, English lessons and things of that sort. Another example is *Museu da Providência*, comprising the historic artifacts that are the city's heritage as a whole. This legacy belongs to the public of Rio de Janeiro.

**CW:** When I visited Rio this past August (2007), the security situation did not permit the tourists to enter.

**LP:** We originally had a partnership with the City's Board of Tourism, with whom we created and traversed a route with executives of theirs who wanted to include it in the touristic Samba City itinerary. After that I spoke with the chief of police to see how we could allow the tourists to come, and he told me: "You can have one day a week for tourist visits. One fixed day!" This did not work for the tourism executives. So, I told the mayor I was throwing in the towel, because when you lose a boxing match, you take the towel and you throw it, right? I gave up.

**CW:** What are the best ways to involve communities in the upgrading of favelas?

**LP:** Beginning in 1988, when I was manager of the Favela Bairro program, we noticed that the community only really got involved after we had launched a Favela Bairro project. We tried a new approach with Célula Urbana, and initiated the Plan of Integrated Social Action before design work started. We promoted meetings to deal with very specific topics. For example, we would have a large meeting about childcare, because it attracted all the women. Then we would have a separate meeting about sport, because it attracted most of the men. When it pertained to sewage, drainage, potable water, the audience's composition varied. The end result was that by the time the designers presented their plans for intervention, the people had already been informed and mobilized.

**CW:** What is the most important quality for a designer to have working in the context of a favela?

**LP:** First, the designer needs to think about sewage and drainage, the distribution of water: this is what is fundamental, not the design of buildings. Brazilian architects think more about the building than the infrastructure. When it comes to the favelas, the architect is working as an urbanist. He may have to change a project because of the natural path of rain water because the route occurs naturally there and not somewhere else, and that will determine where to construct the drainage system. This is the vision that I think informs both the Favela Bairro and Célula Urbana: it is a marriage, a dialectic in which everything is interrelated.

**CW:** I made an observation when I last visited Rio (2007). There was a journalist who walked with me through Morro da Formiga who had been reporting on favelas for more than 20 years. She actually thought favelas were worse off now, because of the worsened security situation.

**LP:** I think so, too. It is important to understand the conflict between drug trafficking and the police that's generating chaos in the favela. I am under the impression that relations amongst people have deteriorated. For example, as recently as two years ago, the ruling drug lord did not allow children to be in drug dealing areas. But what has happened since? With greater police pressure on the dealers and a smaller influx of money, the drug dealers have

**98** ■ *Part II*

allowed crack into the favela. You see queues of 20 kids between the ages of six and 16 years old with little soda cans, smoking crack. I feel that the residents of the favelas are more depressed than ever. They don't have anyone to ask for help and, to some extent, it was drug traffic that inserted some order into the favela.

**CW:** And that's not there anymore?

**LP:** No, because the conflict is tremendous, there are shootings all the time, it doesn't stop. I am not going to say it's the same in every favela, but one can feel it in several of the main ones. I can't generalize it.

**CW:** Did drug trafficking decrease in the favelas following the implementation of a Favela Bairro or Célula Urbana project?

**LP:** No, it doesn't work like that. What we were able to do was to remove the youth from drug trafficking through various other activities. When the young have things to do, they don't make things up.

**CW:** So, as a designer working in a favela, how do you deal with the drug lord?

**LP:** The drug lords have known us for a long time. It is very rare for one of them to speak to me directly, though. They usually send a mediator.

**CW:** Do the drug dealers appreciate the fact that there is a Favela Bairro project or Célula Urbana project in their neighborhood?

**LP:** When they are from the favela, yes, they do. Sometimes, they may ask the contractor to hire someone from within the favela. What always creates trouble is housing, because they always want houses for their various mistresses; a house for the family, for their mothers, dog, cat or bird. The world of the favela is a very complicated one, I wouldn't cover it if I spoke for nothing else for days. It is an intricate universe, and a very large one, impossible to generalize.

**CW:** For more than 24 years, you have worked in poor urban areas. It is hard, dangerous work: why you do it? What motivates you?

**LP:** When I was a child, I lived in Leblon, a middle-class neighborhood in the south of the city, right next to a 100% black favela. One of its exits was on the street on which I used to live, and so we had a lot of contact with its people. I eventually became a left-wing militant and went into exile in Chile. During the Allende Coup I was able to leave Chile and emigrate to Switzerland, thanks to the auspices of the Red Cross. It was not until 1979 that I returned to Brazil, and this is when I started to work with favelas as a matter of ideology. Since we were not able to bring about the socialist revolution, we began to work through social democracy. Working in poor areas gave meaning to my life.

# Note

1. Interview conducted in São Paulo in Portuguese, December 4, 2008; translation into English by Patricia Sakata, edited by Christian Werthmann.

# Case Study III

## São Paulo – Protecting Water

Not unlike Rio de Janeiro, São Paulo underwent various phases of favela initiatives, ranging from attempts at eradication to ongoing large-scale in-situ upgrading programs. According to a 2010 census, 1.3 million out of São Paulo's 11 million residents lived in 1,020 favelas.[1] While the total number of favela residents was roughly the same as Rio de Janeiro's, São Paulo had a significantly lower proportion of citizens living in favelas (10%) than in Rio de Janeiro (22%).[2] The favelas of

Figure 57  One of the reworked creeks in the Guarapiranga Basin Initiative (image from 2007)

99

**100** ■ *Part II*

São Paulo also differ from those of Rio by being mainly located on the periphery of the city. But, in general, many of the favelas in São Paulo share common traits with their Rio counterparts by displaying high population densities, lacking basic infrastructure and services, having little to no rights to the land and being located in environmentally risky areas or on land unsuited for urbanization. São Paulo's *favelados* (Brazilian term for a resident living in a favela) especially suffer long commutes and high transportation costs, as work opportunities are still concentrated in more central areas of the huge metropolitan area.

## Guarapiranga Basin Initiative

São Paulo's first serious and large-scale upgrading program began in 1992 with the Guarapiranga Basin Initiative, in the watershed of a large reservoir in the south of the city. Under the leadership of the urban planner Elisabete França, the Municipal Social Housing Agency (SEHAB) affected almost 27,000 families.[3] The experiences of this groundbreaking program laid the groundwork for a bigger city-wide slum upgrading program in 2005. The team around Elisabete França began to engage large favelas, such as Heliopolis and Paraisopolis, as well as the many small favelas in environmentally sensitive areas to the north and south of the city. Seven years after its implementation, around 130,000 families were touched by the program.[4] An enormous database was created that registered social and physical conditions at household level and guidelines were developed, ranging from community participation to construction standards for all future favela upgrading projects in São Paulo.[5]

For the purpose of this book, with its special focus on landscape, a closer look at the first and older program, the Guarapiranga Basin Initiative, seems most appropriate, because the initiative most vividly reflects the conflict between the geomorphological location of the city, its infrastructural demands and its unequal distribution of wealth.

### Situation

São Paulo has serious water problems: it does not have enough clean water to meet increasing demands, and it has too much polluted water flooding large parts of the city after heavy rainstorms. Both problems negatively affect the residents of São Paulo's informal areas. The history of this relationship can be traced back to the last century.

In the early 1900s, two massive dams were built outside of the core city to catch the clean headwaters of various rivers. Originally built for the purpose of hydroelectricity, both reservoirs eventually became major sources of São Paulo's drinking water. As the metro area's population ballooned from 2.5 million in 1950 to over 17 million in 2000,[6] sprawl and informal urban growth engulfed São Paulo's reservoirs, seriously diminishing their water quality through the unchecked discharge of domestic sewage.

The Guarapiranga Reservoir, constructed in 1906 by damming the Guarapiranga River 20 kilometers southwest of São Paulo's urban core, is second largest in the reservoir system; in 2006, it provided 20% of São Paulo's total water demand.[7]

The 34-square-kilometer reservoir, which holds 200 million cubic meters of water, is part of a substantial watershed that spans 637 square kilometers from the cliffs of the Serra do Mar to the São Paulo plateau. The river valley itself is a sedimentary basin with fluvial deposits, edged by hills of crystalline bedrock of varying steepness, highly susceptible to erosion if deforested. At the time of the reservoir's inauguration in 1906, the hills were still covered by subtropical rainforest that was considered part of the Atlantic Forest ecosystem. Prior to damming, the fluvial deposits of the river valley supported small-scale agriculture: an important food source for nineteenth-century São Paulo. The creation of the large lake surrounded by bucolic hills radically altered the productive nature of this landscape as it became a recreational spot for the growing Metropolis. Being well connected by rail, the lake began to attract more and more city residents. In 1929, a motorway was built between the city center and Santa Amaro, just north of the Guarapiranga dam. The road, marketed primarily to the few privileged car owners, set the stage for the development of the 400-hectare Interlagos satellite city and summer resort. The changes to the area were quite rapidly realized: small agricultural towns like Santa Amaro turned into lakeside resorts, and, in 1937, the Guarapiranga dam was remodeled into a kilometer-long artificial beach. Up until the 1970s, recreational amenities for the upper class were developed in form of yacht clubs, country clubs, lakeside golf courses and large estates and second homes in the surrounding hills.[8]

**Figure 58 The Guarapiranga Reservoir is sometimes visible, but not always accessible (image from 2007)**

**102** ■ *Part II*

Given these conditions, the Guarapiranga Basin was especially susceptible to land speculation and urbanization. Its original denomination as a reservoir intended to generate electricity required public ownership of the lake, but not of its contributing watershed (as water quality was not an issue). It was only a matter of time before the outstanding connections to downtown attracted not just the well-to do, but industrial activity. Beginning in the 1940s, São Paulo experienced a massive growth spurt, with many factories built in the south. These employed scores of low-income workers who tried to find housing opportunities in the surrounding areas. With the further consolidation of industrial activity, the pressure for low-income housing grew to a point when, in the 1970s, the demand could no longer be met through public housing. At the same time, in 1975, the Law of Protection of Water Catchments was enacted, which limited the use of the land surrounding the Guarapiranga Reservoir in order to protect its water quality. The policy had an unintended consequence, however, causing the price of land to drop and incentivizing informal occupation.[9] Unable to afford property in the official housing market, settlers were left to their own devices and began to occupy residual areas that were unsuited for urbanization: much of it protected land that was crucial to the health of the reservoir. In 1992, there were 622,000 people living in the Guarapiranga catchment area; 170,000 of whom lived in the 180 favelas located in the ecologically valuable, but residentially unsuitable, valley bottoms or on steep slopes.[10]

Land speculators would further exploit the situation by illegally clearing forests, parceling large tracts of land and selling the individual lots to low-income citizens. These irregular settlements (*loteamentos irregulares*) are slightly better organized than the favelas described above by virtue of having street systems and a somewhat rational layout of building plots. In 1992, there were 119 such irregular settlements that housed approximately 250,000 people. All in all, more than two thirds of the residents in the Guarapiranga watershed lived in favelas or illegal subdivisions.[11] When industrial productivity in São Paulo declined during the 1980s, many of the factories in the south closed or changed to forms of production requiring less unskilled labor, resulting in the further impoverishment of this population. Currently, some of the poorest citizens of São Paulo may be found in the Guarapiranga watershed, where, in 2000, half of the population's heads of household had no income or income below the poverty line.[12]

The industrialization and modern transportation infrastructure of the basin that triggered the illegal land occupation and subsequent impoverishment of the area seriously damaged Guarapiranga's reputation as a resort. The "beach" became the city's largest pocket of poverty, its surroundings plagued by crime: here was "a population with no short-term employment perspectives, completely absorbed by immediate, day-to-day survival."[13]

Today, Guarapiranga is a patchwork of heavily fortified estates, stagnating yacht clubs, middle-income areas and housing compounds, abandoned factories, dense favelas, irregular settlements and stretches of forest. This quilt is held together by a network of arterial roads that is continuously lined with commercial and retail

**Figure 59** To the left: private recreational club on the lake; to the right: dense informal urbanization further away from the lake (both images from 2007)

buildings catering to the new population. The fact of the matter is: a new city has emerged in the Guarapiranga Basin in the past 40 years. It is characterized by heterogeneity, rapid change and great disparity. Despite its haphazard appearance, the traditional pecking order of wealth still persists, with the poorest populations being disconnected from the lake and lodged in remote areas with densities as high as 500 persons per hectare,[14] with, until recently, no basic services or paved streets, beset by flooding and erosion, while the finest, low-density, lakeside locations are occupied by the privileged.

As a consequence of massive urbanization, the lake as an ecosystem and a potable water resource suffered greatly. With the protective cover of forests being replaced by urbanization, soil erosion set in. Heavy tropical rains gushed through the unpaved favela streets, washing away the naturally unstable soils, silt and trash, and carrying large amounts of sediment into the reservoir. Besides sedimentation, domestic sewage accounts for 80% of the pollutants that are discharged into the reservoir.[15] Only 45% of the basin's population was connected to sewerage systems: the remainder accounted for sewage flowing openly through informal settlements, finding its way into the lake.[16] By 1990, the self-cleaning function of the lake had been destroyed. Large algae blooms gave signs of heavy eutrophication, and the reservoir was at the point of collapse.[17]

## Intervention

In 1992, the Guarapiranga Basin Initiative, funded by a World Bank loan, the State and City of São Paulo, was initiated with a starting budget of US$262 million.[18] Its goal was to improve the reservoir's water quality and to restore its capacity as a potable water source. Since the initiative had to tackle thousands of diverse pollution sources, the sanitation project had to be coupled with an urban rehabilitation project. At this point, there was no question of the removal of informal settlements: from a purely economic vantage, it was obvious that *in situ* treatment of illegal occupation

**Figure 60** Left: creek flowing into the reservoir; right: creek with stabilized banks, promenade and recreational area as part of the Guarapiranga Basin Initiative (both images from 2007)

would be far more cost effective than resettling hundreds of thousands of people outside the basin.

The Guarapiranga Basin Initiative thus consisted of five subprograms: (1) water supply and sewerage service; (2) waste collection and disposal; (3) urban rehabilitation; (4) open space protection and development; and (5) watershed management. The urban rehabilitation program had the largest budget at $114 million; followed by the environmental protection and sanitation divisions.[19] The complexity of the project called for the collaboration of multiple local, federal and national agencies under the aegis of the São Paulo Housing Agency (SEHAB). In just three years, 45 kilometers of sewerage lines, 23 hectares of paving, and 4 hectares of plazas were built.[20] Upon completion of the first phase, project director Elisabete França noted that:

> The projects and works started to focus on the idea of permanence and urban qualification, in a way that, once the works are completed, not only the removal of open air sewage and waste is successfully carried out, but a new neighborhood becomes part of the city and its residents see themselves as participants in the public administration and, above all, responsible for the protection of the region's main assets: the quality of the water of the lake and the privileged landscape of the region.[21]

In cleaning the reservoir, many innovative practices were called for. Agencies with no previous contact with each other had to start working together, exchanging experience and knowledge. The nature of the problem helped overcome traditional municipal boundaries in favor of working on watershed boundaries, so that the territory was eventually subdivided into eight sub-basins. Legislation was changed to allow the development of sanitary work and urban rehabilitation in the favelas built across the basin's no-build zones. Later, the agency transferred the basin-based planning approach to the whole city of São Paulo.[22]

## Process

Once the legislative scene was set, a detailed survey was conducted among the 240,000 residents in the territory. In the pilot stage, seven settlements producing the worst pollution and those with the most precarious housing were selected for upgrading by the São Paulo housing agency. Both the planning and construction phases of this initiative were accompanied by an intensive social program and active community participation. In the first stage, social workers identified the social structure of the selected informal areas, their formal and informal leaders, extant social institutions and the history and dynamics of the particular population. In the second stage, the social team presented the main objectives of the Guarapiranga Basin Initiative to the community, explaining the benefits of the project but also the need for environmental protection.

Meanwhile, engineering and design firms were awarded contracts to develop integrated proposals for projects of urban design and infrastructure. In each of the pilot slums, a detailed survey of risk areas, such as housing on steep slopes, in drainage valleys or on unstable soil, was conducted. Where these risks to the population could not be mitigated, houses had to be removed. Families were, for the most part, moved into temporary quarters and resettled in new houses in the same neighborhood.[23] In the course of the project, social workers developed the following basic principles for this highly sensitive removal process:

> … to remove the smallest possible number of families from the area where they live; to favor the resettlement of families in areas as close as possible to their homes; to give priority to alternatives devised to prevent "informal sales" and the subsequent return of the benefiting families by the Program to inadequate housing conditions.[24]

Following the risk and removal assessments, the engineering companies designed the potable water, drainage and sewerage systems on the bases of the hydrologic and topographic conditions at hand, and the community's size. The new sewerage provision was linked to the basin's main sewerage system, characterized by large collection points and pumping stations for the removal of sewage from the Guarapiranga Basin to the Barueri treatment plant, 47 kilometers north.[25]

Once again, sanitation work in the favelas required innovative practices. The narrow, winding alleyways proved difficult to work with, since sewage pipes, as well as potable and storm water pipes, had to conform to inordinately slim profiles demanding manual labor. Sewerage construction codes had to be altered, to allow the placement of pipes in passages only 1.20 meters wide.[26] Utilities had to be covered with paving to direct surface drainage. Given the large differences in gradient, countless stairways have since been designed to improve access to individual dwellings while diverting storm water from homes. In the valleys and steep hills alike, the large sewage and rainwater pipes run parallel to existing creeks and rivers at the low points of the favelas. Precarious housing over the riverine systems or on their floodplains was removed to make way for these large utilities, which were then covered with roads or promenades to form completely new access systems for the settlement (before this, the urban fabric faced away from open sewers and rivers). These new points of access do not just allow better waste collection, availability of emergency services and surface drainage, they were designed also to provide the sites for new public spaces. Thus, the location of a sewerage system that is governed by gravity, and ultimately by the shape of the land, is the invisible underlying major factor in the urban rehabilitation of the Guarapiranga Basin Initiative.

In the design phase of the sanitation and surface systems, meetings were continuously held with the community and more information was collected. Once a clearer picture emerged, the design proposal was further refined. The proposed work was then presented to the community in several explanatory sessions, with comments being solicited. The scope of housing removal was discussed with the residents, leading to a phase of intensive explanation and negotiation. At this point, a building freeze was negotiated with the population. Once the necessary removals and type of resettlement were defined, the construction sequence was discussed with all participants in further meetings before construction started. In this phase, a social team was on site every day, to oversee the sensitive removal of people from their houses into temporary quarters and, finally, into their new homes. Community meetings kept residents updated on the execution of the works, explained safety issues and attended to conflicts or complaints. The social team was essentially the eyes and ears of the designers and construction companies, giving them regular feedback.[27]

Experience had shown that construction in informal areas requires not merely strategic thinking, but patience. Rapidly changing conditions on the ground often call for the spin-on-a-dime adjustment of design proposals, as designer Marta Maria Lagreca de Sales attests:

> In general, slum areas present extremely unhealthy conditions – open air sewage, landslide risks on slopes and along streams, flooding, low support capacity of the soil and subsoil, shallow underground water, access difficulties; and especially interference in existing homes, very often poorly constructed leading to difficulties in performing mechanical work, often resulting in vertical transport and manual digging of ditches and wedging. Apart from the above described factors, the intense, hectic growth of these clusters, mostly identified from fieldwork and land surveys – when word of eminent works spreads, the engineering quickly becomes obsolete, requiring constant adaptation in scope, both for the work commissioned, and the design itself.[28]

## Post-intervention

The experience of the first seven pilot projects showed that the sanitation and infrastructure program had to be broadened. Community participation indicated that, besides the need for basic infrastructure, the population's recreational requirements also needed to be considered in much more profound ways. When, in 1994, the next round of 30 projects began, great care was taken to develop a new open-space system with residual spaces complemented by the newly cleared spaces created through housing removals and the cleared areas above the utilities:

> The proposals, in general, acknowledged the particularities of each slum area, never considering them a homogenous whole, aiming at exploring the singularity of each site. The projects, other than presenting solutions for problems of stability, sanitation and accessibility, also aimed at integrating empty areas, in order to create social gathering spaces exploiting local topographic contours and relief.[29]

Small green spaces inserted into the fabric of the city, often on vacant lots (pocket parks) and river parks, waterfronts, plazas, sports fields and playgrounds became more deeply integrated into the engineering work, leading to the careful creation of recreational spaces on top of the hydrological infrastructure that characterizes the Guarapiranga Basin Initiative, lending it its distinct quality and making it a significant example in the history of slum upgrading. In placing a high value on the construction of public space, the São Paulo Housing Agency SEHAB committed to following a principle described by Catalonian architect Oriol Bohigas in the reconstruction of Barcelona in the 1980s: "Creating a free space and ascribing signification to it constitute the two fundamental actions for the reconstruction of a neighbourhood."[30]

By fostering these unprecedented, small public spaces and sports-grounds in the favelas, the agency hoped to create a network that had value because it facilitated points of identification in the dense, chaotic fabric of the Guarapiranga Basin urbanization: a public space alternative to wide commercial arteries that would channel the energy of its young population and make room for the cultural expression of the inhabitants. The aspiration was for them to access the advantages and benefits previously available only in the formal city, to enhance their role as citizens and also to facilitate a future partnership for the rehabilitation and protection of the dam.[31]

# Project Credits

## Guarapiranga Basin Initiative

Client: City Government São Paulo
General coordination: Eilsabete França, Housing and Urban Development Department
Geographic information: Ricardo Corrêa Sampaio
Geographic coordination: Violêta Saldanha Kubrusly

**108** ■ *Part II*

Social team: Cleusa Chimelli Mello, Water Resources, Sanitation, and Public Works Department
Managing unit: UGP
CDHU: The São Paulo State Housing and Urban Development Company
SMA: The São Paulo State Environment Department
SABESP: The São Paulo State Basic Sanitation Agency
IBRD: International Bank for Reconstruction and Development
Alto-Tietê Watershed Committee

# Parque Amélia

Out of the 27,000 families affected by the Guarapiranga Basin Initiative, a small upgrading project in a neighborhood of 740 families northwest of the basin is discussed in greater detail.

## *Situation*

The small neighborhood of Parque Amélia is located in the valley of a tributary to the Guavirutuba River, one of the major feeders to the Guarapiranga Reservoir. Before the intervention, the small stream carried the untreated domestic sewage of the informal urbanization to its watershed, contributing to the overall pollution of the dam. Parque Amélia is on the low point that received most of the upstream sewage. Families were reportedly washing their dishes and pans with wastewater. As with many other favelas, some houses were also built directly above the stream. Last, but not least, the neighborhood was also disconnected from the road network and only accessible by foot.

## *Intervention*

Through the sanitation project, all 740 households were connected to sewage pipes. The main collecting trunking was run at the lowest point parallel to the stream, with the stream itself being diverted into a 2 x 2-meter culvert. A road was built over the culvert and the sewage collecting trunking. São Paulo's sanitation standards allow for a 4-meter-wide road next to or over main sewage collector lines, and so this maintenance road is also the major access to the neighborhood. While the São Paulo Housing Agency tries to keep streams open whenever possible, because of the tight conditions and the desire to curb housing removals, the road could not be placed next to the stream in this case.

A half-acre lot beside the river that was covered with housing was removed because it was in a location that could not be served by the new sewerage system. Its residents were relocated to new housing in the neighborhood, creating the opportunity to establish a public space in the removal area. The design team, led by architect Marta Maria Lagreca de Sales, integrated a sports court, a skating rink and a playground into the hill. Three natural springs were caught in a little pond from which they traverse the park, and then reconnect to the stream at ground level. A large and highly visible

**Figure 61 Skating rink at Parque Amélia, eight years after its completion (image from 2007)**

eucalyptus tree was preserved as a landmark. Great care was taken to detail surfaces with a high degree of craftsmanship. Streets were neatly paved with cobblestones; sidewalks and alleys were surfaced with concrete; stairways and drainage channels have been painstakingly inserted into the newly paved access ways. Thirty-seven families in total had to be resettled close by to make way for the roads in the park.[32]

## *Process*

Parque Amelia was part of the third wave of upgrading projects in the Guarapiranga Basin. The managers, designers, social workers and construction companies involved

**110** ■ *Part II*

in the initiative had already gained valuable experience in the more than 30 upgrading projects undertaken in the six years before. A key lesson learned was that the initiative had to transcend sanitary clean-up and the provision of basic infrastructure, and aim for the creation of high quality public spaces. Parque Amelia is the product of this insight.

The implementation process followed the recipe of other Guarapiranga Basin Initiative projects. A technical survey was conducted; risk areas identified; a team researched the social structure of the neighborhood and negotiated the resettlement of the 37 families living in high-risk areas above the stream or in locations that could not be connected to sewerage. In a system known to them as "chess," SEHAB's social team identified residents who were both willing and able to afford replacement housing (the baseline is being able to pay rent). People living in high-risk areas marked for removal who could not afford to cover replacement housing rent were then moved into the empty dwellings of those who had already moved into the replacement housing. The chess system is quite common to São Paulo's upgrading projects and essential in allowing the poorest inhabitants to stay in their neighborhood.[33]

An urban design team under the guidance of João Walter Toscano Arquitetos y Associados developed the layout of alleyways, roads and the location of replacement housing. When the half-acre lot along the stream was opened for development, project coordinator Marta Maria Lagreca de Sales designed the park with the help of a few young architects. Having supervised many other upgrading projects in the basin, she emphasizes the flexibility and quick reaction time designers need in order to erect these projects. Surveys cannot cover every square foot of favela, and one must be able to anticipate unforeseen circumstances, such as difficult soil conditions, the presence of old landfills, or the varying qualities in housing structure. Plans have to be modified on the fly, in ways that sometimes challenge the full-scale capabilities of a designer when decisions are made on-site and executed there and then. Lagreca compares favela upgrading to a "maneuver" based on the tactical and indeterminate nature of the endeavor at hand.[34] One can have a plan, but must expect the final product to differ substantially. As with an obstacle course, the designer has to maneuver around suddenly emerging challenges to attain a common goal. Some of these obstacles can also be rephrased as opportunities, with a case in point being Parque Amélia: when more housing than anticipated had to be removed, new ground was opened for the creation of public space. During construction, the removal zone was surveyed and quickly redesigned as a park, incorporating the springs that were discovered on site. As Parque Amelia demonstrates, a project manager can quickly become a designer due to the shifting terrain of the favela.

## *Post-intervention*

A visit in 2007, eight years after the intervention, revealed that the small park had been well maintained by a caretaker from the community and seemed to be used as a general meeting point. No trash could be found in the park or in the spring-water system (since our visit was announced, everyday conditions might differ). Children

*Case Study III: São Paulo* ▪ 111

**Figure 62** Public space with spring in Parque Amélia (image from 2007)

**Figure 63** Playground in Parque Amélia (image from 2007)

**Figure 64 Drainage and spring details of Parque Amélia (both images from 2007)**

and teenagers used the playground and soccer field intensively. Trees and plants had grown up and were well cared for. Several buildings around the park had been upgraded by residents. A consecutive visit ten years later (2017) was impossible due to security reasons, since the municipal housing agency had stopped working in the area and had lost their contact persons in the population.

## Conclusion

Second in scope only to the Favela Bairro Program in Rio, the Guarapiranga Basin Initiative was, at its time, an outstanding example of a large government-led program that improved the lives of thousands of people. Its scope went far beyond the protection of water resources and encompassed an intensive urban rehabilitation program. The Guarapiranga Basin Initiative is exemplary in its achievements, given the scale of the undertaking; it went beyond similar efforts in China, India and Mexico, as a World Bank review of 2007 attests, and was an award winner for UN Best Practices in 2004.[35]

Despite the positive reviews, there is room for improvement. In the realm of water infrastructure, the sewage treatment facilities in the basin are severely limited, since it was never supposed to hold urbanization. According to Brazilian law, sewage must not be treated inside the watershed of a drinking-water reservoir. Currently, sewage has to be pumped out of the Guarapiranga watershed to a centralized treatment plant. It is understandable that Brazilian authorities are worried about potential contamination of the reservoir by improperly treated sewage. But the disadvantages of its sewage exports are obvious. It is fairly energy consuming to pump sewage for 47 km while risking losing some on the way through leaky pipes. One wonders if São Paulo should start experimenting with cleaning Guarapiranga's sewage to drinking water standards and reinserting it locally into the aquifer.

On the neighborhood scale, one also finds situations inside upgraded favelas where classical civil engineering solutions are applied and valuable open space rendered unusable. Similar to the examples in Rio de Janeiro, houses on erosion-prone hills are typically demolished and its inhabitants located in new buildings at safer places. After demolition, these hills are often coated with shotgun concrete, so called because it is fired onto rocky slopes to eliminate further erosion, which at the same time makes them inaccessible and unusable. Since open space in favelas is so limited, it would be more appropriate to insert programs in the hills that can provide a service to the community, such as terraced community gardens for food production. For less costlier solutions, one could at least stabilize the slopes by soft engineering means with plant material; a solution that would also improve microclimatic conditions by providing shade in the hot Brazilian summers. As in many of the government-led approaches, there is an opportunity for the informal city to upgrade to a smarter and resource saving infrastructure than that of the formal city.

As a further point of criticism, a 2007 review by the World Bank noted that "the bank gave too little attention to educational and behavioral issues of low-income residents affected by the projects."[36] Modern-day projects with similar scope spend up to 25% of the project cost on social programs, whereas, in Guarapiranga, only a much smaller percentage was budgeted. A six-month investigation by Ivo Imparato and Jeff Ruster came to the same conclusion: "The absence of environmental education after the works were completed proved to be a constraint of the development of a wider social awareness about the importance of environmental protection and conservation."[37] Through numerous interviews with program managers and favela leaders, the team stated that the sustainability of the infrastructure works is jeopardized by the absence of post-implementation programs. They finally noted:

> All those interviewed, representing the institutions involved in the Guarapiranga program, conveyed a single overarching lesson. The improvement of the physical environment can produce a very positive impact, but the engine of change is the community, which must be mobilized to continue the development process. Without a strategy for long term participation, no project will be truly sustainable.[38]

It is revealing that the same criticism was directed at the first round of Favela Bairro projects in Rio de Janeiro. It drives home the point that only an integrated approach of well-balanced physical and social interventions can lead to real improvement for favela residents.

Beside these future challenges, it is clear that the Guarapiranga Basin Initiative has set records at many levels: it was the largest favela upgrading project in São

**114** ■ *Part II*

Paulo at the time; it introduced the necessity of planning on the watershed level, independent of municipal boundaries; it forced isolated city and state agencies to collaborate; it addressed more issues than just sanitation; it proved that the development of high quality and carefully designed public open space, together with targeted public infrastructures (schools, health centers, community centers, etc.) is a key ingredient of favela upgrading; and it gave a whole generation of contractors, civil engineers, social workers and designers an unprecedented level of experience for working in low-income areas that is much needed in the other informal settlements in São Paulo. It was the basis for a second wave of upgrading programs being implemented in the largest and most complicated favelas of the city. After 2012, the Social Housing Agency redirected its energies to the construction of new housing as part of a federal push to reduce the housing deficit (*Minha Casa Minha Vida Program*). Thus, municipal favela upgrading efforts were downgraded.[39]

Overall, the combined experience of running the Guarapiranga Program (1992–2005) and São Paulo's city-wide slum upgrading program (2005–2012) gave its long-time executive director Elisabete França and her team invaluable insights. In summary, Elisabete França listed two main issues that are critical for its success:

1. respecting the existing community and their accomplishments
2. qualifying public space.[40]

Finally, Elisabete França came to the following conclusion:

> We no longer conceive of the existence of a formal city that is legal, and another that is informal and built outside the law. We can no longer see slums as sub-normal buildings that need to be evicted, but as communities that have invested their lives and savings in securing a space in the city, in the only locations to which they had access. Their social networks have allowed them to survive the hardships of their daily lives and represent the greatest wealth of their settlements. These communities are building the true contemporary city, albeit lacking the mechanisms to access proper land tenure, housing, public facilities, and educational and economic opportunities.[41]

After 25 years of favela upgrading and being exposed to an enormous diversity of conditions, Elisabete França came to understand informal neighborhoods as an essential building block of our contemporary cities. Her insight is not novel (it has been voiced by others before, most prominently in the 1970s by John Turner), but França's message carries special weight as the director of one of the largest slum upgrading programs in the history of Latin America. Her message contains not only a valuable insight into São Paulo's specific urbanization history, but it also holds great relevance for the future of a rapidly urbanizing Asia and Africa, where informal urbanization rates are higher. França's conclusion reinforces the notion that rapidly growing cities with limited financial capacities need to change their attitude towards poor, rural migrants. Instead of blocking and forcing them into illegal housing construction, they need to integrate and harness their proven neighborhood-building capacities. Instead of repeating the mistakes of the past, these cities need to devise anticipatory strategies of land acquisition and urban expansion that channel self-construction into safe, healthy and affordable neighborhoods. This behavioral change from prevention to allowance is one of the most demanding challenges for the future.

# Project Credits

## *Parque Amélia*
Client: City Government São Paulo
Coordinating architect: João Walter Toscano
Landscape architect: Odiléia Helean Setti Toscano
Architects: Massayoshi Kamimura, Guiherme Filipe Toscano
Park designers: Marta Maria Legreca de Salles, Marcos Boldarini, Stetson Lareu
Survey: Leopoldo Barica
Geotechnical engineer: Antonio R.C. Iglesias
Sanitation, channeling, drainage, water supply, sewers: Nelson Seiji Fukai
Electrical: Minoru Sato
Structural engineer: Koji Nakatani

# Notes

1. Instituto Brasileiro de Geografia e Estatistica, *Censo Demográfico 2010: "Aglomerados subnormais: Informações territoriais*, 2010.
2. Elisabete França, "Slum upgrading: a challenge as big as the city of São Paulo," *Focus* 10(1): Article 20, 75.
3. Elisabete França, *Guarapiranga: Urban and Environmental Rehabilitation in the City of São Paulo* (São Paulo: M. Carrilho Arquitetos, 2000), 33.
4. França, "Slum upgrading: a challenge," 78.
5. Ibid., 80.
6. Regina Maria Prosperi Meyer, Marta Dora Grostein and Ciro Biderman, *São Paulo Metrópole* (São Paulo: Editora da Universidade de São Paulo, 2004), 58.
7. Monica Porto, "Sustaining urban water supplies: a case study from São Paulo, Brazil," *Stockholm Water Front* 2 (2000): 6.
8. Denise Mendes, "The occupation of the Guarapiranga Basin area: historical and urban planning perspectives," in *Guarapiranga: Urban and Environmental Rehabilitation in the City of São Paulo*, ed. Elisabete França (São Paulo: M. Carrilho Arquitetos, 2000), 39–65.
9. Ivo Imparato and Jeff Ruster, *Slum Upgrading and Participation: Lessons from Latin America* (Washington, DC: The World Bank, 2003), 332.

# 116 ▪ *Part II*

10. Ibid., 332.
11. Ibid., 332.
12. Caroline Moser, "Urban violence and insecurity," *Environment and Urbanization* 16(2) (October 2004): 205.
13. França, *Guarapiranga*, 34.
14. Imparato and Ruster, *Slum Upgrading*, 332.
15. França, *Guarapiranga*, 97.
16. Ibid.
17. Monica Porto, "Sustaining urban water supplies: a case study from São Paulo, Brazil," *Stockholm Water Front* 2: 6–7.
18. França, *Guarapiranga*, 28.
19. Ibid., 29.
20. Ibid., 122.
21. Ibid., 33.
22. França, "Slum upgrading: a challenge," 80.
23. França, *Guarapiranga*, 115–125.
24. Cleusa Chimelli Mello et al., "The social aspect of the improvement works in the slums and involuntary resettlements," in *Guarapiranga: Urban and Environmental Rehabilitation in the City of São Paulo*, ed. Elisabete França (São Paulo: M. Carrilho Arquitetos, 2000), 222.
25. França, *Guarapiranga*, 97.
26. Ibid., 125.
27. Chimelli, *Guarapiranga*, 221–231.
28. Ibid., 122.
29. Ibid., 117.
30. Oriol Bohigas, *Reconstruccion de Barcelona* (Madrid: Ministério de Obras Públicas y Urbanismo, 1986), 18.
31. França, *Guarapiranga*, 189.
32. França, *Guarapiranga*, 188, 192–193. La Biennale di Venezia, *Brasil Favelas Upgrading*, 2002.
33. Conversation with Marta Maria Lagreca de Sales, São Paulo, 2010.
34. Ibid.
35. World Bank, Project performance assessment report, 2007, Brazil – Water Quality and Pollution Control Project (loans 3503-br,3504-br, 3505-br to the states of São Paulo and Paraná), 2007, 6, 9.
36. Ibid., 10.
37. Imparato and Ruster, *Slum Upgrading*, 359.
38. Ibid., 359.
39. See interview with Elisabete França, pp. 117–122 in this volume.
40. França, "Slum upgrading: a challenge," 76.
41. Ibid., 81.

# Interview with Elisabete França (EF) and Marta Maria Lagreca de Sales (ML)[1]

## Interviewer: Christian Werthmann (CW)

Elisabete França (EF) is the Secretary of Mobility and Transport of the City of São Paulo. Until recently she was the Director of Planning and Projects of the Housing and Urban Development Company (CDHU) of the State Government of São Paulo. From 2005 to 2012, she was the Deputy-Secretary of Municipal Social Housing Secretary, City of São Paulo (Secretaria Municipal de Habitação, SEHAB 2005–2012) where the Guarapiranga work was performed

Marta Maria Lagreca de Sales (ML) is Co-Director of Lagreca. Sales Arquitetos Associados and former project manager at the Guarapiranga Basin Initiative (1997–2000). Professor of Urbanism, Escola da Cidade São Paulo. Temporary professor (2016–2018) of Faculdade de Arquitetura e Urbanismo, FAU/USP.

**CW:** SEHAB (Municipal Social Housing Agency) has worked for almost 30 years in the Guarapiranga Basin, where most of the improvement work was done in the 1990s. Is the agency still operating in the basin and, if so, what sort of projects is it pursuing?

**EF:** We continued to work in the Guarapiranga Basin until 2012. Thereby, we have improved our methodology. The projects became more complex: we worked with the municipality, the building regulations and other infrastructures, such as water, drainage, sewerage and paving. We incorporated some projects into other sectors, such as the linear parks, the systems of sewage collection and public services like health and open spaces. We integrated other municipal public works. By 2012, a considerable number of actions were implemented in the favelas located in Guarapiranga territory and expanded to Billings.

**118** ■ *Part II*

The urbanization program was integrated into the Córrego Limpo program, coordinated by SABESP [the São Paulo sanitation agency], aimed at cleaning up 100 streams in the city of São Paulo. Another important advance was the integration with the program of linear parks, coordinated by the Municipal Secretary of Green and Environment. In total, 59 precarious settlements were urbanized, benefiting 75,000 families.

**CW:** Did the work continue in Guarapiranga?

**EF:** A third phase was to be started with funds from the PAC (Program for Growth Acceleration), coordinated by the Federal Government. At that time the Program adopted the name of Mananciais, to include the precarious settlements of Billings Reservoir. As the Municipal Housing Plan (2009–2024) was under discussion, we adopted a methodology of work, from which the contracting of works was defined by the Integrated Action Perimeters (PAIs).[2] The priority perimeters contracted in the third phase of the program were planned for another four years and the total number of interventions needed for another eight years.

In 2013, SEHAB concentrated its actions on the search for the implementation of the *Minha Casa Minha Vida Program* [MCMV, a federal housing program], in light of the goals established by the 2013–2016 management to construct 55,000 homes of social interest. This new priority, due to the concentration of federal resources offered to the municipalities, disregarded the programs in progress. Unfortunately, few units were built by the *Minha Casa Minha Vida Program* in the city of São Paulo, because of the cost limits established by the federal program.

In 2013, the new municipal administration faced budgetary problems, as the economic crisis accelerated and the federal resources promised for continuing the program were not made available. Since then, the actions planned for Phase three have been halted.

**CW:** Has the financial structure changed for this later phase? Are there still funds from the World Bank or is it all Brazilian?

**EF:** The resources used for the few actions developed in the water source program, since 2013, only use funds from the municipal budget.

**CW:** Can you give us an overview of the effects of your work, on the social effects for communities, and the environmental effects for the Guarapiranga Reservoir?

**EF:** A long time ago, we did a study with the organization of homeowners. The results were good. Unfortunately, since 2013, the social actions and monitoring of results have not continued, perhaps due to the discontinuity of the works.

**CW:** In regard to the environmental effects of the Guarapiranga Basin work, is the reservoir water now cleaner? Is there any effect on the reservoir?

**EF:** In 2008, the water company, SABESP, put in big sewage collectors. It should be better, but I do not have new numbers on water quality. However, irregular occupations grew exponentially, as a result of the interruption of the control of new occupations. There has also been an accelerated process of vertical extensions of the favelas, which can be attributed to the deepening of the economic crisis and the difficulty in paying rent by the poorest families. In a 2017 visit to the region, it was possible to observe that streams had a high rate of sewage loading.

**CW:** Maintenance of new public spaces is always a big issue. How is the housing agency now approaching the topic of maintenance of public spaces?

**EF:** Yes, maintenance is the biggest issue. You understand that after the conception of the public space, the users are responsible. In general, the community is most interested in the maintenance of the public spaces and our social team was trying to organize the community. Between 2010 and 2012, we were working on training the local population to coordinate maintenance work on the implanted spaces. We have been very successful in the areas, where environmental maintenance was implemented, with the hiring of residents. Unfortunately, as of 2013, this work has been paralyzed, probably due to budget constraints.

**ML:** The question of maintenance is difficult. When the public authority goes away, the population remains subjected to the same rules of management as the rest of the city. It is important that the public sector incorporates these new spaces with the services of the city. It is difficult to convince the administrators in the city that the new public spaces in favelas need the same services as any other public space in the city. It is a cultural problem throughout the city, but it is slowly changing.

**CW:** Before 1970, the Guarapiranga Basin was an area of recreation. Then public perception declined with urbanization, industrialization and with the increase of informal settlements. I am wondering if the Guarapiranga rehabilitation project improved the public perception of the basin and the lake?

**EF:** Oh yes, I believe that is true. When we began the work in the 1990s, every day we looked at the lake and our dream was to destroy the wall surrounding the lake. Then the environmental department opened all the spaces on the left bank to the public. They destroyed all the walls. The view of the lake is totally open now. We wanted to construct more than four or five big parks. Unfortunately, the implantation of the parks was paralyzed and the maintenance of the existing ones was weakened with the economic crisis of 2013.

**CW:** What are, in your eyes, the successes, but also the failures, or deficiencies, of the Guarapiranga project? Is there anything you would do differently today?

**ML:** Guarapiranga's works, in general, permitted a new sensibility for the large scale. Perhaps one of the biggest challenges, as the program unfolds, is to study and design the territory of the basins, Guarapiranga and Billings, in an integrated way as a single system in all urban and environmental aspects. It needs to include geomorphology and environmental protection, mobility and accessibility systems linked to different territories, their centralities and dynamics.

**120** ■ *Part II*

It needs to integrate network action, while respecting the singularities and diversity of social practices in each territory. In this context, the types of maintenance and appropriation of interventions by communities can be expanded.

Looking at the 20 years that have passed in between, the interventions of the Guarapiranga Program have made progress beyond the challenges of the integration of urban and environmental disciplines and legislation, and the laws of land use and occupation of the municipalities that have their territories in the basins.

On another scale, the continuous dialogue between the project and the technical standards, originally developed for the *formal* city, produced significant adjustments and advances. Technical standards were adapted to new challenges in situations of extreme precariousness or through collaboration with lawmakers to create standards appropriate to the forms of occupation of this territory.

A relevant fact in this historical perspective was the development of a technical culture in addition to the vision of architects and their performance in these areas. It has been greatly expanded since then, also, with the development of several courses teaching this approach, like the postgraduate course at Escola da Cidade implemented by Elisabete França, more than ten years ago.

**EF:** Unfortunately, favela urbanization programs have lost ground in the country due to the concentration of federal government efforts to implement the *Minha Casa Minha Vida Program* (MCMV). The resources for the municipalities were constrained by the rules of the federal program, based on the contracting of construction companies directly through the Federal Savings Bank. This caused a mismatch between the municipal public policies and the resources offered. Few municipalities integrated urbanization and construction via MCMV. Obviously, urbanization was eclipsed and the already urbanized areas ceased to be the focus of action by the municipalities.

We lost, in a few years, a whole collection of good practices and we can see that the results were perverse. Slums are growing, mainly vertically, public services do not respond to the needs of the residents and, worst of all, crime is advancing at frightening rates. In 2016, there were 60,000 violent deaths, mainly in poor communities, affecting mainly the young and black population.

**CW:** Is it now fairly normal for architects in São Paulo to work in favelas or is it still only a few specialized architects?

**EF:** I believe that the interest of architects, especially the new generation, is more concerned with public spaces and new forms of mobility. From 2013 onwards, and from the great street manifestations, it seems that the architects agreed with the importance of public spaces, but still focused on the richest regions of the city, Paulista for pedestrians, Parque Minhocão, Largo da Batata. The intellectual and physical distance between architects and poorer neighborhoods is still enormous, although academic debates are always present. Between 2013 and 2016, the views of the architects who consider that the urbanization of favelas is not housing policy was resurrected.

**CW:** Basically, in the past you have connected with universities abroad, not only Harvard University, but also with Columbia University and ETH Zurich. You started a postgraduate degree program in favela upgrading in the Escola da Cidade, and you are training a new group of young designers in favela upgrading. I wonder if these collaborations have changed how you work? Or what are the important lessons for you out of these collaborations?

**EF:** Well, I think that these collaborations are important to us. They help us to improve certain things. We incorporate ideas that the students of Harvard and Columbia discuss in their projects. In my opinion, the stimulation of information and the interchange of words and ideas are good for us. It is very important, because slum upgrading is a new issue in the world. So, everybody who works in this area needs to exchange ideas and knowledge.

**CW:** Have any experiences of other countries influenced you in any way?

**EF:** We exchange ideas, but Brazil was leading in slum upgrading. We began work in the 1990s, a lot of activist work on big projects, and Guarapiranga began in the 1990s too. I think Brazil's experience influenced other countries rather than other countries influencing Brazil. The world of slum upgrading is really a big operation.

However, as I mentioned earlier, unfortunately we abandoned all pioneering learning in shantytown development. Since the launch of MCMV, architects and public managers have been discussing ways to "improve" this program. Academic production almost entirely turned to this debate. And, meanwhile, favelas have been growing, access to basic sanitation has worsened year by year and urban violence has reached unimaginable levels.

I believe that the recovery of all this abandoned knowledge will take decades. We have to think about future public programs from new perspectives that face these new challenges that Brazilian cities face.

**ML:** In addition, a new collective political actor, represented by the militias, entered these territories. Initially as representatives of the state in favor of the communities, and later some of them became partners in the [narcotics] traffic, or power on other fronts such as gas supply, informal collective transport, implementation of clandestine digital networks, as well as construction and rental of properties.

**CW:** Can you give us an outlook for your aspirations for the São Paulo housing agency SEHAB?

**EF:** The future I want for SEHAB is that it will regain its ability to plan and operate in the priority areas of the city and to recover its ability to integrate actions with other secretariats and levels of government. Above all, its central position in relation to the municipal budget is currently limited to less than 1% of total investment, whereas in 2010 it was 4%.

**CW:** What kind of projects do you want to pursue in the future? What kind of collaborations do you want to implement? What are your goals? What do you want to reach?

**EF:** In 2013, after leaving the City Hall of São Paulo, I spent a sabbatical year doing a specialization course in art curatorship. But, in 2015, I was invited to join the cadres of the CDHU [Housing and Urban Development Company of the State Government of São Paulo], as director of planning and projects. A new challenge was posed and in line with the challenges that Brazilian society faces in this moment of deep political and economic crisis. The public sector needs to be restructured, and we must redefine the size of the state that society can support. We need to fight corruption, as it is a rampant attack on our society.

I am implementing these reforms in the company and seeking to structure new housing programs that are more appropriate to the current situation. In this sense, we launched the first public–private partnership for the production of housing in the central region, with a focus on low-income families. We are monitoring the first results to see if it is possible to scale up the program. And, we continue searching for ways to recover the precarious settlements of the metropolitan regions of the state of São Paulo.

**CW:** That sounds like a good plan. Thank you very much for the interview.

## Notes

1. First Interview conducted in São Paulo, October 2010, revised in August 2017 and in September 2020.
2. São Paulo City Hall, "Municipal housing plan: the São Paulo experience," in *Municipal Housing Policy: A Collective Construction* (São Paulo: Secretaria Municipal de Habitaçao, 2012), www.habitasampa.inf.br/documentos/pmh/2012/pmh_vol1_eng/index.html (accessed August 25, 2020).

# Case Study IV

## Medellín – Scaling Mountains

By 1991, Medellín had a homicide rate of 381 people per 100,000: a total of 6,329 homicides a year. It was the most dangerous city in the world, with violence springing from the battle waged between the central government, rural guerrillas and powerful drug interests, mostly in the informal areas of a city that was already in a state of serious deterioration. In the course of the next two decades, however, Medellín experienced a gradual reduction in crime so that, by 2005, the homicide

Figure 65  Public stairway leading to Juan Bobo creek, built in 2007 as part of PUI Nororiental (image from 2019)

**124** ■ *Part II*

rate was down to 37 homicides per 100,000 inhabitants: a rate comparable to that of Washington DC. While homicides spiked again due to turf wars between drug gangs in 2009, the numbers went down again by 2014 and it can be categorically affirmed the city is far safer now than it was at its low point in the early 1990s.[1]

This remarkable recovery comes as the result of many factors. Drug cartels and paramilitary forces have been heavily combated by the federal government, while the poorest, most neglected areas of the city have been physically and socially regenerated. The combination of crime reduction, urban regeneration and educational opportunities established the ground for the relative peace being currently enjoyed.

The history of Medellín and its informal areas differs from that of other cities. Since 1938, Medellín's population grew 15-fold from 140,000 inhabitants to more than 2,000,000 people in just the past 60 years.[2] At present, the entire metropolitan area has some four million dwellers.[3]

Medellín's rapid growth was fostered by the rural exodus to the city brought on by the asymmetrical armed conflict that began in the 1960s and continued up to 2016 (the effects of the historic peace-making agreement are still to be seen). During that period, large numbers of rural citizens tried to escape the escalating violence in the countryside by migrating to Medellín, a city that, despite its burgeoning prosperity in the 1960s and 1970s, could not provide so many newcomers with work. Inequality peaked, dividing the city into poor, middling and wealthy areas. A further wave of rural refugees arrived in Medellín throughout the 1980s, pushed to move by yet another spike in combative activities in outlying areas. As opposed to other cities, which experienced large influxes of hopeful rural populations in search of new opportunities, most of Medellín's new citizens had no choice but to flee their homes. By that same token, hundreds of thousands of people were unable to afford urban housing and forced to build their own dwellings on the steep, peripheral hills on the edges of Medellín. In 1997, the city published an official number of 250,000 people (14% of the total population) living in "subnormal" residences; some scholars estimated that number to be four times higher once all land invasions and illegal subdivision were accounted for.[4]

These informal neighborhoods were disconnected from basic infrastructure, economic opportunity and social services. As with Rio de Janeiro, drug traffickers turned them into their theaters of operation, and, as such, breeding grounds for criminal activity. Soon enough, the poorer half of Medellín's extremely polarized population occupied the north of the city, with its wealthier counterpart retreating into heavily fortified communities in the south. As a result, the city is, up to the present day, socially and physically segregated.

# PRIMED

Medellín's management of informal urbanization underwent several phases, from eviction in central locations in the 1960s to *in situ* improvement strategies for larger peripheral settlements in the 1990s. The first coordinated approach to *barrio*

**Figure 66  A public park by PRIMED (both images from 2011)**

(the local expression for a low-income neighborhood) upgrading was developed at the peak of violence during the early 1990s, when the mounting problems in Medellín's *comunas* (urban districts) finally received the federal government's attention with the creation of the *Consejería Presidencial para el Área Metropolitana de Medellín* (Presidential Council for the Metropolitan Area of Medellín). In 1993, the Consejeria installed the *Programa Integral de Mejoramiento de Barrios Subnormales en Medellín* (Integral Program for the Improvement of Subnormal Neighborhoods in Medellín, PRIMED), a pilot program supported by a diversity of agents, among which were the City of Medellín, the Federal Government of Colombia, the United Nations Development Program (UNDP) and the German government, as represented by the Bank for Reconstruction (KfW) and the Agency for Technical Cooperation (GTZ). Up to this point, sporadic initiatives had been undertaken in select informal neighborhoods, but PRIMED was the first program to develop a strategic framework for intervention in large settlements. It also differed starkly from previous attempts at urban regeneration by accepting informality as a given, and by closely bonding social elements into its physical interventions.[5]

PRIMED formed a new unit in the city government with direct access to the mayor of Medellín and the Colombian president. It collaborated with established agencies within the municipal government and with city-wide institutions, such as NGOs and community organizations, metropolitan planning agencies, national institutes and international entities, planning, coordinating and administering improvement projects in two phases between 1993 and 2000 in the barrios. The physical implementation of the work was conducted by municipal agencies, NGOs and community organizations, with the first phase executed in 15 communities between 1993 and 1997, benefiting some 51,000 residents, or about 20% of the total informal population of Medellín. In 2000, a second phase, planned to assist another 60,000 people, was cut short when the program was dismantled by new political leadership, a short-sighted decision if we consider that PRIMED was a major step forward in the comprehensive tackling of informal urbanization.[6]

PRIMED's goals were ambitiously exhaustive, including strategies as diverse as new planning and implementation mechanisms, citizen participation, physical improvement of the barrios, home improvement and relocation, legalization of tenure and mitigation of geological risk. While these objectives are not easy to meet

# 126 ■ *Part II*

in a climate of organized crime and violence, underemployment and an ingrained mistrust of governmental agencies, PRIMED met almost all of its stated purposes. In his 2007 review, Colombian planner John J. Betancur pointed out that the program was somewhat more successful in its physical than in its social aspects. The legalization of tenure and issuance of land titles, for example, proved to be a more protracted and involved process than originally stipulated. PRIMED's aspirations to build up strong community organizations, raise residents' awareness and create a sense of ownership for the improvement works also fell short of its objectives in the first phase of the program.[7]

Other aspects of resident engagement also furbished important lessons, because community participation is so critical to the redevelopment of informal areas. Initially, PRIMED set out with good conditions for community work through its rejection of political favoritism. Its neutrality allowed it to commit to community organizations in an unencumbered manner. During its first phase, nevertheless, some residents did not feel fully involved in what they perceived as predetermined planning decisions; while others disagreed with sweat equity contributions, where people who cannot afford to buy a house in government-built social housing projects, could help in the building work instead. In some cases, community groups were short-lived and vanished as soon as a project was built. In his assessment of PRIMED's community work, Betancur concluded that:

> it is rather unrealistic to expect that these communities will either work under highly formal frameworks and requirements or that they will follow passively the lead of institutions even as well intentioned and down to earth as PRIMED. Rather, projects and programs need to meet them at their level, take into account the real possibilities of their organizations and then, lend them the support necessary to grow.[8]

PRIMED was eager to address its weaknesses. Its second phase included a more progressive citizen program in the planning, implementation and post-implementation processes. Its ultimate goal was to treat the community as an equal partner by developing the capacity of community organizations, creating more feedback loops in the design process; collaboratively identifying priorities; triggering participatory budgeting procedures; starting up community subgroups to study specific aspects of the work and allowing the community to choose among different scenarios. Regrettably, the sudden termination of the program in 2000 did not permit much time in which to field-test these improvements.[9]

## EDU

Despite its premature cessation, PRIMED laid the groundwork for a radical expansion of Medellín's upgrading efforts when, three years later, a new mayor, mathematician Sergio Fajardo, was voted into office. In 2003, Fajardo initiated a massive reshuffling of public funds towards strategic investment in the poorest zones of the city. He explained his approach with meridian logic:

> I like to think about this as a mathematical problem, to establish and resolve an operation: first major social differences with a huge accumulated historic debt; and second, violence. So, take away the violence, and for every slice you take out, you bring in a new social opportunity: that is the challenge.[10]

The new mayor wanted to re-establish peace through educational opportunities, adhering to his campaign's slogan "Medellín, la más educada" (Medellín, the best educated):

> How can we diminish violence every day but also deliver social opportunities with each individual elimination of violence? Many people in our society have a solid wall in front of them: at one end is a door to enter the world of illegality. Drug trafficking has taken on extraordinary dimensions, more so in Medellín than anywhere else. Another door leads to informality and homelessness. Our challenge has been to open doors in that sealed wall, doors through which people can pass and continue participating in the construction of hope. What is hope? Hope is when someone in the community sees a path they can follow. If they are living with only a wall before them and can't see any options besides than illegality or informality, they have no real alternatives.[11]

During his tenure between 2003 and 2007, Fajardo broke many new openings into that wall. Five library parks (a cross-over between a library and a community center); a science museum; many new schools and school renovations for thousands of students; several major sports facilities; many new housing projects; several parks, including a large forest reserve; the renovation of the botanical garden; a cable car system and uncounted new pathways, streets, pedestrian bridges and plazas were constructed in the poorest neighborhoods of the city. These projects are the built testament of a massive expansion of social, economic and educational programs, which, under Fajardo's leadership, came to be known as *urbanismo social*.[12]

Fajardo's vision was enacted by a multi-sector, multi-scalar planning approach known as *Proyecto Urbano Integral* (Integrative Urban Project, PUI) administered by a newly founded unit: the municipal planning agency *Empresa de Desarollo Urbano* (Company for Urban Development). EDU's origins can be traced back to 1993 as an urban development agency in charge of executing projects in the same vein as PRIMED. In 2004, Mayor Fajardo restructured EDU and assigned it a new director, Medellín architect and academic Alejandro Echeverri. Following Fajardo's

## 128 ■ Part II

command to become active in the poorest and most violent areas of Medellín, Echeverri developed the PUI and defined five zones in it, on the grounds of a detailed analysis of the city and supported by the mayor's knowledge of the terrain:

> We knew the needs of all the city's spaces because we practiced politics on our feet. I myself walked Medellín from side to side geographically; it wasn't like I arrived in an armored car and got out on a certain block to look around. Our way of doing politics consisted precisely in coming into direct contact with people and their communities in all of their spaces. That is very powerful; I had the city under my skin, in my heart, and in my mind.[13]

As with PRIMED before, EDU pursued a holistic approach, the goal of which was to combine institutional coordination with social and physical improvement. In 2004, Echeverri created interdisciplinary teams, comprising ten to 15 architects, engineers, social workers and communications specialists, for each of the five established zones. Each of these teams worked together, from design to project implementation. Communication, agency coordination and the active involvement of the beneficiaries were critical objectives and the team leaders of EDU were closely connected to the residents of their respective zones, as well as to public agencies, NGOs and the private sector. Once again as with PRIMED, the agency made great efforts to involve the community at every phase: so much so that a special form of community participation, the so-called *talleres imaginarios* (imaginary workshops) were developed to include residents from all walks of life. These workshops were held to look into the dreams and aspirations that each and all had for their neighborhood. A participatory budget system was implemented to allow residents to decide on priority measures; a move that greatly enhanced community trust in governmental agencies. Job training and placement programs were created for the

| PLANNING | | | | | | | | | |
|---|---|---|---|---|---|---|---|---|---|
| DIAGNOSTIC | | | | FORMULATION | | | | | |
| MANAGEMENT | | | | | | | | | |
| DESIGN | | | | EXECUTION | | | ANIMATION | | |
| Stage 1 | Stage 2 | Stage 3 | Stage 4 | Stage 5 | Stage 6 | Stage 7 | Stage 8 | Stage 9 | Stage 10 |
| Social - Physical Acknowledgement | Project Profile | Architectural Preliminary Design | Architectural Design | Contractual Supplies | Contracting | Construction Work | Proposition | Management | Execution |

**Figure 67 The transformation of Medellín, a social action (a). Diagram by EDU, City of Medellín (redrawn for this publication)**

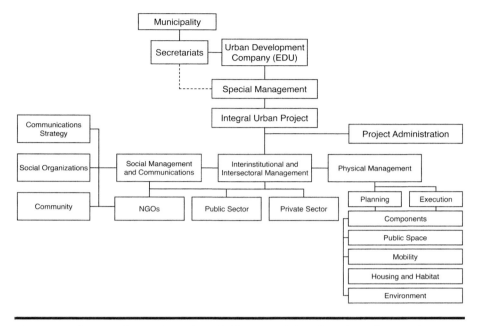

Figure 68 The transformation of Medellín, a social action (b). Diagram by EDU, City of Medellín (redrawn for this publication)

incorporation of former drug soldiers into the program, all of whom were amnestied upon admission.[14]

PUI sought to combine the social goals of education, job creation and community emancipation with the physical intervention of public infrastructure in the line of educational and transportation facilities, public parks and spaces, and environmental restoration. EDU's specific goals involved the improvement of extant public spaces and the construction of new ones, the introduction of public transport systems and the improvement of existing pathways and roads. It also homed in on building new housing for residents of high-risk areas prone to flooding and landslides, and strived for already available housing to be improved and tenure legalized. The same approach towards improving the given and improving the new was extended to public facilities such as schools, and to degraded environmental systems such as mountain creeks, ameliorated through linear parks.[15] For ex-mayor Fajardo, the esthetic impact of the interventions played a crucial role in raising the self-esteem of Medellín's citizens. He mandated that "the most beautiful buildings […] be in the poorest area of our city" and a process was accordingly initiated to select the best architects of the country for this work through public competitions.[16]

Figure 69 The world-famous Metrocable of Medellín, Linea K (image from 2011)

## PUI Nororiental
### Situation

The first PUI was executed in the *zona nororiental* (Northeastern Zone) of the city, where most of Medellín's low-income residents live in steep, mountainous terrain. The area comprises about 347 hectares and around 170,000 residents; it had high levels of violence, gang and drug activity; unemployment ranged around 60% and public space was four times scarcer than in the rest of the city.[17] Many residences are in landslide-prone zones. When PUI began operations, it had the distinct advantage of improved accessibility to the area via a recently built cable car line (Linea K) connecting the hillside barrios with the highly efficient Metro system of Medellín. The notion of the *Metrocable*, a cable car system, had first been conceived in the 1990s, and Línea K was the first to be in inaugurated in 2004.

Figure 70 Calle 107 below Linea K with widened sidewalks and increased businesses activity (left image from 2011, right image from 2019)

**Figure 71** Puente Mirador Andalucía, completed in 2007 as part of PUI Nororiental, rises high above the Herrera creek and connects the neighborhood to the Andalucía Metrocable station (both images from 2019)

## Intervention

The two-kilometer line tremendously improved accessibility for northeastern residents with negligible disturbance to the city fabric. It transports up to 3,000 residents per hour and substantially reduced the absurdly long commutes between the zone and Medellín's center. EDU's northeastern integral project used the four Metro cable stations as natural ancillary points from which to connect the hillside homes with a network of well-designed pathways, pedestrian bridges, public squares, linear parks and playgrounds. Simultaneously, energy and water provision, sanitation, drainage and communication systems were improved by Empresas Públicas de Medellín (Public Works of Medellín, EPM). Along treacherous creeks rushing down steep hills, endangered dwellings were removed and their residents moved to airy six-storey towers in the same vicinity. Extant urban nodes were reinforced through the renovation of schools and deteriorated public spaces and a new iconic hub in the form of the much acclaimed Spanish Library was built and well connected, through a series of clearly defined public spaces, to the nearby cable car station of Santo Domingo.[18]

**Figure 72** The promenade along Juan Bobo creek 12 years after construction (both images from 2019)

**132** ■ *Part II*

## *Post-intervention*

The work of PUI Nororiental has been widely divulged and celebrated as being among the most astonishing urban transformations in recent history. The Spanish Library and Metrocable are not just the most visible symbols of this metamorphosis, they also perform very well. The library receives many visitors and hosts a large assortment of programs and facilities: from municipal offices to a daycare center, passing through adult education courses, it was designed to accommodate a panoply of cultural events. Its building differs so starkly from its surroundings that some residents felt initially inhibited to enter it in the first weeks following its opening, assuming it was not intended for their use. Four more library parks have since been created in other neighborhoods.

Cable car ridership is high. The transfer from the rail-based city Metro to the Metrocable of Línea K is simple. Long queues can form during peak commuting times, which only further demonstrates the usefulness of this novel public transportation system. The gondolas are not only used by barrio residents, but also by many Medellín locals and tourists, all of whom use the system to make the most of its spectacular views over the city. It is worth remarking that the owners of homes below the cable lines have made efforts to improve their houses, and their roofs especially, now that they have become more visible. The success of Línea K spurred the construction and planning of several more cable car lines under the subsequent mayor Alonso Salazar (2008–2011), who continued to endorse *urbanismo social*. In 2010, a new 4.5-kilometer cable car system connected the Santo Domingo station to the 1,700-hectare natural reserve of Parque Arvi. The new Arvi line gives northeastern residents ready access to one of the largest recreational areas outside the Aburrá Valley, lending additional incentives for Medellín's citizens to venture into the former no-go zone of the Northeast. Since 2008, a new 2.7-kilometer Metro Cable (Línea J) is serving low-income communities westside of the valley. Medellín's success with Metrocable has been resonant enough to lure other cities, such as Rio de Janeiro and Caracas, to install their own cable car systems.

While the improvements attained in education and transportation are indeed impressive, the fundamental success of PUI Nororiental resides in the decrease of violence and the return of public life to its streets. Formerly among the most dangerous neighborhoods in Colombia, Santo Domingo can be now be visited and reached. Today, the carefully designed public space and circulation system serve as a platform for the safe gathering of residents; a simple act of civilized society that is often taken for granted, but that was rendered physically impossible in the crowded quarters of the Northeastern zone by organized crime. The network of pathways, bridges and plazas negotiate the meandering and steep topography remarkably well, with transitions between neighborhoods being smoothed out. Pedestrian plazas weave around the hill as ramps and functional stairways grant exciting views of the city. Countless new pedestrian bridges span deep gorges, connecting neighborhoods that were once completely separated. Sometimes, the bridges curve to adjust to the shape of the land, and their heads function complementarily as playgrounds or as public housing. The new, slender replacement housing integrates into the small-scale fabric of the barrio due to its small footprint and a façade treatment that uses the same orange brick as the self-constructed dwellings around it. As opposed to conventional public housing projects, the five-storey towers have verandas, balconies and public passageways that invite one to move through them, and which join with the path system along numerous creeks that were once open sewers and garbage dumps. Streets have been designed to maximize pedestrian comfort. In Calle 107, for example, a steep road below the cable car line, a traffic lane was removed to broaden the sidewalks and small platforms raised to allow the spillover of businesses into the public space. Accordingly, business in the district has increased.[19] It comes as no surprise that PUI Nororiental's success spurred EDU to expand the PUI method to more zones in the city.

**Figure 73** The curved Puente de la Paz spanning Juan Bobo creek at Carrera 48a, 12 years after its construction (image from 2019)

134 ■ *Part II*

# Conclusion

Medellín's resurgence from violence and civil war is an uplifting case that made headlines all around the globe and gave a positive example for the potential of good planning and design. Today, many foreign city officials visit the city to study, and strive for, the so-called *Medellín Model*.[20] At this point of official endorsement, the basic question arises: can the Medellín Model be replicated or is it an irreproducible alignment of fortunate events?

It is true that many factors coincided favorably in Medellín: a deep communal longing to overcome suffering, a consecutive series of visionary political leaders (Perez, Fajardo, Salazar), a traditionally strong design and planning culture and an administration that could successfully channel its sizable income stream. In contrast, earlier and equally valuable efforts, such as PRIMED, suffered from a weaker economy, a spike in the crime rate, endemic corruption and less supportive political leadership.

Medellín's recent transformation was assuredly a fortunate constellation of auspicious circumstances, but it was also the result of a series of deliberate actions that led to a specific outcome. The architect and activist Teddy Cruz argues that a fundamental political re-orientation laid the foundational core of Medellín's transformation:

> The key is to build a new political reality, to reimagine governance, to engage the complexity of process, and to sustain all of this through collaboration with communities over time [...] From the perspective of participatory democracy and social justice, Medellín is a story about how a public restored urban dignity, activated collective agency, and reclaimed the future of its own city.[21]
>
> He distinctly warns against the fallacy of just copying cable cars and library parks by other cities as outward symbols of transformation when there is no political and procedural transformation at its core. The Venezuelan urbanist David Gouverneur underlined this argument in his comparison of the cable car systems of Caracas and Medellín. Despite the original intentions of the designers, the intervention in Venezuela's capital city was not embedded in an equally ambitious upgrading program of its San Agustín neighborhood. It remained reduced to the introduction of a novel transport system. Thus, its impact has been very limited.[22]

The urban researchers Peter Brand and Julio D. Dávila described the Medellín Model in a similar, but less groundbreaking way: "The [Medellín] model itself is a conventional but well executed formula of good urban governance practice, comprising good governance (planning, fiscal discipline, transparency, participation and communication) and stressing education, inclusion, culture, conviviality and entrepreneurship, as well as social urbanism."[23] They attributed the successful implementation of the Medellín Model to three basic aspects:

1. "an extraordinary capacity for project management, centred on the Urban Development Agency (Empresa de Desarrollo Urbano, EDU)"
2. the self-financed works independent of outside donors (in large parts coming from Medellín's own successful public utilities company EPM)
3. the "functional coordination and spatial coherence" of the projects.[24]

When comparing the Medellín Model with other programs, such as Favela Bairro in Rio de Janeiro or the work of the São Paulo housing agency, a picture begins to emerge: the best upgrading programs are holistic, multi-sectorial and multi-functional; they closely combine physical and social actions and actors in carefully staged phases; they offer economic and educational opportunities; they deeply engage residents and various stakeholders and are intricately woven into the morphology of the land. But for all of this to work at all, capable governance structures have to exist. In summary, the Medellín Model is not unachievable or irreproducible, but it truly looks daunting for other cities to gather all these elements in place.

Besides these basic preconditions, I would like to highlight two more aspects that make the Medellín case special: its deliberate use of esthetics and its strong focus on public space.

Former mayor Sergio Fajardo always demanded a high esthetic standard in all of the urban interventions. It was meant as a tool to raise the self-esteem of barrio residents, who, in general, feel treated as second-class citizens. And indeed, the high quality design of the interventions is truly striking and has taken on a symbolic role alongside their utilitarian function. Especially, the iconic value of the Metrocable has nearly outweighed its function as a means of transportation. It is now a symbol of the rebirth of Medellín and regularly pictured on postcards, graffiti and city brochures (it features prominently in the airport). The cable cars, together with the etched cubes of the Spanish Library in *Communas 1* and *2* are now the main identifiers of the city, in much the same way. The pride these interventions instill in residents can be powerful and a new narrative of the city has unfolded: the *Medellín miracle*.[25] According to a field study by Françoise Coupé, one of the most frequent statements by citizens living in the vicinity of the cable cars was that the Metrocable made them finally "visible" to the rest of the city.[26] This psychological uplift should not be underestimated in a population that has been discriminated against for most of their existence.

The second factor that distinguishes Medellín is the understanding that public space is the physical platform from which democracy may once again spring. While the landmark buildings and cable cars work as galvanizing signifiers of change, the less iconic construction of uncounted small streets, plazas and linear parks on the "skin" of the city is the actual workhorse of Medellín's transformation. For Echeverri, the creation of public space is the original design act from which civility and democracy can be re-established in the context of a traumatized society.[27]

It may seem impossible to verify this statement. Which, of all the measures taken at the federal, regional and municipal levels in the fight against drug cartels, militias and general criminality, had the greatest impact on the decrease of violence and the reinstatement of civility and democracy? At the time, one can only assume (and hope) that the integrated combination of urban, economic and social interventions, together with police operations, played a critical role in this. But Echeverri's claim touches a deeper, oft unmentioned, function of public space: namely, the expression of civil life. Of course, the most beautifully designed public plaza cannot function under a reign of terror (as some projects in Rio's favelas have already proven). But once terror subsides, a physical receptacle for the expression of citizenship outside the private home is called for. The Medellín projects reveal the archaic function of public space. Its networks of streets, plazas and sidewalks are more than just paved areas for the management of business and traffic: they are the physical basis for civility and democracy.

In the realm of spatial transformation, the Medellín Model has highlighted the esthetic and democratic role of public space. Its transformation is still young and it remains to be seen if it will be sustained. Factors hard to predict and control, such as gang activity, political leadership and overall economic development may have an adverse effect. Beyond maintaining what has already been done, there is still considerable work to conclude: tens of thousands of homes are still found in high risk areas on the unstable northeastern slopes, constantly threatened by devastating landslides in the rainy season. These hazardous conditions will only be exacerbated by future informal growth. Medellín is expected to continue to grow in the future. Many will not be able to afford a home and will informally settle on the treacherous hills. It is clear that the city must add a series of relocation and stabilization projects, as well as anticipatory growth perspectives, to its current strategies.[28]

Indeed, there is still lot of work to do, because the Medellín Model is not perfect. The geographer Peter Brand claimed that the Medellín Model, despite its high acclaim, actually brought very little direct economic improvement to its low-income residents:

> … although the Metrocables/social urbanism appear to have contributed to improving living conditions in the areas of influence, they have done nothing to contain the increasing socio-spatial inequality of the city. In fact, whilst the Metrocables were being introduced Medellín became the most unequal city of Colombia as measured in terms of income distribution.[29]

His observation underlines the fact that the combating of inequality will take much longer than the duration of any single administration and will require strategies in addition to *urbanismo social*. Unfortunately, there is a danger that Medellín's high visibility projects, such as cable cars and library parks, will seduce future mayors anywhere to focus on showy projects instead of on less glamorous, but equally important measures. Brand observed that "Contemporary urbanism, including the Medellín case, has become increasingly inclined towards the spectacular and its marketing potential, caught up in a dizzy spiral of competition and the short-term logic of capital."[30]

Indeed, the Gaviria administration (2012–2016) unsuccessfully pursued a magnetic rail project (Tranvia) as a lateral connection in the steep slopes bordering the valley,[31] – a spectacular notion whose cost–effect ratio and general benefits can be very much doubted compared to more humble projects, such as enabling hillside communities to simply plant trees and clean out drains.

# Notes

1. The Atlas, "Medellín homicide rate, 1975–2015," 2016, https://theatlas.com/charts/Syhv4LhXe (accessed April 23, 2021).
2. John J. Betancur, "Approaches to the regularization of informal settlements: the case of PRIMED in Medellín, Colombia," *Global Urban Development Magazine* 3(1) (November 2007): 2.
3. World Population Review, "Medellin Population 2020," https://worldpopulation review.com/world-cities/medellin-population (accessed August 20, 2020).
4. John J. Betancur, "Approaches to the regularization of informal settlements," 14.
5. John J. Betancur, "Approaches," 2.
6. Ibid., 2.
7. Ibid., 7.
8. Ibid., 10.
9. Ibid., 11
10. Sergio Fajardo, lecture, Wentworth Institute of Technology, Boston, September 22, 2008.
11. Sergio Fajardo and Giancarlo Mazzanti, "Interview: Sergio Fajardo and Giancarlo Mazzanti," *Bomb* 110, 2010, https://bombmagazine.org/articles/sergio-fajardo-and-giancarlo-mazzanti/ (accessed August 25, 2020).
12. Alejandro Echeverri and Francesco Orsini, "Informalidad y urbanismo social en Medellín," in *Medellín: Medio Ambiente, Urbanismo, Sociedad*, ed. Michelin Hermelín Arbaux, Alejandro Echeverri Restrepo and Jorge Giraldo Ramírez (Medellín: Universidad EAFIT – Centro de Estudios Urbanos y Ambientales, Urbam, 2010), 130–152.
13. Fajardo and Mazzanti, "Interview," 2010.
14. Conversation with Alejandro Echeverri, 2010.
15. Echeverri and Orsini, "Informalidad y urbanismo social," 130–151.
16. Fajardo, lecture, 2008.
17. Empresa de Desarrollo Urbano, *Modelo de transformación urbana–Proyecto Urbano Integral PUI zona nororiental* (Medellín, 2014), 163–188.
18. Echeverri, "Informalidad y urbanismo social," 140–143.
19. Ibid.
20. A term that was coined by the Interamerican Development Bank in 2009 to disseminate the Medellín experience in a structured manner.
21. Teddy Cruz and Fonna Forman, "The Medellín Diagram," www.youtube.com/watch?v=z89ixMyyE1o (accessed August 25, 2020).
22. David Gouverneur, *Planning and Design for Future Informal Settlements: Shaping the Self-Constructed City* (New York: Routledge, 2014), 107–111.

## 138 ■ *Part II*

23. Peter Brand and Julio D. Dávila, "Metrocables and 'Social Urbanism': two complementary strategies," in *Urban Mobility and Poverty: Lessons from Medellín and Soacha, Colombia*, ed. Julio D. Dávila (London: Development Planning Unit, UCL, 2013), 47.
24. Ibid., 52.
25. Kate Maclean, *Social Urbanism and the Politics of Violence: The Medellín Miracle* (London: Palgrave Pivot, 2015), 2.
26. Françoise Coupé, "The Metrocables: risk, poverty, and inclusion," in *Urban Mobility and Poverty: Lessons from Medellín and Soacha, Colombia*, ed. Julio D. Dávila (London: Development Planning Unit, UCL, 2013), 74.
27. Personal conversation with Alejandro Echeverri, May 13, 2012.
28. Joseph Claghorn and Christian Werthmann, "Shifting ground: landslide risk mitigation through community-based landscape interventions," *Journal of Landscape Architecture* 10(1) (2015): 6–15. See also Gouverneur, *Planning and Design*, 105–110.
29. Peter Brand, "Governing inequality in the south through the Barcelona Model: 'Social Urbanism,' in Medellin, Colombia," paper presented to conference *Governance, Contestation, Critique* (Leicester, De Montfort University, 2013), 8.
30. Ibid., 11.
31. Eventually, a more effective alignment was chosen that connects the city center at the valley bottom with middle-to-low-income neighborhoods to the East (from San Antonio to Oriente); its inauguration was in 2015.

# *Interview with Alejandro Echeverri (AE)[1]*

## Interviewer: Christian Werthmann (CW)

Alejandro Echeverri was the Manager of Empresa de Desarollo Urbano (2004–2005, Director of Proyectos Urbanos Integrales (2005–2008) and is currently the Director of the Centro de Estudios Urbanos y Ambientales (Urbam) in EAFIT University in Medellín.

**CW:** Alejandro, the projects you led as director of EDU are well known. PUI Nororiental won many awards and in 2009 you became a recipient of the prestigious Curry Stone Design Prize. Since then, the transformation of Medellín is famous in the planning world. Many people wonder, though, how was it economically feasible? Every city with high crime and poverty rates would love to follow this example, but how would they pay for it?

**AE:** The funding for the projects in Medellín comes mostly from the city's municipality and complemented by national resources. The problem is not generally one of resources but of investment: how to put the money to good use. The major cities of Colombia have a wide spectrum of range when it comes to their ability to collect and invest taxes. In the context of Colombia, Medellín is economically very powerful. Not only is it the second largest city in the country, it also has Colombia's largest economic cluster, with major cement industries and as the center of the coffee economy, so it was generally sound in terms of monies. The most important policy that it enacted since 2004, however, was one of efficiency in its handling of money. Out of every peso that a person pays in taxes, 82 cents go to investment projects and only 18 cents to the administration. In 2008, the city updated its property tax, something politically very difficult to achieve in terms of our community and people, but this allowed for an increase of more than 23% in city revenues. The city government is also

**140** ■ *Part II*

**CW:** How was it that this money was not used prior to the Fajardo administration? Was it a political decision to have it otherwise invested?

more efficient and transparent, with financial institutions ranking it as a triple A. In brief, my answer could be summarized as investing wisely and managing resources with efficiency.

**CW:** How was it that this money was not used prior to the Fajardo administration? Was it a political decision to have it otherwise invested?

**AE:** The money had been used before, but not in the same way. The answer is a bit circuitous because things changed, in term of national constitutional laws, in 1991, giving the cities more autonomy to administer their money. A chapter in the book *Medellín: Medio Ambiente, Urbanismo, Sociedad* gives precise information about these legal reforms.[2] To put it briefly, the two administrations prior to Fajardo's had already started to use public funds for major investments in the city. They banked on different projects, sometimes quite successfully. But these were isolated interventions without a "big picture" frame, as with a system; nor with the purpose or direction of investing foremostly in the poorest areas of the city. Earlier investments at the hands of prior administrations kept to the more traditional line of staying within consolidated areas and neighborhoods. Fajardo changed this by fostering investment of the highest quality into the poorest areas.

**CW:** When you began this series of projects – the schools, the library-parks, the linear parks – how did you convince the architects and designers of Medellín to work in the most dangerous parts of the city?

**AE:** We didn't ask them *[laughs]* … First came the political decision, with the endorsement of the technical groups, that is to say, the architects. One of the main successes of the Fajardo administration involved its inviting top-tier agents from different professions to work with it; whether it be in culture, in security and the social sciences, in architecture or in urbanism. The administration started to work within the public sector hand in hand with architects and planners who were already recognized and well respected, working under Fajardo's orders. It just so happens that Fajardo himself was already quite close to architecture and urbanism because his father was one of the most important architects of Colombia: he grew up with it, as it were. What we did was put together a quality team of young architects, the best of whom were graduating from university at the time, to define an overall strategy. We decided to invite the finest Colombian designers through national public competitions, and I use the word "invite" because it was not any one architect's decision to choose which project to participate in at the time: these were merit assignments. The bases for the competitions were punctiliously drafted, with the support and credibility lent them by the organizers of the contest. Some of the best architects that participated in these competitions won, and they comprised an excellent group of designers that began to look at things differently and to take in the informal sectors with fresh eyes. The process had begun some seven or eight years before we came into office; in our case, it extended to the universities where we were doing very serious work in the crafting of tools and resources

Interview with Alejandro Echeverri ■ 141

through which to intervene in the informal areas. The most important thing was for us to count with a large pool of people training at the undergraduate and graduate levels who would then come to work with us in the municipality.

**CW:** And so, the universities were among the first to work in the *Comunas*?

**AE:** Yes, that was the key. In the middle of the crisis in the 1990s, a different process of innovation started in the comunas, led by social actors, NGOs, and private initiatives, but not by the local government. But it was also coincidental that the universities happened to be conducting very interesting research projects when the political decision to change things finally was made.

**CW:** Many projects were built during your tenure as director of EDU. You designed and built a fantastic science museum, for one. Which projects rank as your favorites?

**AE:** Perhaps the project that excites me the most, because it was a dream come true, began many years before working ith Fajardo, when significant research on the matter had already been done. It is the PUI or *Proyectos Urbanos Integrales*, which cannot be defined as a work of architecture but, rather, as a series of urban interventions. The PUI is a very simple way to implement an appropriate environment in marginal areas through a combination of well-understood local, physical and social conditions, and a proposal of well-defined and sequentially small and large operations: a bridge here, the improvement of a school there, the recovery of an environmental issue through symbolic work such as a park, a library, a transportation system. The project changed how we understood architecture, even as it was important to see how architecture could be an application of social impact in Medellín. At the time, people did not like the name *Proyecto Urbano Integral*, it meant nothing to them; the term was very technical and didn't sound well in the frame of political speeches. At first no one understood or accepted that the PUI was a comprehensive urban project in and for the city. I remember the first year in which I served as manager of the EDU, the home for all strategic urban projects, where we put together managers and technical teams. I invited the press and some members of the community to talk to them about the PUI, which we proceeded to describe in 3D renderings in an effort to get the concept across, but no one understood and no one cared. Both the journalists and the community seemed skeptical and everything was still on paper. Today, the PUI take up entire newspaper pages, people talk about them, and the term has become colloquial.

**CW:** Within this integral approach, which is the most important element to you?

**AE:** The integral approach has some very specific projects, with architecture being applied at different scales. For example, some bridges are very powerful in the context of the city, to the point of having changed the way in which people relate in their communities. Before, they used to live apart and now the bridge connects them. But it is not the bridge alone that is powerful, even as it connects the community to the new transportation system, the pedestrian street, or to a new school. It is these links that give the bridge its power. There are

**142** ■ *Part II*

other projects that function in this way; the Orchard Hall in the Botanical Garden is an instance of a wonderful piece of architecture with great spatial qualities. But the PUIs are my favorite projects: they are my, and our, dream come true.

**CW:** When I talk to the managers of Favela Barrio in Rio, or to the São Paulo housing agency about their projects, one of their biggest problems involves the maintenance of the public spaces they have built: the upkeep of the schools, having sufficient janitors or teachers, having someone to look after the trees. So how does it work in Medellín? You've accomplished so much in such little time. How can you guarantee the long-term management?

**AE:** I cannot answer this question just yet. Allow me to explain. Thus far, everything with these projects is fine, but they are very recent. The first critical consideration is involving the community in the design process and in the discussion of public spaces, but the quality of the final products is also very important. Medellín is developing the best designs with the help of the best architects and technicians. The people of Medellín, however, have an incredibly staunch self-esteem, and the best example through which to show this is that of the Metro. In Medellín we have what we call *metroculture*: the people love the Metro. And we have learned a lot from this. The Metro began to operate 12 years ago through a most interesting process involving a public campaign in the city, and now you can see how the people take care of it. You will not find a [single piece of] paper on the Metro floor today.

**CW:** But is that because people don't drop anything in the Metro or because it is cleaned very well?

**AE:** It is both, because while it is certainly very well cleaned, it is also the case that no one drops paper or makes pencil-marks where they should not. At first we worried about what could happen to our public space, because we thought, for example, that if you have a house without a floor beside new pavement, perhaps you would want to take the pavement of the public space for your own house. But nothing like that happened. Of course the city has to decide on a new budget for that, but quality is paramount. Another important point is that public spaces must be used intensively: if this happens, then people will care for those spaces. We have some instances of other public spaces that were not too judiciously located and they start to deteriorate quite rapidly, but spaces that are well integrated into the living structures of the people are flourishing.

**CW:** The Medellín project was completed in such a short period. How can you ensure successful community participation when projects are moving so fast?

**AE:** The manner in which we involve the community have different dimensions and timings. Some work on some projects is obviously best left to the technicians and not to the community, so you don't have to discuss a lot with it. To give an example: there is the public space where the community takes the bus, the bus stop, where commercial activities happen. Now, all of the informal neighborhoods have one street that means something to everyone, and it is clear that if you improve that street, then everybody will be happy. We set out on those projects fast and work with the community to develop a more complete image of how and where and what that street should be connected with in terms of other public spaces, of other meaningful places that are important to the community. It is in this combination between the more direct projects and the more unknown structures that the community becomes involved.

**CW:** Who addresses the community: is it the social workers, is it the architects, is it both? Who defines the program of the project?

**AE:** They all do, but each project has a face, a person in charge, and a leader; every project its own interdisciplinary team of social workers, architects and technicians. But there is always one person who calls the shots and who has immediate access to the mayor, because these are very complex interventions. If you are going to say to the community that you will have a design ready for discussion in two months' time, then you better have it ready if you want to earn their trust. That is why it is important for the project to have a face and for the team to be 100% dedicated to its territory. That specific team cannot be doing ten other projects in the city. But this tends to be uncommon in the public sector, where people generally have to grapple with all the city's problems simultaneously. So we chose to separate each team in the EDU, to put a leader in charge of it, to lend him/her all of our support and to coordinate every different line of public administration. And the assigned territory must be walked through every single day: one has to be there. So that is where you will find them: not in the municipal tower, but with the community. The architects' workshops are very close to the community.

**CW:** That means the architects have an on-site office?

**AE:** Not in every project, but in some of them, yes.

**CW:** Some of the PUI, such as the Zona Nororiental, are very large. You said that one covered some 100,000 people or more. How can you connect with 100,000 people?

**AE:** We only work in a strategic structure of the territory that is used by 100,000 people, but we can't actually reach 100,000 people: it's impossible. And yet, the PUI and the transport system are providing services to a territory that size. One of the key issues, and one of the great risks, of the PUI is that of size. Now that, on account of the success of the first intervention, we are going through a second wave of PUIs in Medellín, the political decision has been taken to implement a huge PUIs strategy. I used to say that to redefine urbanity one must look at the places people use and live in every day: the path they take when they go from their homes to the bus, to take their children to school, to buy something, to connect with another neighborhood. This is a defined and scaled structure that can translate into a strategy for the improvement of a larger area. But fast change, if you can call it fast, will take years to come to fruition through concentrated strategies. Neighborhoods of this sort require a

**144** ■ *Part II*

lot of this type of work, and it impinges on how the city supports the improvement of housing, of services and so forth.

**CW:** Let's say you want to build a library-park in a certain area and to work in close contact with the community in the area. How do you define your strategies for a PUI?

**AE:** A specific decision we took was to provide some strategies for the entire city: say, we are going to build a new network of public services revolving mostly around cultural education, and we will take those public buildings to operate as new nodes for activities in the poorest neighborhoods. We did a study of the city as a whole and then defined a large-scale strategy. We also singled out the most dangerous informal settlements in Medellín to decide precisely on the size and limits we were going to set between the physical and social problems. After that we started to implement the PUI strategies in those areas. Our method turned out to be a combination of the PUI and the Library-Park strategies: once we have a big picture of the city, we can get a big picture of every PUI territory. We conducted a very serious and exact study of the territory of 100,000 people and defined a strategic view with highly punctual interventions, but we also started work with the community.

**CW:** How did you work with the community?

**AE:** In some ways, we helped it make the right decision. The people that live in these neighborhoods have quite elementary needs; they don't think in terms of big structures, because, to their minds, those do not exist. They do, however, have a great deal of useful information, which helps a lot with strategic decisions. You have to work in both directions and combine the two of them because each gives feedback to the other. As I see it, you can't take every decision on the grounds of the community alone, you have to combine and balance.

**CW:** So what are those two directions: listening to the community's basic needs and developing a strategy for the city as a whole?

**AE:** What we see is how the community improves its understanding of its territory in a process that's incredibly fast. Today, the people can accurately explain to you what the PUI strategies are; we don't have to explain them anymore. But you have to build one first: this helps a lot. In undertaking a second PUI, we put the community where the PUI is going to begin in contact with the community where the PUI has already been built, this has helped a lot …

**CW:** In terms of earning credibility?

**AE:** In terms of earning credibility, exactly; now they know what is going to take place in their neighborhoods.

**CW:** In your lectures you show slides of the Library-Park España, you show the cable car and improved streets, but you also say that the most important parts of the project are invisible. Can you explain this?

**AE:** Yes. The magazines communicate that change came from the library-parks because they are beautiful and visible, but the project itself was just as important to the minds of the local people. Design quality must not be taken lightly: it makes people proud, and many good things can happen because of this. But the Library-Park is, in fact, the last step in the intervention because it takes more time to develop and, in some neighborhoods, it is the largest element of infrastructure. Yet, different kinds of interventions at a very small scale that connect with one another are extremely relevant, and so we have the small street, the small stairway, the small bridge; the improvement of small playgrounds for the kids; trees; a sidewalk here, a streetlight there; and all of this in the frame of the social and cultural work that is also taking place in the community. Our investment is four or five times greater in these small projects than for the Metrocable or the Library-Park, and when you walk into the territory you will see everything at once, but the pictures won't show it all if they are taken from afar. I used to say that the most important things happened on the skins of neighborhoods, and not just physically but socially as well, even as a combination of dimensions really does matter. In many parts of the world, traditional improvement is perceived as being merely elementary improvement. But if you effect that elementary improvement with quality, while also adding infrastructure, the whole place will be better.

**CW:** You already mentioned that one specific aspect of the Medellín project was the impact of beauty on the dignity of people. Fajardo is often quoted as saying that "our most beautiful buildings have to be in the poorest areas." Can you elaborate on that? Did beauty have an effect on the community? Did it improve its self-esteem?

**AE:** The first question you asked was how to connect social and spatial segregation, because in Medellín we have two, three or more, but mainly three, separated cities. You have to work with their physical forms but account for their mental forms, too. Medellín, for example, has 2.5 million inhabitants within the boundaries of the municipality, but 3.5 million people in the actual metropolitan area. Because our society is so segregated we have a lot of differences. In the case of the middle and upper classes, the city that the people have in mind comprises just 30% of the real city; the rest doesn't exist for them, it's nothing. And the other people, the people who live in the poorer areas, occupy 50% of the territory: they can move around the entire city. So how do you not only expand the size of the city, but make rich and poor alike – and not just the poor – more aware of its real dimensions? The quality and quantity of the buildings and public services that we are raising in marginal areas, for instance, has helped us address the wealthy, so that currently all the different "cities" in Medellín are using those buildings and services. So to the people that already live there we may add people from outside who are coming because of the good connections afforded by the transportation system and the quality of the new buildings and cultural programs. People are actually going to the Comuna Nororiental in the Santo Domingo neighborhood, something completely unimaginable just ten years ago. So, it has been critically important to change the minds of the people that make up these communities. Since they are proud

## 146 ■ *Part II*

of their space and feel they have the best buildings there, their services are more complete and better than ever before. Quality of space, quality of design, connections, integral and complementary services: all have been crucial.

**CW:** As a designer you were probably not trained to work in the informal areas.

**AE:** Not at all! When I was a student of architecture in 1985 no one talked about them.

**CW:** But you are also an educator. You have served as a professor and you run a design research institute in Medellín. What would you say for the future education of architects and designers regarding informal city upgrading?

**AE:** When I was a student, some of Medellín's greater problems began to arise because of drug money. Like any other city in Latin America, and many cities in the world, we have inequality, but there was an additional dimension to our problem. Medellín had to deal with enormous safety concerns and an internal war. What happened to me happened to many people, and we sought ways in which to change the situation. The issues that we faced back then and that we face today were taking place in the informal city. I used to work on private projects, but from the time I taught at the university, other aspects of the territory became of interest to myself, to other architects and friends. We were trying to see the complete footprint of Medellín. The first thing that took us to the comunas was water: it was interesting to see how the creeks and other such natural systems defined the structure of the city. When you realize these creeks and ravines are among the most troubled parts of the city and found there where communities have the most problems, you start to understand quite a few things. And so we began to work in the informal spaces, right along the creeks. We thought one of the keys through which to better grasp our territory would involve connecting these natural systems with the human and physical settlements around them, and so we needed a better understanding both of systems and communities alike. So if you ask me about the future of Medellín, my answer will depend on how we start to treat these systems and to work with them. At the time we were only conducting some well-timed, mostly physical, interventions, and though the natural systems are by no means unknown, they must be pushed further. I think we architects have to work with interdisciplinary teams to get a better grasp of natural systems.

**CW:** What do you think about the continuation of the PUI model?

**AE:** Because of the first one's success, politicians think they can expand the model: "If it helps safety and we have this huge area, let's implement a PUI." However, one of the cores of the PUI is to work within complete, precise and limited boundaries. Where and what you are working on matters, because you are building defined and connected structures in the combination scales that I mentioned. But if you deploy this in a more disperse, atomized territory, then the strategy is not all that effective. Technicians don't have all the answers, and many of these decisions need to be made at a higher level. This is one of the main reasons why the mayor needs assistance, someone at a high level working close to him to help him define strategies. When political decisions come only from above and technical ones only from the lower or middle echelons, the ensuing gap affects the project's success.

**CH:** How relevant was the precedent of PRIMED to Fajardo's work?

**AE:** Fajardo was not aware of PRIMED, but those who worked with him were: we knew it very well. The first steps of what would be known as "The North Urban Project," with the north of the city as its target, were taken through a workshop and a research group at a private university, EAFIT. We understood the problems from a theoretical, rather than a real-world, vantage. PRIMED was a national effort: funding was provided by the German and Colombian governments, and some of the people that worked for PRIMED came from the national, hence public, university, which had a very good research department. I looked for some of these people to join my group, and two of them were invited to do so in the context of the "North Urban" workshop. We got to learn about the logic behind PRIMED, and they learned something from us, too. Later, Fajardo got wind of our work and invited us to join him in the municipality. He knew and shared our interests, and from the very start we involved people that had worked for PRIMED, which was unfortunately brought to a complete halt because of a political decision, but also because it was not deeply ingrained at a municipal level, with the assurances of greater institutional independence that this represents.

**CW:** I have one last question. There have been reports that crime in Medellín is on the rise again. Are you concerned about this, or do you see it as a transitory phenomenon?

**AE:** I am worried, but optimistic. There was a rise in 2010, 2011, but from then it went down again; in the medium and long term the numbers continue to decline, but in comparison to other parts of the world they are still high.

The improvement of safety is a combination of many variables. It is not just social and/or physical improvements that account for a change in conditions, and timing is of the essence when it comes to programs seeking to reinsert people into society. In 2003 and 2004, there was a huge national program in which the militia surrendered their arms and began to do just this. In Medellín alone, 4,000 people who used to partake in guerilla groups joined it. The militia reached an agreement with the government, and the latter granted 3,400 people the opportunity to start their lives again, even as the remaining 600 individuals continue to live on their own, violent terms. Not coincidentally, safety improved in the neighborhoods where the presence of the public sector ran parallel to the aforesaid social and physical interventions. At the time, we worked a lot with those projects and we came to involve every part of the community: the leaders, the housewives and mothers, the former militiamen, all sat at the same table collaborating, and that was critical to us and to the process's success.

Let me tell you a story. A community leader who is also a mother in the Santo Domingo neighborhood told us, in tears, how the initiative was

**148** ▪ *Part II*

magnificent, but also very difficult. On the very first day on which it started, which was a Saturday, someone knocked on her door, and there were two guys, one of whom turned out to be the man that had killed her son two years ago. But they had now gone to her house to invite her to the discussion on the Library-Park project. She cried as she told us that, after a year, she and those two men were leading projects together. Stories of reconciliation such as this one are happening all the time. The attitude being struck between the former militia, community leaders, public workers and the local police is deeply important.

**CW:** Do you think the improvement of the public space can decrease crime?

**AE:** Yes, locally. Where we transformed space, current crime indicators are completely different. We don't have exhaustive studies about it, but people tell us. And it's not just the public space, either, but, rather, public space that is extremely well connected and intensely used. I am certain that the improvement of public space benefits the community and can have an impact on the diminishment of crime, but this is only one of the many instruments that have to be deployed for this to happen. You need to have the presence of police: not in a confrontational manner, but you need to have it, like in any city, everywhere. You have to ensure that trash has been collected in an orderly manner, and so on and so forth.

**CH:** Are other cities following the Medellín model?

**AE:** Medellín became an example for other cities in the world with similar challenges. Sometimes it is good if those who come understand the reality and the complexity of the processes. Other times it is very bad, if what they take from here are simple recipes and iconic images. But the most important thing is that the attention helps us to continue a process that we have just started. We ourselves learned a lot from the first steps taken at Favela Bairro, which served as one of our earlier models. But I think that every city must enact change in its own way because of varying political contexts.

**CW:** Thank you very much for the interview.

## Notes

1. First Interview conducted in Medellín, October 8, 2010, revised in September 2020.
2. Santiago Leyva Botero, "El proceso de construcción de estatalidad local (1998–2009): ¿la clave para entender el cambio en Medellín?," in *Medellín: Medio Ambiente, Urbanismo, Sociedad*, ed. Michelin Hermelín Arbaux, Alejandro Echeverri Restrepo and Jorge Giraldo Ramírez (Medellín: Universidad EAFIT – Centro de Estudios Urbanos y Ambientales, Urbam, 2010), 271–293.

# AND NOW?

**150** ■ *Part III*

This book sought to explore the process and perpetuity of landscape transformation in informal neighborhoods in Latin America. Three large-scale, government-led projects (Rio de Janeiro, São Paulo and Medellín) and one small designer-initiated project (Buenos Aires) were chosen. As urban transformation takes decades, only projects were selected that allowed a longer time frame of observation; the selected cases in Rio de Janeiro and São Paulo are now (2020) over 20 years old, and the work in Medellín and Buenos Aires over ten years. The observation supported the notion that public space and landscape is indeed an essential element for improving living conditions in informal urbanization; at its best it can contribute to better infrastructure, environmental risk reduction, economic opportunities, community cohesion, civic self-esteem and democratization in general.

However, it also became clear that the transformation of public space is insufficient if it is not embedded in a multi-sectoral and multi-scalar process that continues beyond election cycles. Landscape and public space should be manipulated in tandem with short- and long-term actions that have to be performed by many actors with shared goals in a fundamentally democratic way. In that integral process, issues of landscape are pervasive; landscape is the stage and the ground, but also threat and opportunity; its necessary manipulation supersedes by far the out-of-date notion of "urban greening" as a luxurious decoration for recreational gains.

If this integral long-term procedure can be achieved not only in a single neighborhood, but for all marginalized neighborhoods of a city, the individual and common gain should be great. But, as the study of the four cases has shown, these instances are rare to find, very hard to do and very difficult to sustain. Progress is fragile, setbacks are common (Rio de Janeiro), and many aspects have to be met or coincide to make an initiative successful (Medellín). Even if a project shows signs of success, a new political leadership with a different mindset can wipe out the gains (Rio de Janeiro). Positive and negative cycles do not exclusively occur in informal neighborhoods, but in cities in general; downward trends such as economic disruption, social conflict, gang wars, disasters and political discontinuity are part of the urban condition. However, in the fragile settings of informal neighborhoods these ups and downs can be more pronounced, with harsher repercussions for its residents (i.e., loss of home, loss of livelihood, loss of life). Therefore, designers and planners working in informal settlements have to learn to navigate this heightened volatility; they have to ask themselves: how can improvement efforts in informal neighborhoods be more effective and resilient?

I would like to put forward four recommendations:

## *Choose Carefully Where and with Whom You Work*

*Observe governance*
*Avoid the pitfalls of government-driven projects*
*Avoid the pitfalls of community/NGO-driven projects*

### Pursue an Integrative Improvement Process

*Connect physical to social improvements*
*Develop better community participation, collaboration and co-creation models*
*Apply a telescopic approach*
*Combat the stigmatization of informal neighborhoods*
*Develop a specific design approach for public spaces*

### Use Landscape as Infrastructure

*End the "upgrading" of informal neighborhoods through wasteful infrastructure*
*Use landscape and public space as a platform for integrated infrastructure*

### Increase Knowledge of Designers and Planners

*Train planners and designers differently*
*Pursue a global exchange of knowledge*

# Choose Carefully Where and with Whom You Work

As the four cases have shown, a project's success is largely dependent on how well it navigates the specific social, economic and political dynamics. Obviously, a designer has to know the local political landscape and has to choose very carefully whom he or she wants to be aligned with and how he or she operates. For example, many residents of informal neighborhoods are wary of governmental projects, as they have been mistreated or misled in the past. Full transparency about dependencies or alliances of the designers is foundational for maintaining the trust of a community. But the designer has not only to know the political landscape of a city, but also of the whole country.

### Observe Governance

A designer working in a country with a relatively stable democratic government has to employ different methods than in a country where the government is in constant disarray. A designer in Argentina, Brazil or Colombia may have to navigate cases of political willfulness, economic crises, government corruption, gang or police violence; however, this designer is still in a less volatile situation than he/she would be in a severely impoverished country without an elected government, warring factions, famine or under the constant threat of natural disasters.

The four case studies in this book have been purposely selected from young Latin American democracies. This is not only a matter of comparability. The emerging democracies of Latin America made city-wide governmental upgrading programs possible in the 1990s. They at least aspired to a democratic implementation, imperfect as it may appear. In contrast, in an autocracy, a democratic process of urban improvement is not even a possibility. Though anything can happen, one would hope that these young democracies have now been long enough in place to weather inevitable political and economic setbacks. It helps that Brazil, Colombia and Argentina are working themselves up the economic ladder. They are emerging economies whose Gross Domestic Product is in the upper to middle ranks globally. Their basic problem is a highly unequal distribution of wealth (the mere existence of self-constructed neighborhoods is evidence of this imbalance).[1] A designer working in stable democracies can at least choose to work in larger government-led projects without fully compromising democratic principles. However, when democratic principles are violated in a massive way, a designer might have to choose smaller independent initiatives (bottom-up).

Even in democracies, urban transformations that have been co-produced with residents are the exception. In the past, large-scale municipal programs have often been in the cross-hairs of critique for being too inflexible and authoritative. A closer look at the government-led case studies, Rio de Janeiro, São Paulo and Medellín, gives a mixed impression. In their best form there is a face-to-face process with affected residents; in their worst form, there is none.

## *Avoid the Pitfalls of Government-driven Projects*

This is unfortunate, because government-led projects promise, in countries with *in situ* upgrading policies, the coordinated large-scale and multi-sectoral improvement of informal and underprivileged neighborhoods. The strong involvement of the government at every level can, in theory, facilitate fundamental progress for a large number of the population. However, as the study of programs in Rio de Janeiro, São Paulo and Medellín has shown, democratic progress is hard to achieve and can be fragile.

Medellín's transformational success could only be achieved through the rare alignment of visionary political leadership, rising economic development and improved security. It was only then that its strong design culture, experience in community design processes and capacity for swift execution proved effective on the multiple fronts of physical and social improvement. If just one of the basic pillars of leadership, economy and security had been deficient, Medellín's transformation would also have been far less comprehensive. The continuation of the Medellín miracle is far from certain. Some critics claim that the city is now embracing the short-term logic of global city branding by betting on shallow, high cost, high profile and high visibility projects while informal settlements are growing by the day.[2]

São Paulo's steady progress since the 1990s towards improving its informal sector was also not immune to the ups and downs brought about by political change or adverse economic circumstances. The relative continuity of the program up to 2012 has largely depended on the unusually long tenure and influence of one visionary urban planner, who could garner political backing from its respective administrations.[3] The experience of 20 years of upgrading culminated in a comprehensive set of urban guidelines and large-scale programs. After 2013, a change in political priorities and a stronger alignment of the city with federal initiatives moved favela improvement into the background. The new focus was on the construction of new housing as part of the large federal *Minha Casa Minha Vida Program*. The unfolding national political and economic crisis (2017) made conditions worse. The most recent shift of the federal government to the far right (2019) effectively erased all hopes for new federal initiatives that low-income citizens of the favelas could benefit from.[4]

Rio de Janeiro has shown that well-intended government-driven projects can fall prey to political clientelism where much is promised before an election and little is delivered ever after. Mega-events such as the 2014 Soccer World Cup and the 2016 Olympics have led to a frenzied cleaning-up of the city, with informal neighborhoods clearly in the way of the glossy appearance favored by international capital. Indispensable features of a democratic improvement process, such as community participation and the building of public consensus, were quickly annihilated when deadlines loomed. These dismal experiences destroy the little trust in government these communities might ever have had. Consecutive efforts will be much harder.

In large-scale government-driven projects, larger dynamics are in play that typically lie outside the reach of a single designer. Being involved can be a double-edged sword. Large-scale initiatives are preconditions to large-scale accomplishment, but can also lead to large-scale failure. They are never linear enterprises, but more like a roller coaster with the designer strapped into the seat. The most important decision for a designer caught in the middle is when to hold on or when to jump ship.

## *Avoid the Pitfalls of Community/NGO-driven Projects*

As described, integrative, well-coordinated and enduring large-scale initiatives are rare to find. In many, if not most, places on the planet where self-construction can be found, one often encounters weak governments, feeble economic progress or problematic safety conditions. These conditions do stymie large-scale programs. Bottom-up or grassroots approaches by the communities themselves, or by individual designers, NGOs or religious organizations, seem to be more promising under these circumstances. In very desolate conditions, these organizations can be the only help that residents of informal neighborhoods will ever receive. In the absence of effective government programs, designers are sometimes forced to take a more activist or entrepreneurial approach, generating theoretical projects or funding their own initiatives. The work and engagement of these designers is highly admirable, when they have to play several roles for little to no financial reward (as it was in the Buenos Aires case). True bottom-up projects are actually initiated by the residents themselves, for example, through the formation of community-based organizations (CBOs). More often than not, small-scale projects will be initiated by NGOs with a specific focus. In most small projects, one typically finds a mix of all, an amalgamation of designers, residents, NGOs, CBOs, academia and governmental programs.

Despite the limited scale and scope, there are actually many positive aspects of small and incremental projects. Foremost, if the community is driving the

## 154 ■ *Part III*

transformation, there is a higher likelihood that the community accepts the results and cares for them. In an ideal scenario, a designer can develop close ties to the community and intimately understand the place, its problems and social dynamics. During the design and implementation process, designers can work collaboratively with the community, earn their trust and receive instant feedback. The incorporation of feedback permits higher satisfaction and ownership by the residents. In small, community-driven projects, there is typically room for innovative solutions tailored to the specific circumstances of the local conditions. Implementation times can be shorter and, as implementation occurs in stages over longer periods, future interventions can "learn" from the existing ones and there is the potential of permanent improvement. Ideally, the designer coordinates with local authorities and their planning intentions (as weak and imperfect as they might be) as well as other small-scale initiatives in order to avoid conflicts with other interventions. In ideal conditions, the designers have the chance to work on a long-term basis with the same community and are not bound to the typical two to three year funding cycle of donors. Then, many small-scale projects may lead eventually to larger change.[5]

The potential downsides of small, bottom-up projects are also well known. A small project can remain a singular occurrence and not lead to larger change. The small-scale interventions might legitimately be criticized as donor appeasement instead of substantial improvement. When not well coordinated, small projects might conflict with larger scale initiatives or with other small-scale initiatives. Especially when one thinks about landscape scale and systems, a larger coordinated approach is often needed. When outside funding plays a dominant role, there can be conflicts with the government of a country. In the worst case, many small projects funded by foreign sources might annihilate a weak state's planning authority (as happened in the case of reconstruction efforts in Haiti).[6] There is also well-founded suspicion that foreign aid makes governments dependent and may be counterproductive for progress in the long run.[7] Another problem is potential discontinuity and fragile longevity of small privately funded initiatives. Urban transformation takes a long time in general, but privately funded enterprises might come to a sudden stop when donor money runs out, or when there are suddenly other priorities inside the foundation. Built products are typically more appealing to donors than their care and maintenance, which tend to be underfunded. Sometimes, capacities might be simply too small for the size of the problem. For example, the time intensive negotiation process between many diverse community voices can quickly overwhelm designers among the many tasks they face.

But, in many cases, there is no other choice than to pursue small projects. For example, a micro-strategy that is employed in a massive informal neighborhood quarter, such as Kibera in Nairobi, may lack large-scale coordination, but, in Nairobi, the political ruling class forbids profound structural change, forcing designers to adopt "stealth" strategies.[8] In most instances where government is absent or ignorant, quick local interventions can be the only feasible *modus operandi* for a designer.

One should also get used to the thought that not all small projects have to necessarily inspire large upgrades. In the case of Caracas, the initial small-scale interventions and propaganda activism of the well-publicized Venezuelan-based design initiative, Urban Think-Tank (UTT), fostered the implementation of a cable car system with infrastructural nodes. But, for larger political reasons, it did not lead to a comprehensive upgrading project for the whole neighborhood of San Agustín as it did in Medellín. This shortcoming does not necessarily discredit the earlier smaller acupunctural interventions by UTT.[9]

As mentioned above, working in informal cities is inherently a long and unpredictable process. Improvement comes in stages. Setbacks occur on a frequent basis. Well-organized, democratic and integrative government initiatives are more the exception than the rule. Therefore, small-scale independent projects, despite all their shortcomings, will still be needed and should still be pursued or nothing happens at all.

There is general agreement among planners that linking top-down to bottom-up initiatives might eliminate the weaknesses and combine the strengths of both approaches. Indeed, significant improvement in low-income communities can be achieved only through a combination of small-scale, local initiatives and massive upgrades to sanitation, transportation, and employment infrastructures, which have to be orchestrated at the municipal, regional and sometimes national levels. Designers disappointed by large government programs and favorable to small-scale approaches should not forget that many of the most successful larger programs – such as *Favela Bairro* in Rio or the *Proyectos Urbanos Integrales* (PUI) in Medellín – started out with boutique-sized pilot programs. Both programs could actually be described as an assembly of smaller projects, with the added bonus of being coordinated. The genesis of the more successful governmental programs suggests that the difference between top-down and bottom-up is actually not as large as is frequently purported. If a municipal project is actually well coordinated and operates in an open, democratic and participatory manner, it has the chance to foster widespread improvement and should be preferred over a series of small uncoordinated initiatives.

Funding for much of the small-scale work in informal neighborhoods is sporadic. When federal or municipal programs or large international lending agencies are involved, the work can be more remunerative but, in the absence of that, it is fair for designers to wonder if they will ever be adequately compensated for their time and effort, especially given the amount of political and community outreach work that is required. For the time being, young designers test new models under the auspices of NGOs or urban think tanks that creatively obtain their funding from a variety of sources –universities, municipalities, private donors or private clients – sometimes all at once.[10] This appears to be the only way for them to work on problems that the regular for-profit design firms cannot tackle. In order to meet the challenges of the biggest urbanization wave in history, many more resources need to be put into democratic large-scale government-led programs that can award contracts to a large number of design firms.[11]

## Pursue an Integrative Improvement Process

Much knowledge has been accumulated in the past 30 years to improve living conditions in informal neighborhoods in Latin America. Particularly laudable is the fact that the focus has shifted towards programs addressing multiple needs and conditions. Whereas designers and public officials may once have thought in terms of mere housing provision, it is now widely recognized that housing by itself is not an adequate response: it must be paired with improvements in public space, infrastructure, education, job training, health, and safety. Ambitious upgrading projects have been undertaken in almost every major Latin American city, with some of the most outstanding being Favela Bairro in Rio de Janeiro, the work of the Social Housing Agency in São Paulo (SEHAB) and the PUI program in Medellín. In their ideal form (rarely achieved) they share in the idea of upgrading informal neighborhoods in a participatory manner with a minimal amount of displacement, inserting strategic improvements in basic infrastructure (electricity, potable water, sewerage), transportation elements (alleyways, stairways, bicycle paths, pedestrian promenades, streets, roads, bus systems, cable cars), social and educational infrastructure (day care centers, schools, libraries, hospitals, community centers, nurseries), recreational and cultural infrastructure (parks, plazas, playgrounds, sports fields, sports centers, performance spaces, community gardens, river promenades) into the urban fabric. In each of these programs, the goal was the improved integration of informal neighborhoods into the polis at large and the provision of residents with equal access to social, recreational and educational services. All of the aforementioned programs focused on the creation of high-quality public spaces, not just as platforms for the functions of daily life, but also as a basic symbol of democracy. It has become increasingly apparent that landscape is a crucial aspect in these projects. After all, upgrading is less a matter of individual buildings than of creating habitable environments and improved urban ecologies.

Designers in Latin America have accumulated ample knowledge for working in informal neighborhoods. Based on the four case studies, I would like to put forward five observations for a better improvement process.

### *Connect Physical to Social Improvements*

"Cities are not only made of bricks and mortar" is a commonly heard notion, and I will not go into too much detail on this point. But, designers in improvement initiatives had to quickly learn about the limits of their physical interventions. For example, after the first wave of Favela Bairro projects, designers came to realize that new public amenities, such as a new soccer field, were welcome additions to the neighborhood, but did not help much to combat illiteracy and unemployment of the players on that field. Experience has shown that physical interventions must be equally paired with strategic social programs or they are bound to fail. The improvement of informal neighborhoods is a multi-sectoral enterprise and no profession should feel superior. Besides designers and builders, a successful improvement project has to employ social workers, anthropologists, community organizers, engineers, lawyers, artists, educators, entrepreneurs and businessmen, to name but few. The most important collaboration is, however, with the residents of the community itself.

## *Develop Better Community Participation, Collaboration and Co-creation Models*

There is a wide spectrum of strategies around which community participation and collaboration can be structured. In our case studies, some designers conducted extensive interviews with residents (as in the case of Villa Tranquila in Buenos Aires), others bring psychoanalysts into the community's discussion (as with Mario Jauregui in Rio de Janeiro) and large programs like the São Paulo housing agency train a sizable number of local residents as social workers that go from door to door to reach all community households. Beside different procedures, all four case studies concurred with the notion that residents cannot be treated as passive subjects of investigation and the receivers of interventions. They must be considered as equal partners throughout the entire transformation process, from its conceptual stages through post-implementation. The notion of mere participation (letting them be part of the process) has to be overcome in favour of an understanding of collaboration and co-creation. Co-creation processes work better with communities that are already well organized and have a functioning leadership structure, but capacity building has to occur with communities that are not yet structured well or where leadership is corrupt and undermined by organized crime. This is one of the most complex but also important subjects for informal neighborhood upgrading.

Major areas for improvement lie in the creation of more and better feedback loops during the design process; in the collaborative identification of priorities; the engagement in participatory budgeting; the development of community subgroups that study specific aspects of the work and the option to let the community develop and choose among different scenarios, to name a few. That being said, many designers are already remarking that community participation is not a one-way street in which designers only serve to channel the desires of the community: their role is also to bring new topics and considerations into the community discussion, because "the residents can only ask for what they know." Community participation and collaboration has to be a two-way street.[12]

It remains a problem that community participation can be very exigent for low-income residents. Many of them have little time and energy left for long participative sessions.[13] A number of them handle several jobs, deal with excruciating commutes and tend to the needs of large families. Innovative models must be found to build up the capacity of community organizations that enable their members to actually serve as equal partners in a time-consuming redevelopment process. It is clear that if residents' associations remain weak and underfunded, the goal of a face-to-face process will remain unfulfilled.

## 158 ■ *Part III*

On the other side of the table, community participation can prove exhausting for the designers, as well. Professionals such as Flavio Janches and Max Rohm in Buenos Aires, who, like many of their peers, had to make do without government support, can attest to this.[14] They had to handle every aspect of participation – what typically amounts to most of the work – all by themselves. In fact, it seems that once everyone is in agreement, the construction process is the easiest part of the process.

If municipal programs are involved, community engagement in large informal neighborhoods can be successful when professionally structured with a sizable group of well-trained social workers, who proceed with respect for the citizens and clear notions of engagement. Even then, community involvement would be intensive and time-consuming: in a one-year period: the São Paulo housing agency performed literally thousands of meetings in Paraisopolis – a large favela of close to 60,000 residents harboring more than 70 civil society organizations – alone.[15] The intensity of the communication processes and long-term continuation of the process is critical, too. Experienced community organizers confirm that it can take more than half a decade to gain the trust of a disenfranchised community, a time frame that stands in stark contrast with the shorter turnover periods of design contracts and political leadership. And that is just the start: once this trust has been carefully earned, it needs to be cultivated.

Obviously, proper community involvement is the core issue when dealing with low-income settlements. There is still ample room for new, creative ways in which to work with communities. Urban politics professor Phillip Thompson (MIT), for example, calls for new financing models that empower low-income communities to steer their own neighborhoods through the select investment of union pension funds in local businesses in the United States. Strategies could be developed to harness the allure of worldwide youth cultures, such as rap and hip-hop, to draw the otherwise elusive young population of informal neighborhoods into the redevelopment process.[16] Modern information technology for residents' involvement could be mined far more, if we consider that most informal dwellers own cell phones and internet access is increasing.[17] For example, organizations such as Slum Dwellers International (SDI) started the campaign "Know your city," which fosters the mapping of informal neighborhoods by volunteers.[18] All the data is given to a database and made publicly available. Currently, SMS technology is dominant, but once smartphones with internet access become ubiquitous, the possibilities of outreach should substantially increase, taking community input to another level.

## *Apply a Telescopic Approach*

A truly integrative design process develops holistic strategies in various scales and sectors. Unfortunately, the terminological segregation between informal and formal neighborhoods has led designers to focus mostly on the problems within the low-income neighborhoods. This areal approach has been the practice in many informal upgrading programs in the past. In contrast, future upgrading programs have to improve the interaction between low-income communities, the entire urban territory and the hinterland. Cities, whether formal or informal, are the nexus for material, energy, water, goods and demographic flows. Instead of an area focus, dendritic strategies must be applied to improve infrastructural, economic and ecological systems such as water, energy, transport, food, industrial production and recreation throughout a much larger territory. Simultaneously, the focus on the particularity of each neighborhood should be maintained. That means a telescopic approach that is capable of oscillating between small, medium, large and global scales is needed. Examples of this telescopic approach are still few, as they go against the traditional subdivision of design disciplines by scale[19] and against the nature of micro projects. However, landscape architects especially, who are used to operating at all scales, are naturally suited to this work.

## *Combat the Stigmatization of Informal Neighborhoods*

The bad reputation of a neighborhood is hard to shake. It lingers in the public consciousness. The stigmatization of informal settlements already manifests in its denominations – whether these be *slum, bidonville, shantytown, favela, comuna* or *barrio* – that can be painfully felt by residents long after conditions have changed. Despite physical and educational improvements, public acceptance of informal cities as regular parts of the city still remains elusive. In the case of Rio de Janeiro, even substantially upgraded favelas are still called *favelas*, conjuring up the negative connotations that cariocas have internalized for decades. In Rio, favela residents are still *favelados* and at a disadvantage when it comes to securing a job in the formal economy.[20] Potential employers are nervous about hiring somebody who could have a criminal background or be even peripherally connected to organized crime. Despite the fact that only a minimal percentage of favela dwellers are involved in illegal activities, unemployment in Rio is sadly on the rise. The stigma of living in a favela cannot be erased in a decade, and it might take generations for a once poor and violent neighborhood to be thought of as safe in the public's opinion. Given these facts, the question designers need to ask themselves is whether this recuperation process can be helped.

Judging from the four case studies in this book, the key ingredients for broader public acceptance seem to be a safer public environment and an element of attraction. The transformation of Medellín has shown that safety, and the mere existence of a space for public use, are the basis for recovery. It is only once the majority of citizens feel comfortable with entering a once inaccessible neighborhood that the process of de-stigmatization can be claimed to have begun. A feeling of personal safety is obviously the foundation of this experience. The example of Medellín has shown that overall attractiveness helps. If other residents have an interest in visiting a certain neighborhood because of a certain attraction – beautiful views, good food, inexpensive shopping or art festivals – the positive individual impressions can mount up over time to a larger public awareness of improvement. It is, therefore, important for outsiders feel drawn to an area, to reclaim a segregated piece of city as their own again.

**160** ■ *Part III*

Medellín's carefully designed, if not spectacular, interventions did not only raise the self-esteem of residents, they also spiked the curiosity of other citizens to venture into the area.

### *Develop a Specific Design Approach For Public Spaces*

But one wonders if there is also a design mode that allows the inherent expression of a certain place. Although most upgrading programs seek to integrate informal settlements into the formal city, this need not mean that the elements of the formal city have to be brought to the informal. Informal settlements have a different genesis, their own identity and an entirely separate set of strengths such as independence, entrepreneurship and neighborhood cohesion that can be jeopardized through formalization. One must question the assumptions on which this very work is based. For instance, is public space – as conceived in the formal city – relevant to the informal settlement? Should it be reconceptualized?

Passive recreation of the sort that characterizes landscapes in the formal city is not a priority in informal contexts, where public space can even be considered dangerous.[21] Facilities for active recreation are usually more suitable to informal settlements than spaces for passive occupation, especially in places with large adolescent populations with limited access to work and education. For example Michael Mariott's study on Favela Formiga's public spaces in Rio de Janeiro has shown that they are used in a very particular way.[22] He found that much more attention needs to be dedicated to the role of the street and alleyways, where most of the informal gathering occurs, while the new, formally introduced spaces by Favela Bairro were not used as much. Informal gathering is the basis of the much-cited community cohesion of informal neighborhoods. There is a danger that the formalization of public spaces destroys these very qualities. A design approach that brings the idiosyncrasies of informal settlements to the forefront must be developed. One may have to push conceptions of public space towards a notion of productive spaces that include market facilities, community kitchens, laundries and places for cultural expression, as with Rio's samba schools.

## Use Landscape as Infrastructure

Even if seemingly obliterated, every city landscape pervades everything; it is ground, livelihood and threat, all at once. Landscape is invaded by urban settlers, and reinserted into crowded public space when these settlements improve. Landscape is a fabric that bears a host of operations: social transactions, cultural events, moving vehicles, playing children, provisions of food, yielding of water, offering of construction material, and so forth. The formal city has perforated its urban landscape with pipes and conduits to facilitate exchanges of clean and dirty water, bring electric power and communication, connect to distant landscapes on the periphery of the city, pave it over to carry the movement of goods and people and channel rivers to control flooding. Cities are the nodes of a steady flow of goods and people that manifest at an opportune location in a certain landscape. But the "mastered" landscape that enables urban life is so familiar to us that we do not even refer to the final plumbed and paved product as a landscape anymore. It is a *city*. Landscape lies buried beneath, both physically and mentally. It is preserved in pockets as a culturally adapted notion of landscape or as a conserved artifact of a previous biological regime in the guise of designed parks or ecological reserves that satisfy the mental craving for landscape. The true unconquered landscape only emerges in disasters, when cities are flooded, buried by landslides, shaken by earthquakes or run out of water.

With regard to the industrialized and post-industrial city, the relationship between informal neighborhoods and their landscape is more primal. Whereas the industrialized city fits its landscape with plumbing and paving to receive future houses, the informal dweller builds his or her house without machinery directly onto the unprepared landscape's fabric. He or she is confronted with landscape mostly as a nuisance in the form of obstructive vegetation, bare soil, unchanneled water streams, unstable slopes, flooding and landslides. Naturally, residents urgently wish to receive the same services enjoyed by the industrialized city in order to tame this raw landscape. If the city denies them these services, they resort to connecting illegally to existing water mains and electrical poles. When the city proves more amenable, improvement projects insert basic infrastructure into informal settlements, as in the cases of Rio, São Paulo and Medellín. Upon inspecting these improvement projects more closely, one notices that the newly inserted landscapes and public spaces are disconnected from the underlying infrastructure. The new public spaces are essentially recreational spaces cosmetically laid over engineering projects that attempt to control the volatile landscapes below while bringing underground services to the city. Not much evidence exists to show that the improvement of public space and landscape can, in itself, be a form of infrastructure.

## End the "Upgrading" of Informal Neighborhoods through Wasteful Infrastructure

So far, the goal of municipal infrastructural upgrades has been to provide informal settlers with the same infrastructure as the formal city. Unfortunately, the infrastructural concept of most industrialized cities is based on a resource-inefficient model. In most cities, garbage (if collected) is trucked to faraway overflowing landfills. Recycling schemes are in their conceptual stages and are often better handled in the informal economy of the settlements. $CO_2$-emitting power plants are on the brink of capacity; new power plants in distant locations have to be built to satisfy customer demand, losing much energy on the way. Sewage, if treated at all, is pumped over long distances to large plants in remote locations; energy is expended, much is lost on the way and water bodies remain polluted. New drinking-water reservoirs are constructed in far-flung areas, while once-remote reservoirs have been engulfed (and polluted) by rapid urbanization (see São Paulo). Food is shipped over enormous

## 162 ■ *Part III*

distances, while industrial food production techniques lead to loss and erosion of fertile soil. Tragically, in many cases, upgrading today means that informal neighborhoods, once characterized by their resourcefulness and inventiveness, are hooked up to the wasteful infrastructure systems of the formal city. As with most cities on the planet, these centralized infrastructural systems rely on the externalization of problems. They aggressively secure and negatively impact distant landscapes to serve their growing needs. The wisdom of conventional upgrades during a time of climate change is questionable. If we bring electricity to thousands of self-constructed areas, for example, should it come from coal-fired plants? The urgent question arises: does the upgrade of informal neighborhoods always have to lead to the import of resource-wasting infrastructure of the formal city?

It is common knowledge that, in the face of climate change and environmental degradation, major changes need to occur globally in how cities are served by infrastructure. Wide agreement exists that cities are not the problem, but the solution, for a growing population. There is another growing conundrum. For some years, the combined total output of greenhouse gases in the developing world has been higher than that of all industrialized nations.[23] With the hopeful prospect of greater prosperity, greenhouse gas emissions will only rise more in developing countries. The per capita emissions of developing countries, however, are a fraction of those in industrialized nations: obviously, Western societies that achieved their prosperity through $CO_2$-emitting industrialization have no moral ground from which to demand that developing countries cut theirs. If the common wisdom of the Kuznets curve – according to which countries which are poor, but fairly low in harmful emissions today, will gain prosperity only through emitting more – prevails, the global climatological effects of this will be disastrous.[24] This leads to a central question. How can prosperity rise without an increase in emissions? Given that informal settlements have little to no infrastructure to begin with, there should be, in theory, an opportunity to skip antiquated technologies and make low-income settlements models of sustainable development.

## *Use Landscape and Public Space as a Platform for Integrated Infrastructure*

Although a strong desire exists for greater effectiveness, the development of closed-loop systems, more decentralized infrastructure and the maximization of local resources is still in its infancy. Many of the best practices of an energy-efficient and resource-saving urbanism are still being defined and final solutions have yet to be tailored to individual communities. However, an overall tendency is visible. One major principle of environmental urbanism is to create more closed-loop cycles by using waste as a resource and reducing the amounts of consumed materials and energy. This principle has led to favoring small, decentralized infrastructure over big centralized infrastructure. In the few available examples of environmentally conscious communities, energy is created closer to the user, storm water is handled locally, sewage is treated near to the source, potable water is recycled several times before being sent to treatment, more food is grown locally, local employment is favored to cut commuting distances and mass transit is favored over individual transport.[25]

The decentralization of infrastructure holds great promise for informal cities. But, why should anybody whose main concern is to put food on the table be concerned about his environmental footprint? The most voiced concern in low-income communities is the wish for a proper job. Environmental concerns are low in priority. And, indeed, the best long-term way to improve the lives of low-income settlements is by creating jobs that allow families to have a steady income and to pay for housing, food and the education of their children. It follows that the redevelopment of wasteful and resource-inefficient cities has to go hand-in-hand with the creation of jobs. If prosperity should rise without raising emissions, the sustainable improvement of informal cities has to be coupled with income generation for their residents. It is an ambitious project to foster green economy in informal neighborhoods, but one can already find encouraging examples. For example, in São Paulo, the NGO Cidades sem Fome (Cities Without Hunger) converts leftover parcels of land into productive farmland through community cooperatives.[26] In the same city, the municipal initiative *Connect the Dots* seeks to enable small organic farmers on the urban fringes to produce food for public schools.[27] If we look beyond Latin America, one can also find innovative examples in Asia and Africa. For example, in Kolkata, thousands of families live by cleaning urban sewage through fish farming.[28] In Bangladesh, the NGO Waste Concern employs previously informal trash collectors to gather organic waste in cities for compost production.[29] In Nairobi's largest informal neighborhood, Kibera, the Konkuey Design Initiative (KDI) develops with residents new public spaces by engaging waste and flooding problems.[30]

These few examples expand the notion of a decentralized infrastructure to a more integrated approach that operates on multiple scales, spans various sectors and incorporates a multitude of actors. Their driver is income generation for the residents, while their platform is public space and landscape.[31] If one wants to expand the notion of landscape from an element to restrain, perforate and pave over to an element of shared opportunity in informal neighborhoods, a complex challenge arises. A truly integrated infrastructure approach needs to perceive landscape as a dynamic and living entity where collaborative, culturally fitting, economically rewarding, ecologically sensitive, resource-efficient and spatially delightful actions are enabled. A distant dream?

## Increase Knowledge of Designers and Planners

### *Train Planners and Designers Differently*

A small but growing group of landscape architects and landscape planners are currently engaging in the improvement of low-income neighborhoods.[32] Given the magnitude of the informal condition, their numbers have to grow. Fortunately,

**164** ■ *Part III*

more and more design schools are engaging the topic of self-constructed cities in research and curricula, but considering that one fourth of our urban population lives in informal areas and that a revolution is needed to work out how these cities are sustainably serviced, the curricula and foci of the world's design schools have to be refocused, not only for landscape architects. Architects, landscape architects, urban planners and urban designers have to be trained to better understand the complex sociology of low-income communities; to better work with disenfranchised communities; to engage new professional fields such as environmental engineering, urban biology and industrial ecology; to better understand and manipulate processes and systems. Prototypical projects have to be developed in which new approaches can be initiated, adapted and evaluated. This restructuring of curricula needs to start in the design schools of the countries that have self-constructed neighborhoods and informal growth on their doorsteps.[33] Pedagogy needs to be retooled, to shift more educational focus from the formal to the informal, from the developed world to the developing, especially in those areas of Africa and Asia where growth in the informal sector is highest.

## *Pursue a Global Exchange of Knowledge*

As there are more planning and design professionals per capita in highly industrialized countries, one might wonder what their role is in fast growing informal cities worldwide. One would think their knowledge could be useful. Some highly industrialized countries have been pushing for decades for more resource-efficient infrastructure in their own cities. Designers in Europe and, increasingly, in North America, have gained significant experience in the development and integration of decentralized infrastructure systems such as green roofs, stormwater and sewage treatment wetlands, urban farms and solar applications into dense urban fabrics. Pretty much every design school in Europe and in North America discusses models for a more sustainable urbanism. Emergent theoretical frameworks such as *Ecological Urbanism* or young disciplines like *Industrial Ecology* offer fresh approaches to reading and modifying the modern city, deeply enmeshing cultural and ecological processes.

But, can there be a truly productive knowledge exchange between cultures? Can principles and technologies that were developed for highly industrialized cities even be helpful in a different context? Can designers provide socially and culturally appropriate solutions in cultures they know little about? Is there a danger that European city models will be forced onto disparate contexts, resulting in a new form of design imperialism? Is it even possible that a designer can earn the trust of a low-income community thousands of kilometers away? Is there even a role for designers of highly industrialized countries, or should they rather stick to their own culture?

These are valid questions, but they are somewhat moot at this point. Whether one likes it or not, globalization has made international design practice already an integral part of many medium-sized and larger design firms. European and North American design offices increasingly pursue global projects (mostly in East Asia),

And some of them support substantial parts of their operations with foreign contracts. At the present time, these commissions are mostly in areas of the formal city, but, given the global proliferation of informal urbanism, this will change. Especially when it comes to master planning in larger metropolitan areas, designers will have to deal with all levels of society: a global expert knowledge of designing for low-income communities is both urgent and necessary. If this global expert knowledge is not developed in the coming years, international design professionals will not be successful and can even cause damage.

Therefore, a truly productive and respectful exchange has to be structured between designers globally, no matter where they are from.[34] Informal urbanism, as the dominant mode of urban growth on the planet, deserves a global discussion. In order to have partners for this discussion, the planning, landscape and urban design capacities will have to be strengthened in countries where the most urban growth will occur. In the coming decades, immense metropolitan areas will form predominantly in Africa and Asia; design and planning will be challenged to engage problems of water, energy, food and infrastructure on top of growing inequalities under a changing climate. If the design and planning profession in these countries is too small and of weaker influence, more mono-functional engineering projects that exclude ecological, social and cultural aspects will be devised. The challenges that lie ahead require a more equal distribution of planning and design intelligence through both a global knowledge exchange and a local expansion of design and planning capacities.

There are at least encouraging trends that acknowledge alternative design practices. Recent prizes in architecture have gone to practitioners who are proactively engaging low income conditions. The highest recognition for architects, the Pritzker prize, went in 2018 to Balkrishna Doshi and in 2016 to Alejandro Aravena.[35] Both are known for their innovative solutions for low-income housing. These choices sent important signals for a whole profession and generations to follow. Also, a whole field (under competing names such as *Social Design*, *Humanitarian Design* or *Collaborative Design*) has developed with its own award culture. For example, the Curry Stone Design Prize annually awards designers and their projects in low-income areas, with categories such as housing, community development, urban strategies, environment, healthcare or conflict and disaster.[36] UN-Habitat has a long-standing tradition of recognizing innovative projects with the World Habitat Awards.[37] All these awards invite designers and planners to gain knowledge and inspiration from these projects; one can only hope that they instigate a larger shift in design education.

# Notes

1. See World Bank GDP (PPP) per Capita. Out of 175 countries, Argentina ranks at 57, Brazil at 73 and Colombia at 77. As these countries display an unusually high Gini Co-efficient, it is more a matter of a redistribution of prosperity. The World Bank, "GDP per capita, PPP (current international $)," https://data.worldbank.org/indicator/NY.GDP.PCAP.PP.CD (accessed August 25, 2020).

**166** ■ *Part III*

2. Peter Brand, "Governing inequality in the south through the Barcelona Model: "Social Urbanism" in Medellín, Colombia," paper presented to conference *Governance, Contestation, Critique* (Leicester: De Montfort University, 2013), 11. Joseph Claghorn and Christian Werthmann, "Shifting ground: landslide risk mitigation through community-based landscape interventions," *Journal of Landscape Architecture* 10(1) (2015): 6–15.

3. Elisabete França led the municipal social housing unit for the Guarapiranga Basin Initiative from 1992–2005 and from 2005–2012 for the whole city. Elisabete França, "Slum upgrading: a challenge as big as the city of São Paulo," *Focus: The Journal of Planning Practice and Education* 10(1) (2013): Article 20.

4. See interview with Elisabete França, pp. 117–122 in this volume.

5. See also the basic tenet of the exhibition "Small Scale, Big Change" at the Museum of Modern Art in New York, curated by Andres Lepik (2010). Andres Lepik, *Small Scale, Big Change: New Architectures of Social Engagement* (New York: The Museum of Modern Art, 2010).

6. A prime example is the reconstruction process undertaken in post-earthquake Haiti (2010), where private aid organizations provided higher funding than governmental institutions. The numerous coordination efforts failed.

7. Dambisa Moyo, *Dead Aid: Why Aid Is Not Working and How There Is a Better Way for Africa* (New York: Farrar, Straus and Giroux, 2009).

8. Adeya, conversation with landscape architect and principal of KDI, a design-based NGO working in Nairobi, 2011.

9. David Gouverneur, *Planning and Design for Future Informal Settlements: Shaping the Self-Constructed City* (New York: Routledge, 2014), 107–111.

10. Examples are MASS Design, KDI, UTT Caracas.

11. The very ambitious upgrading program *Morar Carioca* in Rio de Janeiro started in the right direction when 40 design firms were selected through a public competition to take part in the program (2010). Unfortunately, *Morar Carioca* fizzled out prematurely due to a change of political priorities.

12. Bruno Fernandes (Archi5), conversation with Flavio Janches and Hubert Klumpner (UTT), 2011. See also the experiences described by Ahlert et al., in *Moravia Manifesto. Coding Strategies for Informal Neighborhoods* (Berlin: Jovis, 2018).

13. John J. Betancur, "Approaches to the regularization of informal settlements: the case of PRIMED in Medellín, Colombia," *Global Urban Development Magazine* 3(1) (2007): 11.

14. United Nations Human Settlements Programme, *The State of the World's Cities 2006/2007: The Millennium Development Goals and Urban Sustainability: 30 Years of Shaping the Habitat Agenda* (Routledge, Vol. 3, 2006), 30.

15. Conversation with Elisabete França, 2010.

16. See Phillip Thompson's talk at the Symposium Metropolis Nonformal, 2011, https://vimeo.com/33653056 (accessed August 25, 2020).

17. For example, the Berlin based door2door company developed a *Track Your City* application that maps with volunteers and GPS trackers non-formal transport routes (for example, the routes of the Daladalas in Dar es Salaam). The results are published on open street maps. See "Track your city: help us map your city," Door2Door, www.trackyourcity.org (accessed August 25, 2020). The Kenian company mSurvey conducts simple surveys through SMS technology. See: "Engaging conversations at scale," msurvey, https://mysurvey.solutions/ (accessed August 25, 2020).

18. See "Know your city," sdi, http://knowyourcity.info (accessed August 25, 2020).

19. One good example of a telescopic approach is MMBB's proposal "Watery Voids" for São Paulo's waterways exhibited at the Rotterdam Biennale 2007. 3rd International Architecture Biennale Rotterdam, "Watery Voids," http://archive.iabr.nl/2007/PowerNotes_05/top/126 (accessed August 25, 2020).
20. Janice E. Perlman, *Favela: Four Decades of Living on the Edge in Rio de Janeiro* (New York: Oxford University Press, 2010), 316–341.
21. In Caracas, the residents of San Rafael-Unido conveyed their anxieties that new public space would simply provide more opportunities for vagrants and drug dealers. John Beardsley and Christian Werthmann, "Improving informal settlements. Ideas from Latin America," *Harvard Design Magazine* 28 (2008): 3.
22. Michael Joseph Marriott, "Territoriality and the regulation of public space in Favela Morro da Formiga, Rio de Janeiro," PhD Thesis (Queensland: School of Design, Creative Industries Faculty, Queensland University of Technology, 2015).
23. US Energy Information Administration, "Today in Energy," www.eia.gov/todayinenergy/detail.php?id=26252 (accessed August 25, 2020).
24. Von Weizsäcker et al., *Factor Five: Transforming the Global Economy through 80% Improvements in Resource Productivity* (London: Earthscan, 2009).
25. Thomas Schroepfer, Christian Werthmann and Limin He, "Aspirations and realities of exemplary eco-cities," *DETAIL* Green 2, 2010. Christian Werthmann, "Skipping centralization," in *Global Stability Through Decentralization?*, ed. Martin A. Wilderer and Martin Grambow (Heidelberg: Springer, 2016) 75–80.
26. Cidades sem Fome, "Cities without Hunger," https://cidadessemfome.org/en/ (accessed August 25, 2020).
27. IABR, "IABR and Sao Paulo: connecting the dots," www.iabr.nl/en/project/connect-the-dots (accessed August 25, 2020).
28. Dhrubajyoti Ghosh, "The Calcutta wetlands: turning bad water into good, *Changemakers Journal* (1998), www.scopekolkata.org/wp-content/uploads/2019/05/Dr.-Ghosh_changemaker.pdf (accessed August 25, 2020). Charlie Pye-Smith "Salvation from sewage in Calcutta Marshes," *People & the Planet* 4(1) (1995), www.ncbi.nlm.nih.gov/pubmed/12295819 (accessed August 25, 2020).
29. Waste Concern, "Waste concern models," http://wasteconcern.org/models/ (accessed August 25, 2020). Christian Zurbrügg et al., "Decentralised composting in Bangladesh, a win–win situation for all stakeholders," *Resources, Conservation and Recycling* 43(3) (2005): 281–292. Anne Matter, Martin Dietschi and Christian Zurbrügg, "Improving the informal recycling sector through segregation of waste in the household – the case of Dhaka Bangladesh," *Habitat International* 38 (2013): 150–156.
30. One should also add that KDI is part of a new generation of socially conscious designers who intensively studied preceding initiatives and overall NGO conduct in order to develop their own model of approach in the field. For more information see: "KDI," Kounkuey Design Initiative, www.kounkuey.org/mission (accessed August 25, 2020).
31. For example, in 2017, the exhibition "Out There. Landscape Architecture on Global Terrain" at the Architectural Museum in Munich featured five landscape architects (including myself) with ten academic projects. For more detailed information on the projects consult the exhibition catalogue, *Out There. Landscape Architecture on Global Terrain*, ed. Andres Lepik (Berlin: Hatje Cantz, 2017).
32. Ibid.
33. Many Latin American schools are already in a process of reorientation. A good example is *Escola da Cidade* in São Paulo, where young professionals are specifically

trained to work in non-formal areas. Another good example is the *Maestría en Procesos Urbanos y Ambientales* of EAFIT University in Medellín.

34. Results from this discussion can be found in Christian Werthmann and Jessica Bridger, *Metropolis Nonformal* (San Francisco: Applied Research + Design Publishing, 2015).
35. The Pritzker Architecture Prize, "Laureates," www.pritzkerprize.com (accessed September 8, 2020).
36. Curry Stone Foundation, "Curry Stone Design Prize Winners," 2020, https://currystone foundation.org/design-prize/design-prize-winners/ (accessed September 8, 2020).
37. World Habitat, "World Habitat Awards," https://world-habitat.org/world-habitat-awards/ (accessed September 8, 2020).

# Afterword

## Anticipation

This book has been concerned with the experiences of improving informal neighborhoods through landscape and public space in Latin America. Another book could have been written about landscape and public space strategies for anticipating the next wave of informal urbanization.

It is estimated that there will be nine billion people on this planet in 2050. In the next three decades, the UN expects that an additional 2.5 billion people, or a total of seven billion, will live in cities. 90% of the urban growth will be concentrated in Asia and Africa.[1] There are currently no reliable estimates of how many of the new city dwellers will fall under UN-Habitat's category of a slum household, but one can safely assume that the numbers will go up further, as they have done so in the past 15 years.[2]

With this prospect, there is an urgent need to develop revised urban growth models. Conventional models of the past that focused on slum prevention have failed. Models of housing provision for the poor have failed. Exploratory models of *Sites and Services* of the 1970s have, unfortunately, failed to find wider acceptance. Since most of the urban growth will occur in low-income countries of Africa and Asia, strategies of urban expansion have to be developed that do not rely on the provision of housing, but on embracing the self-construction capacities and entrepreneurship of the incoming populations. There will be no other choice, as these countries will not be able to afford fully built houses for all their citizens (which tends to result in very monotonous expansions that have created their own problems in the past). Instead of blocking the newcomers, they need to be supported. Instead of improving informal neighborhoods after the fact, a supportive self-construction process needs to be initiated before the influx. It could avoid the worst hardships for informal dwellers, such as building in risky terrain or having no to little infrastructure. If the urban pioneers of the future are given a safe environment to roll out their activities supported by necessary infrastructure, better cities will arise.

Examples for a change in attitude exist. In Chile, some of the most recent examples of incremental housing developed by Pritzker Prize winner Alejandro Aravena

# 170 ■ *Part III*

and his team can be visited (Elemental 2016).[3] In Egypt and El Salvador, the positive gestation of 30-year-old Sites and Services projects has been documented by MIT scholar Reinhard Goethert.[4] Shlomo Angel, of New York University, has proposed some very simple rules for city expansion through dirt grids.[5] The urbanist David Gouverneur, of Pennsylvania University, has put forward a well thought-out growth strategy that fuses formal and informal activities; he proposes a smart system of robust "informal armatures" consisting of corridors, patches and stewards "to plan for future informal settlements." In these armatures, landscape and infrastructure plays the most prominent role.[6]

Much stands in the way of a different approach; rarely does any city want to attract large low-income populations by setting aside ample land for poor people to build their shacks. Conservative politicians and their constituencies who view informal neighborhoods more as breeding grounds of crime than places of hope will further pursue strategies of deterrence. Often willful ignorance is at play, when a city just ignores its incoming stream of migrants and does not engage in an active growth strategy. With increasing migration, xenophobia is on the rise as well. Newcomers will face more hostile treatment than in the past.[7] The major battle will be to convince city governments and their leaders that managed self-construction can produce functional neighborhoods. Arguments will have to be made that a co-produced city is better and less expensive than "fixing" informal neighborhoods after the fact, and that it produces a more functional city where important infrastructures such as transportation, education, health, recreation, energy and water can grow organically with it. Once this attitude has changed and a proactive growth strategy by city governments is pursued, further hindrances, such as corruption and land speculation, have to be tackled in order to really implement it.

Given the continued speed of global urbanization and foreseeable migration waves triggered by climate change, it is clear that we need nothing short of a revolution. It will need all sectors of society to initiate and maintain change on all levels. As designers, we have to contribute to the holistic development of more equal and sustainable living. As landscape architects and planners, we have to use the potential of landscape and public space to improve the living conditions of many more informal neighborhood dwellers. Our task is unambiguous. In the intersection between a more sustainable metabolism and an increased quality of life for everybody lies the greatest design challenge – and opportunity – of the twenty-first century.

## Notes

1. United Nations, *World Urbanization Prospects: The 2018 Revision* (New York: United Nations, 2018).
2. While the proportion of the urban population living in slums fell from 28% in 2000 to 23% in 2014, the absolute numbers kept growing: from 792 million in 2000 to 880 million in 2014. UN-Habitat, Sustainable Development Goals, https://unstats. un.org/sdgs/report/2017/goal-11/ (accessed August 25, 2020).

3. Elemental, "Elemental: Quinta Monroy," www.elementalchile.cl/wp-content/uploads/080814_QM_Mark_Magazine_HQ.pdf (accessed August 25, 2020).
4. SIGUS MIT, "Reflection on the la Presita Surveys," workshop report, El Salvador, 2008, http://web.mit.edu/incrementalhousing/articlesPhotographs/laPresitaSurveys.html (accessed August 25, 2020).
5. Shlomo Angel, "Making room for a planet of cities," policy focus reports, Lincoln Institute of Land Policy, 2011, http://sollyangel.com/wp-content/uploads/2013/06/Making-Room.pdf (accessed August 25, 2020).
6. David Gouverneur, *Planning and Design for Future Informal Settlements* (New York: Routledge, 2015).
7. Compare, for example, the riots in South Africa against immigrants from Somalia, Nigeria and others in 2017.

# Figure Credits

**Book Cover** author

**Figure 1** author ......................................................................... vi

**Figure 2** author ......................................................................... vi

**Figure 3** author ......................................................................... vii

**Figure 4** author ......................................................................... vii

**Figure 5** author ......................................................................... viii

**Figure 6** author ......................................................................... viii

**Figure 7** author ......................................................................... ix

**Figure 8** author ......................................................................... ix

**Figure 9** author ......................................................................... xviii

**Figure 10** author ......................................................................... 11

**Figure 11** First version of map composed by Armando Milou and Juliana Silbermins, Harvard Graduate School of Design (2008), updated and reworked by Nick Bonard (2014) and Leonie Wiemer (2020), Leibniz University Hannover. Informal areas courtesy of TECHO-Argentina ........................... 13

**Figure 12** Composed by Nick Bonard (2014) and Leonie Wiemer (2020), Leibniz University Hannover. Informal areas courtesy of DAP, Municipality of Medellín, "Geodatabase del POT Acuerdo 048 del 2014," www.medellin.gov.co/geonetwork/srv/spa/catalog. search#/metadata/1a2ecfe8-d073-45d5-a89c-8dfdf8ff2b28 (accessed September 27, 2020) ...................................................... 14

**174** ■ *Figure Credits*

**Figure 13** First version of map composed by Ahlam Abdulla, Sarah Conyngham and Sarah Van Sanden, Harvard Graduate School of Design (2008), updated and reworked by Nick Bonard (2014) and Leonie Wiemer (2020), Leibniz University Hannover. Favela outlines courtesy of "Data Rio," Instituto Pereira Passos, www.data.rio/datasets/limite-favelas-2016 (accessed September 27, 2020) ..............................15

**Figure 14** First version of map compiled by Jonathan Tate and Anne Vaterlaus, Harvard Graduate School of Design (2008), updated and reworked by Nick Bonard (2014) and Leonie Wiemer (2020), Leibniz University Hannover. Informal areas courtesy of SÃO PAULO, PREFEITURA MUNICIPAL DE SÃO PAULO, GeoSampa, http://geosampa.prefeitura.sp.gov.br/PaginasPublicas/_SBC.aspx (accessed September 27, 2020).......16

**Figure 15** Cartoon drawings by Chelina Odbert and Jennifer Toy as part of the exhibition "Dirty Work: Transforming Landscape in the Americas," Harvard Graduate School of Design, 2008 ..........17

**Figure 16** author........................................................................18

**Figure 17** author........................................................................19

**Figure 18** author........................................................................20

**Figure 19** author........................................................................21

**Figure 20** author........................................................................22

**Figure 21** author........................................................................23

**Figure 22** author........................................................................24

**Figure 23** author........................................................................25

**Figure 24** author........................................................................25

**Figure 25** author........................................................................26

**Figure 26** author........................................................................26

**Figure 27** author........................................................................27

**Figure 28** author........................................................................27

**Figure 29** author........................................................................28

**Figure 30** Flavio Janches ............................................................39

**Figure 31** Flavio Janches ............................................................40

| | | |
|---|---|---|
| **Figure 32** | Flavio Janches | 41 |
| **Figure 33** | Flavio Janches | 43 |
| **Figure 34** | Flavio Janches | 44 |
| **Figure 35** | Flavio Janches | 46 |
| **Figure 36** | Flavio Janches | 47 |
| **Figure 37** | Flavio Janches, Max Rohm, Nobuko Publishers | 48 |
| **Figure 38** | author | 61 |
| **Figure 39** | author | 65 |
| **Figure 40** | author | 68 |
| **Figure 41** | author | 69 |
| **Figure 42** | author | 70 |
| **Figure 43** | author | 71 |
| **Figure 44** | author | 72 |
| **Figure 45** | author | 73 |
| **Figure 46** | author | 74 |
| **Figure 47** | author | 75 |
| **Figure 48** | author | 76 |
| **Figure 49** | author | 78 |
| **Figure 50** | author | 78 |
| **Figure 51** | author | 81 |
| **Figure 52** | author | 82 |
| **Figure 53** | author | 82 |
| **Figure 54** | author | 84 |
| **Figure 55** | author | 85 |
| **Figure 56** | author | 87 |
| **Figure 57** | author | 99 |
| **Figure 58** | author | 101 |
| **Figure 59** | author | 103 |

| | | |
|---|---|---|
| **Figure 60** | author | 104 |
| **Figure 61** | author | 109 |
| **Figure 62** | author | 111 |
| **Figure 63** | author | 111 |
| **Figure 64** | author | 112 |
| **Figure 65** | author | 123 |
| **Figure 66** | author | 125 |
| **Figure 67** | EDU, City of Medellín | 128 |
| **Figure 68** | EDU, City of Medellín | 129 |
| **Figure 69** | author | 130 |
| **Figure 70** | author | 130 |
| **Figure 71** | author | 131 |
| **Figure 72** | author | 131 |
| **Figure 73** | author | 133 |

# Index

Aburrá Valley 14, 15
adolescents 76; *see also* youth
Africa 11
Agency for Technical Cooperation (GTZ) 125
agglomerations 20, 21, 62
aid agencies 31
alleyways 10, 24, 89, 105, 160
Amsterdam 42, 55
Amsterdam Architecture Academy 42, 59
Angel, Schlomo 170
anticipation 31–32
Aravena, Alejandro 32, 165, 169
architects 120–121, 140, 163–164
Architectural Museum in Munich xix
Argentina 56, 58, 151, 152
ARQUI 5 (architectural firm) 68–70
Asia 11
authoritarianism 64

*baile funk* dance parties 77
*Bairrhino* program 63
Bangladesh 163
Bank for Reconstruction (KfW) 125
Barcelona 107
*barrio* 53, 124–125, 135
Barrio Pinazo 46
beekeeping 76
Berlage Institute 46
Betancur, John J. 126
Bohigas, Oriol 90, 107
Braathen, Einar 84, 86, 91
Brand, Peter 134, 136
Brazil 56, 63, 80, 121, 151–152
bridges 141, 145
Brillembourg, Alfredo xviii
Buenos Aires xviii, xix, xx, 2, 39–49, 56;
    mapping of informal urbanization 13–14

cable car projects 83–85, 130–133, 135, 155
Canthino do Céu 19, 21, 23
*Canudos* war 80
Caracas xviii, 134, 155
Carleton University 46
car ownership 10
*cartoneros* 51
Casa Amarela 85
Cascata River 73, 74, 76
Castillo, Jose xviii
CBOs *see* community-based organizations
Célula Urbana (Urban Cell) 63, 80–81, 85–86,
    96–98
chess system 110
children 41, 43–46, 54–57, 60, 76
Chile 32, 169
churches, 42
Cidades sem Fome (Cities Without Hunger) 163
Cimento Social 80–83
Cities Alliance 32
cities: formal 7–9, 17, 60, 79, 120, 162;
    informal 6, 10–11, 17–18, 60, 163;
    population of 2
citizenship 39, 62, 136
Ciudad Nezahualcóyotl (Ciudad Neza) 20
clearances 29–30
climate change 3, 162, 170
co-creation processes 157–158
collaboration 86, 121; community 88, 134,
    157–158; eye-to-eye 88
Colombia 14, 139–140, 151, 152
Columbia University 121
community assistants 64, 66
community-based organizations (CBOs) 31, 64,
    125–126, 153, 157
community cohesiveness 77, 79
community collaboration 88, 134, 157–158

**177**

**178** ■ *Index*

community cooperatives 163
community development 79
community-driven projects 153–155
community gardens 76, 113
community identity 42
community involvement 45, 57–58, 97, 158
community leadership 64, 78
community participation 7, 64–65, 75, 88, 100, 105, 107, 113, 126–128, 142, 157–158
compact developments 10
*Companhia de Desenvolvimento de Comunidades* (CODESCO) 62
Connect the Dots initiative 163
Consejería Presidencial para el Área Metropolitana de Medellín (Presidential Council for the Metropolitan Area of Medellín) 125
"Conservative Surgery" 31
*consolidación nivel 3* 15
contagious diseases xx
Copacabana 7, 16
Coronavirus pandemic xx
Córrego Limpo program 18
Coupé, Françoise 135
crime 7, 29–30, 40, 102, 120, 123–124, 126, 147–148
Cruz, Teddy xviii, 134
cultural differences 44
Curry Stone Design Prize 165

data gaps 11
Dávila, Julio D. 134
deforestation 73
democracy 31
democratic principles 151–152
denial 29
deprivation 11
designer-driven initiatives 31
Dharavi 22
Dias, Giselle 84
Dirty Work: Transforming Landscape in the Non-formal City of the Americas (show) xviii, xix, xx
Doll, Henk 55
Doorn, Alijd van 55
Doshi, Balkrishna 165
drug cartels 124, 136
drug trade 62, 64, 97–98
drug traffickers 64, 70, 75
drug-related violence 77

Echeverri, Alejandro 127–128, 135–136, 139–148
ecological urbanism 164

economic crisis 51
EDU *see* Empresa de Desarollo Urbano
educational programs 85
Egypt 170
electricity 24
emerging economies 152
Empresa de Desarollo Urbano (Company for Urban Development, EDU) 126–129, 131, 135, 143
Empresas Públicas de Medellín (Public Works of Medellín, EPM) 131, 135
energy efficiency 10
entrepreneurship 10
*envión* 53
environmental problems 60
environmental risk 22
environmental urbanism 162
EPM *see* Empresas Públicas de Medellín
erosion 22, 103, 113
Escola da Cicade 120, 121
esthetics 129, 135
ETH Zurich 121
Evangelist churches 53
evictions 29, 30, 84
exclusion 8–9
exteriors 24, *26*
Eyck, Aldo van 42, 55

Fajardo, Sergio 126–127, 129, 135, 140–141, 145, 147
*favela (Cnidosculus phyllacanthus)* 80
Favela Bairro xvii, xx, 31, 49, 62–68, 72, 74–75, 77–81, 85–91, 96–98, 135, 155, 157
favelas: Rio de Janeiro 8, 16, 21, 62–91, 159; safety issues 7; São Paulo 7, 9, 17, 21
favela tourism 86
fish farming 163
flooding xix, xxi, 22, 23
floodplains 22, 23, 30
floors 24
flush toilets 23
foreign aid 154
foreign investment 91
formal institutions 53
fragmented communities 42
França, Elisabete xvii, 100, 104, 114, 117–122
fruits 24
fruit trees 76

gangs 70, 83, 84, 86, 90, 124, 130
Geddes, Patrick 30–31
gender-specific needs 44, 56–57
gentrification 9, 86, 90–91

## Index ■ 179

geophysical landscape xix
Goether, Reinhard 170
Gouverneur, David 32, 134, 170
governance 151–152
government-led projects 31, 49, 152–152
governments: modes of engagement 28–32,
61–62; municipal 31, 40, 46, 52–53, 60,
73, 125; and public spaces 57; *see also*
government-led projects
*Grade Estatística e Atlas Digital do Brasil* 21
Grandes Favelas 63
greenhouse gas emissions 162
green spaces 107
Guarapiranga Basin Initiative xvii, xx, 100–115,
117–120
Guardiões dos Rios program 74, 76

Harvard Graduate School of Design 42
Harvard University 121
Heliopolis 100
Heringer, Anna xix
hills 22
holistic approaches xviii, 88, 128, 135, 158
homicide 123–124
Hora, Mauricio 84–85
housing: Cimento Social program 81–83; public
62, 66–67, 102, 133; social 30, 83

identity building 42
imaginary workshops (*talleres imaginarios*) 128
improvement 30–31
income generation 65, 66
India 22, 30
industrial ecology 164
informal occupation 18
informal settlements: growth of 20–21; mapping
10–17; occupation types 18–19; process of
17–18; recommendations for improvement
process 150–165; sizes 19–20; stigmatization
159–160; wasteful infrastructure 161–162; *see
also* irregular settlements; slums
informal socializing 77
informal subdivisions 18–19; *see also* irregular
subdivisions
Integral Program for the Improvement of
Subnormal Neighborhoods in Medellín
(Programa Integral de Mejoramiento de
Barrios Subnormales en Medellín, PRIMED)
125–126, 128, 134, 147
Integrated Action Perimeters (PAIs) 118
Inter-American Development Bank 31, 62
internet 158
internet cybercafes 96

Ipanema 16
irregular settlements (*loteamentos irregulares*)
102; *see also* informal settlements; irregular
subdivisions
irregular subdivisions (*loteamentos irregulares*)
7–8, 102; *see also* informal subdivisions

Jacarezinho 96
Janches, Flavio xviii, xx, 39–47, 49–60, 158

Keeling, David 41
Klumpner, Hubert xviii
knowledge exchange 164–165
Kolkata 163
Konkuey Design Initiative (KDI) 163
Kuznets curve 162

Lagreca de Sales, Marta Maria 106, 108, 110,
117–122
landfills 22
land invasions 18, 30
land ownership 8, 52
land property rights 8
landscape 22; architecture xvii–xix, 1; and
infrastructure 160–163
landslides xix, xxi, 22, 30, 73
land titles 8, 126
large-scale interventions 2, 53–54, 56, 90,
152–155
Latin America 2–3
*Laufen Manifesto* xix
Law of Protection of Water Catchments 102
Lefaivre, Liane 55
legal framework 8
Lepik, Andres xix
library parks 127, 132, 144–145
low-income citizens 8, 11, 22, 31–32, 62, 102,
113, 157
low-income communities 1–3, 155, 158–159,
163–165

magnetic rail project 137
Mananciais 118
Manhattan 21
maps xix, 10–17
marginal lands 1
marginalized communities 42
market-based solutions 3
Marriott, Joseph Michael 77, 79, 160
MCMV *see* Minha Casa Minha Vida program
Medellín xix, xx, 8, 19, 123–137, 139–148,
152, 159–160; mapping of informal
urbanization 12, 14–15; social urbanism 49

## 180 ◼ Index

*Medellín: Medio ambiente, urbanismo, sociedad* 140
Medellín Model 134–136
medieval towns 2, 10
*mejoramiento integral* 15
Metrocable 130–133, 135
metroculture 142
*Metropolis Nonformal* xix
Mexico City xviii, xix, 2, 20
microenterprise 3
micro-strategy 154; *see also* small-scale
    interventions
middle class 10
Minha Casa Minha Vida program (MCMV)
    114, 118, 120, 121, 153
"mixed zones" 10
Morar Carioca 63, 80, 83–85, 90, 91
Morro da Favela 80
Morro da Formiga 73–80, 88
Morro da Providência 80–88, 90, 96
Mumbai 22
municipal governments 31, 40, 46, 52–53, 60,
    73, 125
municipal workers 59
murals 45, 58
Museu da Providência 96
Museu do Amanhã (Museum of Tomorrow) 83
Museum of Modern Art 30
Mutirão Remunerado program 62, 73

Nairobi 154, 163
neoliberal policies 3
NGOs *see* nongovernmental organizations
nongovernmental organizations (NGOs) 12, 13,
    29, 52, 125, 128, 153–155, 163

Olympic Games 2016 83–84, 90, 153
organic farming 163
*Out There. Landscape Architecture on Global*
    *Terrain* (exhibition) xix
ownership: car 10; land 8, 52; sense of 57–58,
    88, 126

PAC program (Program for Growth
    Acceleration) 118
PAIs *see* Integrated Action Perimeters
Paraisopolis 21, 23, 100, 158
Parque Amélia 108–115
Parque Royal 67–73, 88
peaceful coexistence 42
peripheral neighborhoods 62
Petersen, Lu 63, 81, 96–98
physical interventions 88, 125, 146, 147,
    156–157

Pilar 46
pirate development 30
*Plan de Ordenamiento Territorial del municipio de*
    *Medellín* (territorial planning plan) 15
Plan of Integrated Social Action 97
playgrounds 41–46, 55–57, 107
playing 42–43, 54–55
Playspace Foundation 55
Plaza Pinzón 46
plazas 43, 45–46, 77, 79, 89, 107
Plaza Vicente Lopes 45–46
political landscape 151
population density 21–22
population numbers 19
Porto Maravilha 83
post-implementation programs 113
POUSOs (Postos de Orientacao Urbanistica
    e Social, or Posts for Social and Urban
    Orientation) 63, 67
poverty 9, 86, 88, 102
PRIMED *see* Integral Program for the
    Improvement of Subnormal Neighborhoods
    in Medellín
Pritzker prize 165
private–public partnerships 91
Providência Hill 80
Proyecto Urbano Integral (Integrative Urban
    Project, PUI) 127–129, 141–144, 146, 155;
    Nororiental 130–133, 143
public facilities 1
public housing 62, 66–67, 102, 133
public spaces xviii, 10, 39–40, 45, 48–49, 52,
    56–57, 61–91, 107, 114, 120, 135–136;
    and citizenship 39, 62, 136; connectivity 89;
    culture 89–90; development of 88; integrated
    infrastructure 162–163; maintenance 45, 79,
    89, 119–120, 142, 154; materials used in
    construction 89; network of 43; and playing
    42; regulatory structures 77; planning and
    design 89, 160; unbuilt 24; usability 79, 89
public transportation xviii, 10, 129, 132
PUI *see* Proyecto Urbano Integral

rainfall 23
rainforests 73, 76; *see also* reforestation
ravines 1, 22, 146
Reconquista River 41
recreational spaces 44, 89, 101, 107, 132, 156,
    160
recycling 24, 161
reforestation 74, 76, 80
religious organizations 29
relocations 2, 29–30, 62, 76, 84, 136

resident associations 65, 74–76, 78
Riachuelo River 14, 40–41, 60
Rio de Janeiro xvii, xx, 2, 7, 8, 23, 29, 31, 56, 61–91, 153, 159; mapping of informal urbanization 12, 15–16
riparian areas 22
river parks 107
rivers 12, 17, 23, 100, 106
Rocinha 21, 23
Rohm, Max xviii, xx, 39–47, 49–61, 158
roofs 24, 132, 164
Rudofsky, Bernard 30

SABESP *see* São Paulo Sanitation Agency
safety 7, 24, 146–147, 159
Salazar, Alonso 132
San Diego xviii
San Fernando 46
sanitation 2, 66, 103–108
San Martin 59
San Salvador 170
Santa Amaro 101
Santo Domingo 131, 132
São Paulo xvii, xviii, xix, xx, 2, 7, 8, 9, 23, 56, 152; mapping of informal urbanization 12, 16–17; population density 21; water issues 99–115
São Paulo Sanitation Agency (SABESP) xvii, 118
São Paulo Social Housing Agency (SEHAB) 100, 104, 107, 110, 114, 117–118, 121, 135, 158
Second World War 42
security of tenure 8
segregation 145
SEHAB *see* São Paulo Housing Agency
self-construction 30, 32
self-esteem 62, 129, 135, 145
*setores subnormais* (subnormal clusters) 17
sewage 14, 24, 53, 67–68, 97, 100, 103–106, 108, 112–113, 118–119, 161, 163–164
shantytowns 6; *see also* informal settlements; slums
shopping malls 10
Sites and Services project 31, 169, 170
Slum Dwellers International (SDI) 158
slums 2, 24, 50; attitude towards 114–115; definition 6, 11; global numbers 10–11; population of 2; upgrading programs 56, 100, 114; *see also* informal settlements
small-scale interventions xviii, xx, 46–49, 53–54, 153–155
smartphones 158
social cohesion 10

social differences 44
social dysfunction 10
social fragmentation 42, 53, 54
social habits 42
social hardship 29
social housing 30, 83
social initiatives 65
socializing 10, 77, 89
social life 77
social networks 42–43, 62
social programs 65, 88, 113, 156–157
social relations 54, 55
social spaces 41, 54
social urbanism (*urbanismo social*) 49, 127, 132, 134, 136
Spanish Library 131, 132
sport clubs 42
sport fields 62, 68, 107
squatting 8, 18
Starke, Dietmar 63, 77, 96
streets 10, 24, 62, 69, 77, 83, 89, 133
subnormal settlements 63
sustainability 10, 113, 163–164, 170

TECHO 12, 13
telescopic approach 158–159
Texcoco lake xviii
Thompson, Philip 158
Tijuana xviii
Tijuca National Park 15
tolerance 30
Toscano, João Walter 110
tourism 86, 97
toxic sites 1
training 163–164
transportation 24, 43, 49, 89, 100, 102, 129; public xviii, 10, 129, 132
trash collection 24, 148, 163
Turner, John 30, 114

unemployment 41, 90, 130, 156, 159
UN-Habitat 11–12, 165, 169
Unidade de Polícia Pacificadora (UPP) 63, 77
United Nations (UN) xix, 2, 10–11; Development Program (UNDP) 125; Best Practices awards 112; *see also* UN-Habitat
United States 10
University College London 64, 75
UPP *see* Unidade de Polícia Pacificadora
urban agriculture 48
urbanism 63, 136, 140; ecological 164; environmental 162; formal versus informal 7–10; social 49, 127, 132, 134, 136

**182** ◾ *Index*

urbanization growth rates 3, 11, 30
Urban PAC – *Programa de Aceleração do Crescimento*, or Acceleration Development Program) 63
urban planning 10, 30
urban population 11
urban rehabilitation programs 103–106, 112
Urban Think-Tank (UTT) 155
UTMP 13
UTT *see* Urban Think-Tank

vandalism 58
vegetables 24, *27*
Venezuela 134
Villa Independencia 46
Villa Las Flores 52

*villas* 13, 51
*villas de emergencias* xviii, 39
Villa Tranquila *39*, 40–49, 52

Waste Concern 163
water 23, 97; connections 24; mains 23; reservoirs 22, 23, 100–104
waterfronts 107
wealth distribution 152
World Bank 10, 31, 112, 113, 118
World Habitat Awards 165
World Population Review 21

XPEKT 77

youth 41–42, 45, 48; *see also* adolescents